AFTER THE FACT?

AFTER THE FACT?
The Truth About Fake News

Marcus Gilroy-Ware

Published by Repeater Books
An imprint of Watkins Media Ltd
Unit 11 Shepperton House
88–89 Shepperton Road
London
N1 3DF
www.repeaterbooks.com
A Repeater Books paperback original 2020
1

Distributed in the United States by Random House, Inc., New York.

ISBN: 9781912248735
Ebook ISBN: 9781912248742

To my parents, my sister, and my "chosen family"

CONTENTS

Foreword

Dear Reader,

The subtitle of this book, "the truth about fake news", is intentionally playful and light-hearted. But behind this mischievous subtitle is a genuine intention to understand the urgent problems of misinformation and disinformation — the inadvertent and deliberate forms of falsehood — that the phrase "fake news" indirectly refers to.

The most important "truth" about "fake news" is that it is not actually a useful or precise term for talking about misinformation and disinformation at all. As a number of people have pointed out, most notably the communication scholar Claire Wardle (2017), the phrase is not only conceptually uncertain, but fundamentally flawed. There just isn't any single thing called "fake news" — the phrase has simply become a pejorative label for information, misinformation or disinformation we have a particular objection to. After the US election in 2016, Donald Trump and the people working for him became well-known for dismissing unfavourable coverage as "fake news", but this sense of the phrase has since become a common occurrence in political discussion across the English-speaking world. In the UK Parliament in May 2018, for instance, then Secretary of State for Health Jeremy Hunt dismissed claims that the UK's National Health Service was being privatised as "fake news" (Hansard, 2018). This kind of explicit dismissal of factually accurate information heralded an increasingly emboldened refusal to acknowledge or admit basic facts about the world, regardless of the evidence. This kind of factual denial became common not only in the language of certain politicians, but in the thinking and political discussion of the people voting for them as well.

As far as the politicians, CEOs, and other figures in power dismissing information as "fake news" when it was harmful to their interests, this kind of cynical usage of the phrase was only possible because it also had an entirely different meaning. Trump may have been quick to reject unfavourable coverage as "fake news", but after he was elected, there was a panic amongst some of those who had opposed his rise to power that certain types of hoaxes and other deliberate forms of disinformation, published online to look as much as possible like actual news websites, might have been a big part of the reason that Donald Trump was elected at all. Google Trends, the data analysis tool that shows how many people are searching for a given term at any particular time, indicates a huge spike in searches for the phrase "fake news" in the weeks *after* Donald Trump won the 2016 election. It was at *this* moment that the phrase "fake news" really *arrived* in the English language. Just at a time when people were already learning that inconvenient facts could be simply denied, the phrase "fake news" was, in at least two different senses, part of the way the world made sense of this somewhat shocking outcome *after the fact*. But here too, just as with the dismissive usage favoured by Trump, there was misinformation in how this diagnosis was formulated. As we will see in the first chapter of this book, there were numerous, longstanding political and cultural issues, studied by political scientists for decades, that contributed to Trump's victory, and those of other politicians using a similar toolkit. The amplified panic around a malevolent new online phenomenon called "fake news" having largely caused Trump to be elected was simplistic and misleading, in the way that technologies are often blamed for complex political problems. Even worse, normalising this phrase into the language at that moment actually made it easier for political leaders to carry on dismissing inconvenient truths as "fake news", and thereby implying that all journalists were potentially unreliable and deceitful.

Meanwhile, journalism itself was facing its own crisis, and some journalists had become lazy, cynical, out of touch or just plain overworked, so professional journalism wasn't necessarily very reliable either. Even if "fake" wasn't the right term, there was no shortage of bad journalism, which made Trump and others' cynical dismissal of their work easier. By now, with the phrase "fake news" well and truly incorporated into common parlance, even the very best journalism could be labelled as "fake" by politicians who did not want to be held account by it, all because of a simplistic, lazy analysis of how Trump and similar politicians had supposedly been elected because of technology and genuinely "fake" news articles — an analysis that these politicians themselves had appropriated to their advantage in order to attack real journalism. Quickly, the picture gets very complicated, and all because several different phenomena share one simple two-word phrase. The reality is that misinformation and disinformation are everywhere, and the whole idea of "fake news" suggests that even the way we talk about misinformation and disinformation is itself misinformed. Yes, *fake news" is fake news*.

The world should have swiftly moved on from the idea of "fake news", but the term proved remarkably persistent, perhaps because there was no easy way of referring to the prevalence of misinformation and disinformation that had become so conspicuous at that moment. The first step to moving on is finding something better, and so far as the analysis of misinformation and disinformation is concerned, that is the goal of this book. And once we have let go of the unhelpful phrase "fake news", save as a piece of language that deserves a degree of analysis in terms of how and when it is used, far more interesting questions and problems arise.

Some crises produce new understanding. After COVID-19 arrived, the world came to learn at least a little bit more about what a virus actually is and how it attacks the body. But there is another crisis of information that by its very nature prevents us from understanding it, and which has served to obscure and enable the insistent forces that have remade the world around ruthless free markets and also driven us towards fascist presidents, rising seas, raging wildfires and our unpreparedness for the pandemic itself.

This misinformation and disinformation was not simply the fact of people believing inaccurate information they read on Facebook or being misled by some devious Russian government operatives, much as these were a part of the picture. Instead, what we see is a much more complicated and interesting arrangement of deeply held, culturally engrained forms of misinformation that allowed this tension to carry on building until these dramatic results suddenly arrived in quick succession. There is no possibility of understanding "fake news" unless we make sense of this broader crisis.

The book you hold in your hand is about the feedback loop of misinformation and disinformation in the systems that produced that crisis, and how those systems covered their tracks wherever possible. It is my account of what I (and many other researchers whose work has informed this enquiry, to whom I am indebted) have discovered while investigating how we came to live in a world in which "fake news", along with many other distortions to our informational landscape, developed and persist. Overall, it is not primarily a book about journalism, so much as about the cultural and economic context in which the many informational problems called "fake news" take place. The first chapter traces the development of the society that gave us Brexit, Donald Trump, global warming and other related crises. Chapter Two explores how capitalism and the market-driven society that it has created are both dependent on and productive of widespread misinformation and disinformation. Chapter Three examines how a specific form of misinformation — conspiracy theories — arises in relation to power, and Chapter Four examines the phenomenon of so-called "liberalism" as a pervasive form of misinformation. Chapter Five turns to journalism, and Chapter Six closes with an examination of technology platforms both as enablers of misinformation and disinformation, and as manifestations of the market-driven society in themselves. Altogether, it is my hope that these chapters not only provide a fresh mapping of culture and politics onto misinformation and disinformation, but that they will also provide an entertaining and informative read.

Marcus Gilroy-Ware
July 9th, 2020

Chapter One
A Short History of Fake Democracy in Three Parts

Completed in 1926, the St Francis Dam was built to store water for the city of Los Angeles. It was designed by Irish engineer William Mulholland, after whom the famous California highway Mulholland Drive, and well-known David Lynch mystery film, are named. It was part of an ambitious, centralised, publicly funded water system that allowed the city of Los Angeles to grow to the sprawling metropolis that it became. As time wore on however, cracks and leaks had appeared in this particular dam. These flaws were reported by engineers, and Mulholland himself even inspected the dam personally, insisting that the cracks and leakage were not out of the ordinary. But they were, and just before midnight on 12 March 1928, only a day after Mulholland's visit to the dam, it collapsed, releasing twelve billion gallons of water into the canyon below and the towns beyond it, and killing more than four hundred people.

The lesson from this tragic episode is not simply that dams fail, or that human dominion over nature is never entirely secure, so much as in Mulholland's combination of arrogance and reckless naivety in relation to the flaws in the structures whose construction he had overseen. Had Mulholland had the sense and humility to acknowledge those flaws in his construction; had he been open to repairing the dam; had he considered that what was a mere engineering question for him might affect other people's lives in ways it did not affect his, the disaster could possibly have been averted, and lives would have been saved even if the dam had still given way. The lessons of the story of the St Francis Dam are that the longer you ignore the cracks in any unstable system, the weaker that system might become to withstand the pressure it is required to handle, and that the more blind you are to the potential harms that may befall others who depend on that system, the greater and more tragic the price society will likely pay when it all collapses in the end.

These principles don't apply solely to shoddy civil engineering projects. In the years immediately before the COVID-19 pandemic, from around 2015–2016 onwards, the political life of a number of countries habituated to relative stability began to get a lot more volatile. Political outcomes considered to be a virtual impossibility only a few years earlier started to happen. Besides Greece's stand-off with the European Union that nearly saw it leave the Eurozone, these included Britain's vote to leave the European Union, Donald Trump's 2016 victory, Marine Le Pen's progression to the second round of the French presidential election in 2017, Matteo Salvini's success with the once-fringe, far-right party Lega in Italy in 2018, which is consistently commanding the support of between a quarter and a third of voters at the time of writing, and Jair Bolsonaro's victory in Brazil the same year. Alongside these higher-profile shocks, a number of related movements were building in other, lower profile settings. The conservative anti-Semitic party Fidesz came to completely dominate Hungarian politics under the leadership of Viktor Orbán, while far-right or right populist parties sustained double-digit polling in Germany, the Netherlands, the Flanders region of Belgium, Poland, Finland, Austria, Estonia and several other countries.

When the COVID-19 pandemic first hit in early 2020, the most urgent conversations seemed momentarily to turn away from understanding the overall significance of these angry, nationalist elements of the political landscape to focus on the realities of mitigating a global health crisis. There was even speculation that the pandemic had halted or limited these political movements, but they also adapted and responded to the pandemic. The "lockdown" and "social distancing" measures introduced to fight the pandemic, along with the public health officials urging them, became proxies for the institutions of democracy as a whole — these movements' regular targets. While the number of new cases was still growing by tens of thousands *per day*, US flag-waving Trump supporters protested against the restrictions on movement and suspension of most businesses, demanding that the economy be reopened, and frequently referring to outlandish conspiracy theories about vaccination, 5G, or the Federal Emergency Management Agency (FEMA). Even wearing a face mask became a politically charged symbol — were you oppressed by the state, or simply protecting those around you? In the US state of Michigan, armed protesters even entered the State Senate building, and tried to force entry to the floor of the senate chamber, but were prevented. Donald Trump gave these protests his support, saying on Twitter that "these are very good people, but they are angry. They want their lives back again, safely!" Similar protests, virtually always from the extreme right of the political spectrum, occurred in Brazil, where President Bolsonaro, who later contracted the virus, also joined in, and in Germany — again with support from far-right parties (Hume, 2020).

There are a number of pitfalls to be avoided when talking about this wave of political movements, however. It would be a mistake for instance, to believe that this crisis only *began* around 2015. Nationalism, fascism and reactionary politics are old, and had long existed in the political lives of those countries in some measure — particularly for those who were on the receiving end of their Islamophobia, white supremacy, anti-Semitism, or forced displacement and migration. The headlines may have suggested their "shock" arrival, but just like the dam breaking in the story above, it is more accurate to think of it in terms of their sudden disinhibition. As we will see in this chapter, rather than their being some sort of random, unforeseeable crisis, these movements were arguably the result of flaws that were *inherent* to the combination of politics, culture and economics in the societies where they appeared.

It would also be a mistake to imply that there are not important contextual differences between the various places these problems appeared, that all authoritarian populism (for example, the Duterte regime in the Philippines or Erdoğan in Turkey) can be attributed to the same political or economic processes, or that there were not other important political struggles happening concurrently in the world — for example, in Venezuela, Syria, Palestine, Kashmir, Hong Kong, Xinjiang or the Democratic Republic of Congo.

At the same time however, when we take into account the concurrent timing, similar vocabulary and common xenophobic, anti-democratic impulses of these movements, we see clues that these events do comprise a distinct moment that is the outcome of historically specific processes and requires its own analysis. What I hope to offer here is not only an accessible analysis of that moment and how it came about, but also to trace how the same political economic features that made this wave of reactionary politics inevitable also led to the deteriorating environmental crisis, left us disastrously unprepared for the COVID-19 pandemic, and produced the "fake news" crisis itself.

Identifying the development of anything that feels like a singular moment in history is far from straightforward. History is not a neat line like an urban train map, with stops evenly distributed along it, so much as a messy knot that gets incrementally more tangled. One of the most difficult challenges in recounting history is that there is no beginning — you can always go back further to explain whatever starting point you might have identified for a story like the one this chapter will tell.

To explain the crises above, one could go back as far as the dawn of capitalism, during the reign of Elizabeth I of England, to find relevant insight as to how we arrived at the moment of political rupture that I have described. Indeed, the German sociologist Max Weber famously argued that the "spirit of capitalism" had partly developed from the work ethic of the Protestant movement that was sweeping Europe around that time, which not only permitted but encouraged religious devotion through hard work in pursuit of economic gain outside of any explicit religious context. And as historian Peter Linebaugh points out, the sixteenth century was "the beginning of modern capitalism" and also the moment at which privatisation began (2008: 47). As we will see, privatisation — the transfer of public property, institutions and processes into private control and ownership — is indeed a key part of the story of how the world arrived at the moment outlined above.

But in the context of telling this particular story, it would be absurd to try to cover multiple centuries of history in sufficient enough detail to be useful, especially given the limitations on space inherent in such an ambitious task. Even with a more realistic timeframe however, there is no obvious point at which to start. While some people who have attempted to recount aspects of this story choose the 1970s as a starting point, such as the economist David Harvey or the filmmaker Adam Curtis, others — for example, the economist Colin Leys, the political scientist Wendy Brown, the historian James Gleick or the economist Yanis Varoufakis — begin in the late 1940s, just after the end of World War II in Europe.

This post-war moment turns out to be the best place to start a story about democratic decline, because although the "democracy" that is analysed in this story may never have been fully intact or functional, the period immediately after World War II entailed a level of urgency in the Euro-Atlantic world's democratic *aspirations*, at least for its own people. The story that must be told is not only of the degradation of democracy itself, but the loss of this aspiration, to the point that some people became so disenchanted with it as to turn against democracy itself.

The story will be recounted in three parts. The first begins at this moment of recovery after World War II and ends at the dusk of post-war social democracy in the 1970s, where we move to the second part, the dawn of what Colin Leys (2003) calls "market-driven politics". This period of ruthless *hollowing out* of socially oriented post-war democracy culminates around 2000 not only with market-driven politics but an entirely market-driven *society*. We then move to the third "act" in this tragic play — a period of *unmasking,* characterised by steady decline towards the moment of crisis that I have outlined above.

"Market-driven society" is a concept that will be extremely important in this book. Scholars often use the word "neoliberalism" to denote a dominant system of market-based valuation, originated in free-market economics and later incorporated into government policy, consumerism, and culture itself. But it is easy to conflate neoliberalism as an active process with its result. The "market-driven society" is what neoliberalism brings about. It is the captive status of an entire society — from government to popular culture, to health, to creativity, to love, to our collective political imagination, to the future itself — within a paradigm in which free trade, the pursuit of profit and the private accumulation of wealth have been made into the supreme and dominant principles of that society, far beyond the capitalisms of old. As the Italian philosopher Bifo Berardi put it, "the economy has taken the place of the universal grammar traversing the different levels of human activity" (Berardi, 2018: 32). The idea of a market-driven society is as much a social and cultural phenomenon as it is political or economic, however. It is also flexible over time and space, and I use the term "market-driven society" not as a fixed or immutable structure any more than the idea of a society itself is fixed.

Part I: The Post-War Consensus

In the immediate aftermath of World War II, the countries of Western Europe began to take steps to help their populations recover and avoid future conflict on European soil. This recovery was aided by the United States, which loaned large amounts of money and propped up the value of European currencies by guaranteeing their exchangeability with the US dollar at a fixed rate under a system known as Bretton Woods.

In Britain, as in France and other countries, many soldiers had returned from the battlefield to a life very different to the one they had left behind: poverty, injury and rationing of basic supplies such as sugar, clothes and petrol. Thousands more did not even return, leaving behind families who faced uncertain, bleak futures.

It is important to remember how this recovery was implemented, especially when you hear people claim that the free market can take care of everything. In 1942, despite it being far from clear that Britain and its allies would be able to overcome the Nazis and their allies, Conservative Prime Minister Winston Churchill had asked Liberal economist William Beveridge to write a report into how Britain could rebuild itself and look after its population after the war. The result was a brave and ambitious plan: a system of social insurance that would look after everybody, "from cradle to grave", regardless of their wealth or poverty. In a somewhat dramatic plot-twist, Churchill, who had hero-like status after the seemingly victorious outcome of the war, lost the 1945 general election to the self-proclaimed "socialist" Labour Party in a shock landslide defeat, and the quiet but determined Labour leader Clement Attlee became Prime Minister. As journalist Derek Brown (2001) describes it:

> Though Churchill had presided over the planning for radical social reform, though he was a genuine hero of the masses — and though, ironically enough, the Tory manifesto pledges were not all that different from Labour's — the people did not trust him to deliver the brave new world of Beveridge.

The years following this election saw the creation of some of the most well-known and important parts of the British welfare state — institutions that were subsequently imitated in numerous other countries. The National Health Service Act was passed into law in 1946 and the system established in 1948, a nationalised railway company, British Railways, was formed the same year, the legal aid system was established in 1949 and a number of other public services followed. France, under Charles de Gaulle, did similarly.

The reason these establishments and reorganisations of the state remain so important is because they comprise a moment when, in response to great crisis, the collective public good was put ahead of commercial considerations or basic conservatism. It was both necessity and ideology that, in this state of post-war crisis, there was something more important than money or convention for politics to prioritise: the people themselves. In Britain, the Labour Party's nationalisations of the coal industry, the Bank of England, telecommunications, electricity, gas, oil and steel ran counter to Conservative policy, but in the post-war environment they were a lot less radical than they perhaps seem in hindsight. At least as far as the new NHS was concerned however, all the major parties were in agreement. The vision of a state that took responsibility for the health and wellbeing of its citizens, over and above the commercial potential in curing people or selling medicine, or the strict class divide — something that sounds radical in 2019, especially in the United States — was a near consensus in Britain after the war, sometimes referred to as the *post-war consensus*. In terms of understanding what happened to democracy in the decades that followed this period, we need to recognise that in response to crisis there was at the very least a genuine aspiration to build a state that put its people first. As much as the fate of these institutions themselves, it is also the deterioration of this ideal that we must trace over the time since then.

The main opposition to the National Health Service came from the doctors that would subsequently become the face of that service, who were concerned about how the new system would affect their earnings. A compromise was reached that saw doctors employed as relatively autonomous workers, almost like freelancers, instead of as direct government employees. Doctors worried that this experiment would affect their bottom lines were not the only opponents of this new system, however. In April 1947, just as the plans for the National Health Service and the nationalisations of the post war British state were being negotiated with doctors and a record number of babies were being born in the UK — the first of two major baby "booms" — an important series of meetings was taking place in a ski resort town in Switzerland called Mont Pèlerin. Austrian-British economist Friedrich von Hayek, who was based in London at the time, where he taught at the LSE, had organised a conference of like minds to plot the economy that they wanted to bring about after the war, and respond to the policy of nationalisations and state-funded services that were being created by the Attlee Labour government. What they created there was an economic policy organisation — essentially an early think tank — that saw the world in terms of private life, property and free markets. Named after this initial meeting, it became known as the Mont Pèlerin Society.

Friedrich Hayek, Milton Friedman — another economist who was attending from the US — and the other economists who would become the Mont Pèlerin Society itself did not necessarily have a great deal of power in 1947, and their economic ideas had been discredited and were fairly obscure. But these ideas would eventually come to dominate the Euro-Atlantic world. Indeed, one of the people to be influenced by Hayek's work as an undergraduate at Somerville College at the University of Oxford, was a chemistry student with a keen interest in politics called Margaret Roberts. She would later change her name to Margaret Thatcher.

Hayek and the Mont Pèlerin Society's primary concern was trying to prevent totalitarianism, which they equated with the overreach of government. They were horrified at the wave of nationalisations and state-building of the Attlee government, and saw that trajectory as a path to more of exactly the forms of totalitarianism that the world had seen during World War II, and which were still alive in the Soviet Union. Consequently, the bulwark they envisaged against any return of totalitarianism was a system that limited state provision and encouraged unhindered "free" trading between private individuals and companies as the best means to ensure peace and co-operation. Crucial to this theory were the suppositions that private individuals and organisations, and the system of competition between them, could keep each other's power in check, and that government influence and intervention were unnatural distortions in this process. In the classic sense of the word, "liberals" were people who had long believed that personal liberties such as freedom of expression should be unimpeded by any kind of state control. What this "neo-liberalism" did was to foreground private trade and competition amongst these freedoms, as a means to prevent totalitarianism. As Wendy Brown puts it, "Forged in the crucible of European fascism, neoliberalism aimed at permanent inoculation of market liberal orders against the regrowth of fascistic sentiments and totalitarian powers" (2019: 9). Crucially, as Brown points out, their original imagination of this "neoliberal" system was one that assumed that family structures and basic morality could be relied upon to assist with issues such as caring for the sick and preventing anti-social or unconscionable outcomes. They also assumed that participants in this "free market" based society would act rationally and morally. This assumption would later prove to be disastrous.

The development of this trade-based system, and its eventual domination not only of the world's economies but of the cultures of the Euro-Atlantic world, is in many ways a foundation for this story. But there should be no doubt that this system went further than its creators intended in this post-war moment, and a crucial part of the story to come is about how this already discredited ideology dangerously intensified.

By 1951, the Cold War was well and truly underway, and the US had significantly increased its testing of an alarming variety of nuclear weapons — in an arms race with the Soviet Union. Across the Atlantic, in Europe, Britain's population had become slightly more jaded in their democratic aspirations already, and despite Prime Minister Clement Attlee's Labour Party winning the popular vote and achieving their highest number of votes to date, they were unexpectedly defeated by the Conservatives — an indication of the shortcomings of the first-past-the-post voting system. Winston Churchill was elected Prime Minister again in October of that year.

Other aspects of the world that would become foundations for the instability of 2015 and beyond were beginning to form. The gathering in Mont Pèlerin in 1947 wasn't the only attempt to bring people together with the aim of shaping the world that was emerging after the war. In 1954, the year the iconic Fender Stratocaster guitar was first launched, a well-connected Polish operative and Freemason called Josef Retinger was worried about the possibility of future wars on the same scale as World War II. He and a number of other figures, including the Prince of the Netherlands, used their connections to bring together a group of powerful individuals to try to foster greater international understanding, particularly between the United States and Europe. Two people from each country, one conservative and one liberal (in the classic sense) were invited to the Bilderberg Hotel in the last days of May 1954, and the Bilderberg Meetings were born (Wilford, 2003). Over time, the annual meeting would evolve into a gathering of senior politicians and diplomats, academics, lobbyists and the CEOs of various corporations, including arms makers and major banks. The secretive nature of the meetings and the fact that they involved so many powerful people meant that they eventually became a favourite subject of conspiracy theorists — analysed further in Chapter Three — including the infamous US conspiracist Alex Jones, who would not be born for nearly twenty years.

Another influential group was also about to be set up. In 1955, former Royal Air Force pilot and commercial chicken farmer Antony Fisher founded the Institute of Economic Affairs with economist Ralph Harris, to promote similar free-market ideas as those favoured by the Mont Pèlerin Society. But the connection to the founder of the Mont Pèlerin group, Friedrich Hayek, was even closer than this. Fisher was a fan of Hayek's, and had read an abridged version of his book *The Road to Serfdom* in the magazine *Reader's Digest*. After Fisher tracked Hayek down in London — at the LSE, where he was working — and told him of his intention to go into politics, Hayek convinced Fisher to found what we would now call a think tank instead, saying "forget politics. Politicians just follow prevailing opinions. If you want to change events, you must change ideas" (Fischer, 2018). This approach would ultimately be extremely successful. Decades later, the Institute of Economic Affairs' (IEA) brand of free-market fundamentalism would be an important force behind the United Kingdom's vote to leave the European Union.

There is an irony in this connection, however. Just two years after the IEA was founded, in March 1957, European powers felt their influence waning in the post-war era. Six of them — France, Germany, the Netherlands, Belgium, Luxembourg, and Italy — signed the Treaty of Rome, creating the European Economic Community, which would later become the European Union. The new treaty provided for "freedom of movement" for the first time, the ability to move freely between the territories of signatory countries that Brexit campaigners would later fight desperately to get rid of. The great irony is that almost twenty years before, in 1939, Friedrich Hayek had called for freedom of movement, when he wrote that:

> It is rightly regarded as one of the great advantages of interstate federation that it would do away with the impediments as to the movement of men, goods, and capital between the states and that it would render possible the creation of common rules of law, a uniform monetary system, and common control of communications.

In other words, the IEA would later fight for Britain to withdraw from a federation whose core principles were based almost word-for-word on the writings of the free-market economist who had been so influential on the IEA's founder. This discrepancy should be an early clue in our story that just as fundamentalist interpretation of religion is rarely based on an accurate or nuanced understanding of those fundamentals, the already misguided free-market ideals of the Mont Pèlerin group would be significantly intensified and distorted in the years to come.

Before our story advances into the 1960s, it is important to say something about the role of culture in the reconstruction that was taking place. A lot of popular culture that we still celebrate and equate with a certain Western cultural dominance over the world, such as rock and roll, can be traced to the years between the end of World War II and the beginning of the twenty-first century — sometimes called the "late modern" period.

It is crucial to remember that people tend to see themselves and their political choices in the context of the society they inhabit. As we'll explore further in Chapter Two, politics is not just about making the most logical argument. It also needs to be appealing to the imagination and identity of the people it concerns, and is often a case of trying to convince people "who we are" in terms of shared identity and values. The Enlightenment of the eighteenth century, complete with its coffeehouses, rising literacy and new conceptions of citizenship, is often evoked as a moment of great scientific and cultural "progress". There is a case to be made that in the context of reconstruction after World War II, when Euro-Atlantic societies needed especially strong reinforcement of who they were, the increased freedoms and rapid cultural change that characterised this late modern period represented a similarly important cultural threshold.

The culture industries were a hugely important part of this project. In fact for the social theorists Theodor Adorno and Max Horkheimer, writing in the 1940s, there was already something about the way that culture had been turned into an industry of mass production that was itself propaganda for, and a reinforcement of, a certain technologically sanctioned, top-down system of capitalism (1989 [1947]). In the years prior to World War II it had been fascist movements that pioneered the use of conspicuously modern media, technology and even fashion to appeal to would-be adherents, and equate political allegiance with way-of-life (Gilroy, 2000). After the war, however, the ascendant liberal capitalist world needed to do the same. Particularly while forms of government that called themselves communist still had a substantial presence in the world, capitalism had to *sell itself*; to seduce its people into believing that it was best. This meant equating itself with the idea of meeting people's needs and elevating them to a standard of "modern" consumerist living that was fundamentally exciting.

Against the backdrop of this more general process, the 1960s were not just a series of shiny lights, futuristic cars and other subtly pro-capitalist propaganda. The decade is also rightly thought of as a moment of enormous cultural and political transition, and there is no denying that a lot changed in this period, not least in the sense that the cultural conservatism of the earlier twentieth century began to be challenged more explicitly.

But the idea of "the 1960s" as a decade when everything changed is something of a construction, and should be treated cautiously. As the philosopher and cultural critic Fredric Jameson has argued, it is extremely difficult to "periodise" the 1960s, and certainly, the changes that the decade stands for do not fit neatly within those ten years — it is not as though everything suddenly began to change on

January 1st, 1960, and finished on December 31st 1969. As we will see, the 1960s were a period during which a number of important political changes did begin, but overlooked in this counterculture-versus-conservatism narrative is the fact that between these antagonistic extremes fighting it out, post-war capitalism was building an eight-lane highway towards its own cultural dominance and seeming inevitability in ways that would be extremely important in the decades to follow.

As Jameson explores, another essential aspect of this period 1960s is that many of the social and political freedoms won at that time had their origins in the developing world, as former colonies in the British and French empires were gradually gaining their independence. This decolonisation, Jameson argues, was what provided a foundation for the process of allowing "those inner colonized of the first world – 'minorities,' marginals, and women", to begin securing greater freedoms at home (ibid.: 180). Particularly in the United States, it marked "a return to a more internal politics" as far as mainstream political conversations, but paradoxically, the nominal end of European colonialism also enabled a wave of US neocolonialism as the country sought to limit communism and secure petroleum and minerals to fuel the exciting capitalist lifestyle that had become so important.

In Britain, a new band called the Beatles had their first hit, "Love Me Do", in October 1962, just two weeks before the Cuban missile crisis. In autumn 1963 the band began appearing in the US press for the first time, as part of the "British Invasion". That November, President John F. Kennedy was shockingly and gruesomely assassinated in Texas, and Vice President Lyndon B. Johnson took over. Political assassinations are always shocking, but Kennedy was extremely popular as a president. US pollster Gallup reports that his average 70% approval rating over his time as president is the highest of any president since they began measuring approval ratings (Dugan and Newport, 2013) and his untimely death had a major political and cultural impact. It was not just the death of a president, but also the symbolic death of an emergent form of public-spirited sentiment in US politics. As Fredric Jameson puts it,

> "The assassination of President Kennedy played a significant role in delegitimizing the state itself and in discrediting the parliamentary process, seeming to mark the decisive end of the well-known passing of the torch to a younger generation of leadership, as well as the dramatic defeat of some new spirit of public or civic idealism." (1984: 182-183)

Given the overall prevailing wind of anti-state and anti-democratic politics that would come later, this is a significant feature of the Kennedy assassination, even if in reality he was relatively conservative, and had proven extremely reckless during the Cuban missile crisis.

As well as being a political shock, Kennedy's assassination also represented an attack on the intersection of loosening social attitudes and sheer glamour that the Kennedys' inhabitation of the White House had symbolised, and was a moment of major cultural trauma. The incident led to a wave of conspiracy theories about who "really" shot Kennedy, and what their motives might have been — a sign that people have never easily trusted the official line given about shocking events.

On the economic front, Yanis Varoufakis details in his account of the history of the European Union that as early as 1964, France was in secret discussions with Germany about the idea of a shared European currency as they sought to consolidate European power, mostly against the US (2016). At this point in history, most people still did not have bank accounts and were paid weekly in cash, and the first ever credit card had been launched by the Bank of America only a few years earlier.

By the mid-1960s, according to the US think tank the Economic Policy Institute, the ratio of CEO pay to the salary of the average worker in the US was approximately 20 to 1 (Mishel and Wolfe, 2018). At the same moment, the average concentration of carbon dioxide exceeded 320 parts per million for the first time in the history of the planet (NASA, 2011). In the coming pages, we will return periodically to both these figures as a means to understand how the economy and the environment change dramatically over the decades.

1968 is an important year in our story. It is primarily known for student protests, particularly in Paris and across the United States, but a number of other things were happening at the same moment that offer an interesting snapshot of how this post-war modernity was maturing.

The war in Vietnam, a brutal conflict that involved a lot of US deaths and casualties, featured prominently in the nightly news, unlike the thousands of Vietnamese civilians who were killed or maimed in the conflict. Meanwhile, in Britain, the Commonwealth Immigrants Act 1968 was passed, which prevented Commonwealth citizens from claiming the right to live or work in the country unless they had at least one parent or grandparent born there. Cruel as it was, it was still not enough for Conservative MP and fascist sympathiser Enoch Powell, who made his infamous "Rivers of Blood" speech in Birmingham only a few weeks later, warning that if immigration into Britain continued, "the black man will have the whip hand over the white man". In the US, Martin Luther King, who had increasingly focused his attentions on the interests of the poor, regardless of their position in America's ethnic hierarchy, was assassinated in Memphis, Tennessee. Just two weeks before he died, he had told striking sanitation workers in Memphis that "If America does not use her vast resources of wealth to end poverty and make it possible for all of God's children to have the basic necessities of life, she too will go to hell."

Later that year, the Standard & Poor's 500, an index of the stock market performance, would climb above 100 for the first time ever, and in a major development for civil aviation, the world's then largest passenger jet, the Boeing 747, was first produced. Commercial aviation had already been revolutionised by the Boeing 707 and DC-10, but the 747's distinctive shape and size meant economies of scale that would help to normalise long-haul air travel and international commerce for millions of people, and made it a recognisable icon of cultural modernity in the way that earlier commercial aircraft were not. The following year, supersonic passenger jet Concorde would also complete its first test flight in France.

Just as more people than ever were imagining what part of the Earth they might want to visit, one of the most significant cultural events of the 1960s took place: the Moon landing in July 1969 — also an increasingly common subject of conspiracy theories in the decades that would follow. Beyond the sheer engineering feat, the US government, which was already locked in a space race with Russia which had become a cultural proxy for the Cold War, knew the symbolic value both domestically and internationally of getting to the Moon first. Technological progress large and small was an important symbol of the broader cultural modernity that was being assembled. The same year as the Moon landing, the first ever message was sent over the ARPANET, the precursor of the internet, and only two months later in the UK, the BBC and ITV channels switched to full-colour broadcasting.

Part II: Greed is Good

The second part of this story — the years between approximately 1970 and the year 2000 — can and must be seen as a crucial period of transition between the ascendant cultural modernity of the post-war years described earlier, and the ultimate dominance of the market-driven society. What we see throughout this period is a steady thinning of post-war social democratic aspiration and cultural innovation into a ruthless, money-driven, technology-assisted world of dog-eat-dog.

Economically, things started to get bumpy in the early 1970s. With what would quickly come to be known as the "Nixon Shock", US President Richard Nixon issued an executive order in 1971 that effectively ended Western Europe's involvement in Bretton Woods, the post-war system which had kept the exchange rates of the world's major currencies fixed to the US dollar and ultimately to the value of gold. Its end triggered a phase of economic and political instability in which economies that had become accustomed to stability measures after World War II were now standing on their own two feet.

As Yanis Varoufakis has pointed out, the Bretton Woods system ended in part because of the tension that had been growing between politicians who preferred fixed exchange rates for their currencies, and bankers who wanted to be able to trade and speculate on the values of currencies. This antagonism between private sector interests and the public's interests is an old one, as old as democratic government itself, but its intensity grew steadily in the second half of the twentieth century. In fact, it is hard to overstate just how much the Euro-Atlantic world would be reconfigured around this tension in the years following this period of instability, and the contradiction of a society that is both genuinely democratic and faithful to the substantive ethos of capitalism *is* the primary source of tension of this post-war period. The direction of travel was increasingly in the interests of private capital.

As 1973 got underway, the US conservative think tank the Heritage Foundation was founded to drive conservative policies in the United States. Among its founders were Paul Weyrich, a religious conservative who coined the phrase "moral majority" and would go on to set up another organisation by that name, Joseph Coors, an avowed segregationist who was the president of Coors Brewing Company and grandson of its founder, and Edwin Feulner, a devotee of Friedrich Hayek who would later write a foreword for the new *Reader's Digest* abridged version of Hayek's *Road to Serfdom*. The Heritage Foundation would go on to actively support every Republican president, including Donald Trump.

In Italy that April, thirty-seven-year-old Italian property developer Silvio Berlusconi, who would go on to be a populist prime minister and media magnate, was entering the media world for the first time with a fledgling cable TV company called TeleMilano, funded by the profits of a construction project near Milan. At the time, the Italian state had a monopoly on broadcasting, which was only relaxed with a constitutional decree the following year, but this did not stop Berlusconi, who had the backing of a powerful Masonic group called Propaganda Due, or P2, from pressing ahead. Not only the constitutional decree, but the move into television itself were major developments, as the connection between political control and private TV broadcasting started to become more important in the consolidation of power.

In 1976, the UK government, despite being run by Labour, accepted an IMF loan on conditions that saw them forced to replace Keynesianism — which put democracy and employment ahead of the economy — with monetarism, which made the economy central to democracy. The cracks in the dam grew a little bigger.

Meanwhile, biologist Richard Dawkins published *The Selfish Gene*, which not only gave the world the idea of the "meme" for the first time, but was later used by followers of Margaret Thatcher to promote the idea that humans were naturally selfish, and that economic systems should embrace these qualities. The phrase "greed is good", inspired by the 1987 film *Wall Street* about stock market traders, is a later expression of the same ethos. This crossover should be a reminder, lest we need one, that the economic and political changes of this period were accompanied by quite dramatic cultural changes as people were increasingly encouraged to embrace the new forms of consumerism that global supply chains and deregulated markets put in place.

By 1978, the ratio of CEO pay to the salary of the average worker in the US had grown to approximately 30 to 1. The concentration of carbon dioxide in the atmosphere was now 332 parts per million. In China, Deng Xiaoping was opening up the Chinese economy to liberalisation after having taken over from Chairman Mao, and in Britain the following year, Margaret Thatcher was elected Prime Minister, inspired by the ideas of Friedrich Hayek. Other familiar elements were starting to develop in Britain too. Prefiguring Brexit, the far-right had already started pushing for Britain to leave the European single market. A 1979 National Front leaflet included the following top-line policies:

- Stop all immigration and start phased repatriation
- Get Britain out of the Common Market
- Restore our links with the White Commonwealth
- Root out corruption. Restore honest government
- Encourage free enterprise that serves that national interest
- Combat unemployment by buying British

- Create genuine incentives to work hard and invest in our country
- Put National Defence before Foreign Aid

Here we see a similarity over time and space between the far-right in Britain and the US. In hindsight, these policies read like a sort of incoherent, partially realised roadmap for what was to come. All of these positions later became either mainstream Conservative or Republican policies, or the increasingly amplified talking points of much more recent far-right elements such as Britain First, UKIP, or the Trump campaign and subsequent administration. Particularly striking in a European context is the mention of Britain leaving what was then called the "Common Market", all those years ago. The far-right in the UK wanted to leave the EU before it was even the EU! Brexit was always a far-right objective, and those who supported it when it became a mainstream issue more than three decades later were complicit with this, whether they knew it or not. But what is also interesting here is how the language of "free enterprise" appears. As we will see in the pages to come, the degree of affinity between an aggressive free-market approach and the far-right is extremely ambivalent, and varies much more with context, time and location. Sometimes they are against NAFTA or the European Union, and at other moments, as in the case of using a "points system" for immigration or casting certain "others" as "scroungers", they reveal an unmistakeably neoliberal ethos. The instability of this relationship, as we'll see, goes to the very core of the moment whose origins are explored in this chapter.

As far as our story, Thatcher courted the far-right up to a point, but was strongly pro-Europe because it represented a huge market, and owing to the influence on her thinking from the work of Friedrich Hayek, she saw a world in which markets were the basis of everything. This should be another clue about the inherent contradictions in the right's embrace of free-market capitalism.

As the 1980s began, Hayek wrote to Antony Fisher, the founder of the Institute for Economic Affairs, to congratulate him on the success he had had in setting up the institute, as well as a number of other similar organisations in other countries. Meanwhile, yet another secretive political group, The Council for National Policy, was founded in the US by Tim LaHaye, a writer of apocalyptic Christian novels who believed the Illuminati were conspiring to establish a "new world order" (Beirich & Potok, 2016), along with Paul Weyrich, who had co-founded the Heritage Foundation, and several other extreme conservatives with the aim of influencing policy. The group was so secretive that members were asked not to admit membership or name the group, but numerous winning Republican presidents and senators have addressed them, often before seeking election.

In the autumn, former actor Ronald Reagan was elected President of the United States, a role in which he would work closely with Thatcher. Reagan was a very different president to Donald Trump, but there were aspects of his having been known to the US public from the world of entertainment, and for his capacity to *perform* leadership without actually being a strong leader that made him seem like a precedent for Trump years later. He also came up with the slogan "make America great again". His ascendancy attested to the US's capacity to elect an entertainer and be enthusiastically taken in by a kind of fake spectacle that French philosopher Jean Baudrillard, who published a major work of semiotics the following year, might have called a *simulacrum* — it was somebody playing president, and using the power that came with it, but not to deal with any complicated ideas or genuinely serve the people who had elected him.

Reagan and Thatcher partnered to liberalise cross-border capital controls, which meant allowing money to be moved freely between countries by private traders. This may sound trivial, but it is one of the most significant changes to take place in this entire story, and had profound effects on the democracies of the world, as Colin Leys explains:

> The starting-point for understanding the new policy regime is the ascendancy of capital that followed — and was meant to follow — from Thatcher's and Reagan's elimination of controls on cross-border capital movements from the early 1980s onwards. This allowed the financial markets to set increasingly tight limits on the policies that national governments could adopt. (2008: 119)

In other words, allowing money to move around the world more freely would help to clip the wings of national, democratically elected governments. As above, the free movement of capital was an idea that had been suggested by Hayek in 1939. It was already a policy in the treaties of the European Economic Community when it was established in 1957, which Britain had finally joined in 1973 after its two prior attempts had been vetoed by France. However, these relaxations not only meant more global movement of capital, they also saw the beginning of offshore wealth hoarding, as people sought to evade taxes — first in Panama and then in the British Virgin Islands, the Bahamas and other places — accelerating capitalism's anti-state tendencies. Until this point, as far as the distribution of wealth goes, both Britain and the United States had been slowly becoming more economically equal since the 1920s (Dorling, 2010: 256). But in the early 1980s that tide began to turn, in no small part because of the domestic policies of the Thatcher and Reagan governments.

As the 1980s wore on, the pace of media and technology innovation began to increase. In the United States, software company Adobe Systems, which would later produce the image manipulation software Photoshop, was founded. Adobe was the first company in Silicon Valley history to become profitable in its first year, largely thanks to investment from Apple co-founder Steve Jobs. In the UK, the broadcasting environment saw two significant developments. In November 1982, a fourth channel, branded simply as "Channel 4", was launched as a non-profit public service broadcaster to bolster Britain's arts, film and independent TV production. The following year, just a few weeks after the 1983 general election — a Conservative victory — Rupert Murdoch's company News International bought a 65% stake in a company that would later become known as *Sky* and grow into a broadcasting giant. Just like Berlusconi ten years earlier, Murdoch was investing in the political power of privately owned TV networks.

In January 1984, Apple released the Macintosh, to much fanfare. In front of a live audience in a huge auditorium, Steve Jobs removed the little Mac from its carry-bag, inserted a floppy disk, and the machine played "Chariots of Fire" before beginning to speak to the crowd in a computer voice, all to fanatical applause. It is important to realise the ways that technology companies, echoing capitalism itself in prior decades, enticed people to build technology into their lives rather than simply their work. In some ways foreshadowing the adoption of media platforms like Instagram into our kitchens, bedrooms and bathrooms, Apple's real invention was not the Mac, the iPod or the iPhone — it was the idea that digital technology was a part of your life; that it was about what kind of a person you were rather than about what results you could get.

As Mark Zuckerberg and Edward Snowden were born in the mid-1980s, the Euro-Atlantic world saw more steps in the transition to a market-driven society. Prominent amongst these were the dramatic strikes in the UK's coal mining communities, as Margaret Thatcher sought to close the country's pits. Coal may be a filthy fuel that in the long run would have needed to be replaced anyway, but Thatcher was not interested in closing the pits to protect the environment. Her motivation had much more to do with who had power in the British economy — and Thatcher did not want the labour unions to have any. More and more, the political shift spreading across the Euro-Atlantic world — the one advocated for by the Mont Pèlerin group, the Institute for Economic Affairs and everyone else influenced by Hayek and Friedman's ideas — was a swing back in favour of the owners and bosses, away from that post-war consensus and its democratic ambitions. Hayek and his associates had seen the free market as a political solution — a means to keep the balance of power out of the hands of states as a way to avoid the totalitarianism they had seen during World War II. But now, those building the world around their ideas, with Thatcher and Reagan chief among them, were emphasising the project differently. Instead of it being primarily about politics or society itself, it was a moral narrative about hard work leading to upward mobility, with freedom being the freedom to buy and sell, and above all a war of the private against the public. Thatcher herself had a narrative about being the daughter of a greengrocer, and in the new world she was building with Reagan, the idea of hard work producing wealth would be sacred. Ironically, it would also be much more difficult.

Part of that was the right to own your own house. In one of Thatcher's more controversial moves, in 1980 she had introduced a scheme known as the "right to buy", which meant that tenants in local government-owned housing could effectively privatise their own house and buy it as their own property. Houses were not just homes where you could feel safe anymore — to her they were also economic assets. But privatisation was everywhere, and many of the public utilities companies set up by the Attlee government after World War II were made into private companies. For example, December 1984 saw the sale and flotation of British Telecom, which was used as propaganda for privatisation because of the number of BT employees who had bought stock.

Margaret Thatcher made a famous remark in 1987 that there was "no such thing as society", in an interview with *Woman's Own* magazine:

> I think we have gone through a period when too many children and people have been given to understand "I have a problem, it is the Government's job to cope with it!" or "I have a problem, I will go and get a grant to cope with it!" "I am homeless, the Government must house me!" and so they are casting their problems on society and who is society? There is no such thing! There are individual men and women and there are families and no government can do anything except through people and people look to themselves first. It is our duty to look after ourselves [...] and life is a reciprocal business.

This is highly instructive. Here, Thatcher frames both a reduction of what the government should offer poor people and an instruction for people to "look to themselves first" and act reciprocally (rather than generously or in solidarity) in the terms of moral duty. This is a key aspect of the de-democratisation that continued to accelerate, not only in the UK but in the US and elsewhere too. The idea that there was "no such thing" as society was precisely what allowed the society that did exist to be entirely taken over by free-market logic.

By 1989, the ratio of CEO pay to the salary of the average worker in the US had almost doubled to approximately 58 to 1. November of that year saw the fall of the Berlin Wall, a sign that the power of the Soviet Union might be starting to fray at the edges. And 1990 finally saw the end of Margaret Thatcher's reign itself, mostly over the shared European Monetary System which she had bitterly opposed, despite strong support for it from within her own party and from Labour. In her last ever Prime Minister's Questions session in parliament on 27 November, under taunting questions from Leader of the Opposition Neil Kinnock, she told the House that "under that kind of central bank there will be *no democracy*".

As Yanis Varoufakis notes, if she was really serious about democracy, this is perhaps the only thing she ever got right. Reflecting on the end of Thatcher's reign, he observes that "The notion that money can be administered apolitically, by technical means alone, is dangerous folly of the grandest magnitude." (2016) So too was Thatcher's narrow understanding of democracy however, which was expressed primarily in terms of money. Not only did she not believe in "society", but her blind obsession with a "capital-owning democracy" was not actually very democratic if you were poor. Furthermore, some moments later in the same parliamentary session, she also told the House of her enthusiasm for the United Kingdom's "first past the post" voting system, which does not offer proportional representation at all, and produces results that are greatly at odds with the country's actual preferences.

After Iraq had invaded Kuwait that same year, just a few months before Thatcher's departure, February 1991 saw start of the first Iraq War, in which George H.W. Bush — a former oil investor and lifelong Republican who had once campaigned for Eisenhower — sent US forces into the region, in what later became known as the Gulf War. As the late scholar Philip Taylor has written, the Gulf War was notable partly for the ways that the news media helped to provide propaganda in support of the military effort:

> Propaganda known to be such is useless; it is dismissible simply as "propaganda" as it is properly understood. But if it is disguised as news and information, it is more palatable to the by now traditional western notions of the public's "right to know", balanced against the essential military preoccupation with the "need to know". (1992: 25)

In November that year Bush awarded Friedrich Hayek the Presidential Medal of Freedom. Meanwhile, the far-right was gaining momentum across Europe. For example, in Belgium:

> Hostility towards [Flemish extreme right party] Vlaams Blok did not prevent it from increasing its vote share at every election since the beginning of the 1980s. Its breakthrough came with the 1991 general elections, later labelled "Black Sunday": the share of Flemish extreme-right votes more than tripled from 3 per cent (1987) to 10 per cent (1991). (Jagers and Walgrave, 2007)

The End of History

At the end of 1991, the day after Christmas Day, the Soviet Union finally fell, and the Cold War came to an end. After the Cold War, something seemed to change. A system that had been falling over itself to seduce people into believing in what it had to offer using flashy cultural novelties or stock market flotations realised it had won. It seemed to grow complacent and myopic.

In the later years of the Thatcher government, the Conservative Party had campaigned that, as far as capitalism was concerned, there was "no alternative". This slogan was copied in 1994 by the Christian Democratic Union party in Germany, which would later be led by long-time German Chancellor Angela Merkel. As a political approach it became known in German as "*alternativlos*".

At this moment, when communism seemed to have been defeated and there was said to be "no alternative" to the ostensibly liberal forms of "capitalist democracy" in Western Europe and North America, the political philosopher Francis Fukuyama famously argued that this was the "final form of human government" and represented the "end of history". The suggestion was that there no longer needed to be an argument about how human societies should be organised. This was of course wishful thinking, not least because a "capitalist democracy" would ultimately prove to be a wholly contradictory idea.

As the philosopher Nancy Fraser wrote around the same time, "we hear a great deal of ballyhoo about 'the triumph of liberal democracy' and even 'the end of history.' Yet there is still a great deal to object to in our own 'actually existing democracy'" (1990: 56). Fukuyama's claim amounted to a kind of naïve complacency and intellectual bankruptcy that would exacerbate the already-serious flaws in exactly the system of liberal capitalist democracy that had supposedly "won" the Cold War. As the writer and activist Tariq Ali later wrote:

> when the Berlin Wall came down, it was not simply the Soviet Union or the "communist idea" or the efficacy of

"socialist solutions" that collapsed. Western European social democracy, too, went down. In the face of the triumphalist capitalist storm that swept the world, it had neither the vision nor the determination to defend elements of its own past social programmes. (2015)

All the same, the "end of history" and the victory of capitalism it was said to have heralded were pervasive ideas, not confined to political conversations. Nearly twenty years later, the writer and cultural theorist Mark Fisher wrote that "Fukuyama's thesis that history has climaxed with liberal capitalism may have been widely derided, but it is accepted, even assumed, at the level of the cultural unconscious." (2009: 6) This "capitalist realism", Fisher observed, became "more like a pervasive atmosphere, conditioning not only the production of culture but also the regulation of work and education, and acting as a kind of invisible barrier constraining thought and action". This meant that the insistence on maintaining the status quo of liberal capitalist democracy did not come only from official sources and in political language, but once again, via culture. This was a direct legacy of the ways that capitalism had mainstreamed itself in the decades after the war. And it was more than just the liberal capitalist status quo that was enforced by cultural means; it was an entire architecture of disinformation and misapprehension of the world's power relations.

Ironically, this idea that the political argument was over and that no new forms of government would ever be needed is what set the stage not only for the major political reorganisations that followed, but also for the giving way of that metaphorical dam described at the beginning and end of this chapter. It not only prevented the system from being made fairer or more sustainable — it also paved the way for an increasingly aggressive neoliberalism to reconfigure everything away from democracy and towards markets and competition. As Wendy Brown has put it:

> In a century heavy with political ironies, there may have been none greater than this: at the end of the Cold War, as mainstream pundits hailed democracy's global triumph, a new form of governmental reason was being unleashed in the Euro-Atlantic world that would inaugurate democracy's conceptual unmooring and substantive disembowelment. Within thirty years, Western democracy would grow gaunt, ghostly, its future increasingly hedged and improbable. (2015: 9)

It cannot be overstated what a period of technological growth the 1990s were, especially as far as consumer and office technologies were concerned. In the years between 1990 and 2000, the average clock speed of a computer processor grew nearly twentyfold (Tuomi, 2002). Alongside gaming, one of the most important drivers of this increase was the digitisation of professional work, and the arrival of the "world wide web", which was made public by Tim Berners-Lee, a computer scientist at CERN, in August 1991. This was followed by Mosaic, the first modern web browser that could display images and was easy to install on Windows, in 1993. Microsoft licensed Mosaic's source code in 1994, the year that their co-founder and then CEO Bill Gates became the richest man in America, having already used some of Mosaic's code to create their own browser, Internet Explorer. The following year, Microsoft's new user-friendly operating system Windows 95 was released to huge fanfare, featuring the Rolling Stones' 1981 single "Start Me Up", and with New York City's Empire State Building lit up in the same colours as Microsoft's branding. Although Windows 95 was in some ways a pretty boring product in itself, here again we see "cool" cultural elements used to sell products on a massive scale. That same year, Gates crossed a new threshold and became the richest person in the world. Meanwhile, the ratio of CEO pay to the salary of the average worker in the United States had now doubled again to approximately 121 to 1, and the concentration of carbon dioxide in the Earth's atmosphere was recorded as 359ppm.

Against a never-ending tide of technological determinism — the belief that technology is a *primary* driver of societal change — it is worth remembering that technology is actually more commonly an *enabler* that facilitates pre-existing (if latent) cultural, economic and political demands. This is not a new idea. Karl Marx and Friedrich Engels famously wrote in 1848 that:

> The bourgeoisie cannot exist without constantly revolutionising the instruments of production, and thereby the relations of production, and with them the whole relations of society. [...] All that is solid melts into air, all that is holy is profaned, and man is at last compelled to face with sober senses his real conditions of life, and his relations with his kind.

In other words, capitalism requires constant change, and relentlessly attacks and reformulates our societies, our relations to one another, and the technologies we use to carry out various forms of labour. Nearly a hundred years later in 1942, the Austrian economist Joseph Schumpeter wrote approvingly of capitalism's "creative destruction" — riffing on Marx and Engels, except that he thought this constant technological revolutionisation was a *good thing*, even if it put vast numbers of people out of work.

Schumpeter envisioned this process as being slow enough that successive generations could be re-trained, so that the human cost would not be too high. But fifty years later, in an essay for the *London Review of Books* in 1994, the political scientist Edward Luttwak saw two problems that could combine to terrible effect. The first was that, as capitalism accelerated and computers became a fixture of more and more places of work, the quickening pace of technological change shortened the length of time it took to make people's skills completely redundant, to the point that the pressure on individual workers was extreme. More than the much-remarked squeeze on working-class jobs in areas of the economy such as manufacturing, Luttwak saw an accelerated "creative destruction" affecting clerical jobs in white-collar data-heavy industries such as banking that were being disrupted by capital's "Schumpeteresque" technology-assisted modernisation as they were digitised.

The second problem he noted was that the conservative politics of this era was increasingly self-contradictory — celebrating the virtues of unimpeded competition and dynamic structural change, while simultaneously mourning the decline of the family and community "values" that had been eroded by the very market forces it commended, something which he called the "Republican/Tory non-sequitur".

Luttwak warned his readers that the combination of these two issues — the incoherence of standard conservatism that was still praising the market, and the squeeze on middle-class Americans — risked the development of a "product-improved Fascist party, dedicated to the enhancement of the personal economic security of the broad masses of (mainly) white-collar working people". The stage was already being set.

In 1996, Bill Clinton was elected to a second term in the White House, and across the pond the following year Tony Blair became Prime Minister in a landslide victory that humiliated many of the most prominent faces of the Conservative "nasty" Party of the 1980s such as Michael

Portillo. In many ways, however, this would prove a hollow victory, since it came as a consequence of Labour's adoption of the very privatisation-friendly pro-market policies that the Conservative government had spent the prior eighteen years constructing. When Margaret Thatcher was asked at a party in 2002 what her greatest achievement had been, she is said to have replied, "Tony Blair and New Labour" (Burns, 2008). It is not hard to see why. As Colin Leys puts it, "They announced their acceptance of virtually the entire legacy of the Thatcher and Major years — 'pro-business' trade union and employment law, privatisation, a 'marketised' public sector, a no longer universal welfare system, privatised housing, the neutering of local government" (2003: 42–43).

Blair, like Clinton, was a so-called "centrist" in that he contrasted himself with his more overtly right-wing predecessors by using comparatively liberal language and ideas like the Freedom of Information Act 2000 (which he later expressed regret for having introduced), but continued to pursue Thatcher/Reagan-style policies like those of the 1980s on the assumption that as long as prosperity continued, nobody would notice.

Though the rot and resentment alluded to by Luttwak and others had already begun to set in, the gleaming cultural veneer of new technology, pop music, and celebrity only seemed shinier than ever. The Spice Girls were promoting "girl power" dressed in tight clothes and high heels, and Tony Blair and Bill Clinton, the latter having been embroiled in a major sex scandal that saw him lie under oath and eventually impeached, were said to have "jammed" with each other — Blair on his Fender Stratocaster, and Clinton on tenor saxophone.

In 1998, Google was founded and Apple released the iconic teal and white iMac, both of which were intended to capitalise on the public's growing interest in the "world wide web". Mobile phone ownership in the UK nearly doubled in the short period between 1998 and 2001, from 26% of people owning one to 47% (Statista, 2019), with a similar, if slightly lesser growth in the United States (Statista, 2011). Meanwhile, economist Danny Dorling reminds us that "By 2000 the wealthiest 1% of US citizens owned 40% of the wealth and the poorest 40% owned 1% of their country's wealth, that 1% shared out very thinly between them all" (2010: 256). By 2000, the ratio of CEO pay to the salary of the average worker had also soared to a peak of approximately 368 to 1. The total wealth stored in offshore tax havens was estimated to be around $5–$7 trillion dollars, and the concentration of carbon dioxide in the Earth's atmosphere was recorded as 369ppm.

Part III: OK Boomer

The third part of our story is one of decline. It is the period over which the supposed triumph of liberal capitalism once heralded as the "end of history", which some still hold onto, built up over decades and spread across much of the world, truly began to fall apart. Part of this downfall was born of complacency about the seeming progress that, on the surface, those in power felt had been achieved. Economies were booming, a new millennium had begun and the only direction that things could move in was surely upwards. Defining what he calls the "hard centre" of capitalist governance since the end of the Cold War, Tariq Ali writes of this moment that:

In 2000, social democratic parties or coalitions dominated by them governed most of Western Europe, barring Spain. The experience confirmed that none of these parties could deliver effective policies that improved the living conditions of the majority of electors whose votes had placed them in power. Capitalism, intoxicated by its victory and unchallenged from any quarter, no longer felt the need to protect its left flank by conceding any more reforms. Even a marginal redistribution of wealth to reduce inequalities was off the agenda. (2015)

In 2000, after eight years of the pattern that Ali describes, George W. Bush managed to defeat incumbent Vice President Al Gore, a symbol of the "hard centre" Clinton years, in the US presidential election — despite not necessarily winning the actual election. Not only did Bush trail in the popular vote, but the count was so close in the state of Florida, where there were twenty-five electoral college votes to be won which could swing the overall result either way, that a recount was ordered. A month later, the United States Supreme Court stopped the recount before it could be concluded. The eventual result, inconsequential as far as the election was concerned, showed that the state could have been won by either candidate by just a few hundred votes, depending on the standard to which a paper card needed to be perforated in order for it to count — a concept known as "hanging chads".

Less than a year into the Bush presidency, in September 2001, the World Trade Centre — a symbol of American global financial dominance — was attacked with airplanes piloted by suicide bombers, and more than three thousand people were killed. The Pentagon, home of the US Department of Defence, was also hit. Once again, conspiracy theories abounded. Fifteen of the nineteen hijackers of the planes that hit the Twin Towers were Saudi citizens, and the attack was claimed by al-Qaeda, a terrorist group headed by the Saudi radical Osama bin Laden, who had been among the mujahedeen in Afghanistan receiving military assistance from the US to fight against the Soviets in the 1980s, and which followed the ultra-conservative Wahabbist interpretation of Islam also favoured by the

Taliban, and some years later by Daesh, the so-called Islamic State. Despite the Saudi connection, the US did not take any action against Saudi Arabia whatsoever, perhaps partly because Saudi Arabia, seen as an ally, held hundreds of billions of US foreign debt. Some years later, when President Barack Obama considered signing a law that would enable damages to be pursued against Saudi Arabia for their role in the attacks, the Saudi government threatened to sell this debt, which would have devalued the US economy. The attack, which occurred in the midst of a recession in the US and preceded the bursting of the so-called "dot-com bubble", would subsequently be manipulated in order to justify two US-led wars, in Afghanistan in 2001 and Iraq in 2003, both of which were disastrous and led to increased terrorist activity and recruitment (Hasan and Sayedahmed, 2018).

Meanwhile, the battle around climate change was beginning to intensify. Frank Luntz, a Republican communication strategy consultant who had been classmates with Boris Johnson at Oxford, wrote a memo in 2002 for the Bush administration to assist them in fighting the growing awareness around global warming, in which he said, "The scientific debate is closing [against us] but not yet closed. There is still a window of opportunity to challenge the science." He advised the government to avoid allowing the scientific consensus to become obvious to the public, saying:

> Voters believe that there is no consensus about global warming within the scientific community. Should the public come to believe that the scientific issues are settled, their views about global warming will change accordingly.
>
> Therefore, you need to continue to make the lack of scientific certainty a primary issue in the debate.

If this wasn't bad enough, that Bush administration, together with Tony Blair's government in the United Kingdom, was undertaking an even more brazen attempt to manipulate the truth — the plan to invade Iraq. The story is reported in detail elsewhere, so only a very brief summary will be given here, but it surely ranks as one of the most significant and disastrous examples of governmental deceit since the end of the Cold War. In September 2002, under the guise of the "War on Terror" that had started a year earlier on 9/11, and the accusation of a co-operative relationship between Iraqi president Saddam Hussein and al-Qaeda, who had carried out the attacks, the Bush administration made a case to the UN Security Council to invade Iraq. The UK government under Tony Blair was supportive, as was Italy's Prime Minister Silvio Berlusconi, but France and Germany were not. Iraq was known to have chemical weapons, which had been used to kill thousands of Iranians and Kurds, because the US had helped them obtain and develop these capabilities. Eventually, a resolution was passed by the Council that restarted the weapons inspections that had stopped in 1998 during the Clinton administration, and promised consequences if Iraq did not comply. However, United Nations weapons inspector Scott Ritter had already publicly stated that, as long ago as 1998, Iraq had already been largely disarmed. Weapons inspectors returned to Iraq in November 2002.

In January 2003, just as future climate activist Greta Thunberg was born in Sweden and the average concentration of carbon dioxide in the Earth's atmosphere passed 374ppm, her fellow Swede Dr Hans Blix, who had naively underestimated the Chernobyl nuclear disaster when he was the director general of the International Atomic Energy Authority (Willsher, 2019), was now leading the inspection of Iraq's weapons of mass destruction capability. Iraq destroyed a few remaining items left in its arsenal, under the supervision of Blix and his team of inspectors, but Blix declared that Iraq was not complying as quickly as the UN resolution had required. Bush and Blair had an "emergency" meeting, after which Bush declared that diplomacy had failed. On 5 February, in front of the UN Security Council, Defence Secretary Colin Powell delivered a presentation that has become an infamous part of US history, for which even Powell himself has since expressed shame, calling it "painful". Powell presented "evidence" of Iraq actively developing weapons of mass destruction, which was actually "evidence of the Iraqis *doing what they were supposed to do* — i.e. searching their gigantic ammunition dumps to make sure they weren't accidentally holding onto banned chemical weapons — and doctored it *to make it look as if Iraq were hiding banned weapons*" (Schwartz, 2018).

Despite German and French opposition, on 20 March 2003 the US and the UK began bombing Iraq, but the deceit did not stop even there. Remembering how the US public had begun to turn against the Vietnam War effort partly because of the widely reported loss of life and the imagery of flag-draped coffins being repatriated on the nightly news, the Bush administration banned news coverage and photography of dead soldiers' homecomings on all military bases (Milbank, 2003). Later that year, in September 2003, the US Presidential Envoy to Iraq, Paul Bremer, supervised by Defence Secretary Donald Rumsfeld, announced the full privatisation of the Iraqi state, and a special legal provision for businesses to be foreign-owned and allowed to "repatriate" their profits — transferring money back to the US and Europe, and out of the Iraqi economy (Harvey, 2005).

Simultaneous with this moment was a huge development in the ways that people used the internet: an explosion in what came to be known as "user-generated content" on the web. In the late 1990s, the web had been used as a content distribution platform in a more top-down fashion, with an emphasis on e-commerce. But then a new wave of companies realised they could make websites that were services that simply connected people and enabled them to upload their own content. As Nick Srnicek puts it, "In the wake of the [dot-com] bust, internet-based companies shifted to business models that monetised the free resources available to them" (2017: 36). This echoes philosopher and economist Rosa Luxemburg's argument that capital would continually try to exploit new areas of value as it progressed.

The advent of blogging and the establishment of social media platforms together produced a rapid increase in the sheer quantity of content online. Loosely termed "web 2.0" at the time, it was an idiot-proof world of rounded corners, cute logos, made-up words like "Flickr" and vibrant colour palettes that refashioned the web around the content that its users produced, regardless of quality or reliability. Now, anyone with a web browser and an internet connection could publish, and this was heralded as an important democratisation of the media landscape. What we will see in Chapter Four, however, is that there is a common tendency to overstate the ability of technology to solve problems that are political in origin. The new platforms that comprised this user-centric model for the web consisted of a strange alliance between the world of open-source software development and the same rapacious get-rich-quick impulses that had driven the dot-com boom the first time. Between March 2003 and July 2006, the number of active blogs grew exponentially, doubling every six months to approximately fifty million (Technorati, 2006). Much of this growth was facilitated by the open-source blogging engine called WordPress, launched in May 2003.

Commercial platforms YouTube, Vimeo, Twitter, Flickr and Facebook (then "TheFacebook") were also all launched in the same period. As we now know, TheFacebook, founded in 2004 by a joint psychology and computer science major at Harvard, Mark Zuckerberg, before dropping out, would go on to pioneer the ruthless commodification of human sociality and emotion for advertising purposes that now characterises much of social media (Zuboff, 2019; Gilroy-Ware, 2017).

In June 2007, two days before the iPhone was first put on sale, Tony Blair stepped down as Prime Minister, and his Chancellor of the Exchequer Gordon Brown took over, giving his first speech to the Labour Party conference as leader that September. This was the first of several times he would use the phrase "British jobs for British workers", which was considered quite controversial. Although the financial crisis was only just starting, a tide of xenophobic populism was already rising — a reminder that it was long in the making — and the Labour Party used the same rhetoric as it tried in vain to cling to power. The Leader of the Opposition, David Cameron, remarked somewhat disingenuously during a parliamentary debate two months later in November 2007 that:

If we want just one example of the absolute bankruptcy of this Government, let us take the slogan that the Prime Minister wheels out every week: British jobs for British workers. Yes, if only he could see how embarrassed his Labour MPs are, how they shudder when he utters those words. I have done a bit of work on this little slogan of the Prime Minister's. The Secretary of State for Work and Pensions told us that there should be no doubt. It is, he said, "explicitly a British jobs for British people campaign". We asked the House of Commons Library, and it said:

"There is apparently nothing in the detail of the proposals to suggest that foreign nationals will be excluded from any of the initiatives if they happen to live in the area where the locally based schemes operate."

So there we have it: the reality is that the Prime Minister has no intention of providing British jobs for British workers, because he knows that *it would be illegal under EU law*. His proposals will not help British people working in Britain any more than they will help Italian people working in Britain or Polish people working in Britain. That is the truth about British jobs for British workers. I did a bit more research to find out where he got his slogans from: *he borrowed one off the National Front; he borrowed another off the British National party. Where was his moral compass when he was doing that?* (Hansard, 2007; emphases added)

As the added emphases in this exchange hopefully illustrate, it is instructive for a number of reasons. Euroscepticism and anti-EU sentiment around Brexit, nine years after this took place, were associated with Conservatives, while those few left-wing Eurosceptics focused on critiques of the EU as a neoliberal institution, and emphasised how Greece was treated in the years leading up to 2015. But here we see it was also Labour who were guilty of dog-whistling to placate the far-right, adding fuel to the fire of what would become Brexit and promoting a policy that was not only xenophobic, but utterly incompatible with the EU treaties that could be traced all the way back to the Treaty of Rome in 1957. While the far right may have been calling for Britain's exit from Europe for decades, the Labour Party were also complicit in bringing about a standoff between outright xenophobia and the European Union, and peddling the myth that EU migrants were a serious threat to British employment prospects.

Only a month later, the Treaty of Lisbon was signed by all EU member states, which added the famous "Article 50" provision for member states to leave the Union that would be triggered by Theresa May as Prime Minister almost ten years later. Virtually nobody realised that this combination of rhetoric and political-economic tension was already pointed in the direction of what would eventually become Brexit.

By this point, in 2008, the number of billionaires in the US had grown to its highest in history, at 469 (Statista, 2012). Then came the global financial crash — a crisis with huge cultural and political consequences as well as economic effects, which was brought about almost entirely by unrestricted greed and irresponsibility. Tension had been building since the previous year in the United States as a result of so-called "sub-prime" mortgages, which were sold to people who could not pay them back, but the causes go back further. House prices in the United States had been growing for years, but from 2001–2007, they accelerated. This price bubble was driven by the easy accessibility of these "sub-prime" mortgages and a steadily deregulated global financial sector that had been given the nod by successive post-Thatcher governments in the US, UK and northern Europe, to make as much money as possible from derivatives trading. Sub-prime mortgage debts were then packaged up and sold on to other traders as investments, but eventually the number of defaulted mortgages began to affect the value of these investments, and the number of resulting foreclosures saw house prices start to drop again as more and more of these homes were repossessed and auctioned. As property prices fell further and further, it meant that even foreclosing and auctioning the properties did not recover the value of the original debt, meaning that this debt that had been traded throughout the financial system was essentially worthless. Like a nuclear power plant melting down, the system of free trade went into overdrive, before disintegrating and bringing with it the livelihoods and economic security of millions.

Investment bank Lehman Brothers collapsed in September 2008, and a number of major financial institutions, such as the US's largest savings and mortgage bank, Washington Mutual, also went bankrupt and had to be nationalised and bailed out with public money. The corresponding slowdown in consumer spending in the months and years that followed meant that other major corporations also had to be saved by governments, such as the US car manufacturing giant General Motors, to which newly elected President Barack Obama lent $80bn in 2009. An entire generation of people who were starting their careers in those years faced fewer jobs and greater precarity, as their economies shrank. Yet very few people ever faced justice for the recklessness that led to this crisis. The public still barely knows the names of those responsible, yet as historian and philosopher Philip Mirowski recounts, "they were bailed out by the taxpayers, and went on to enjoy their most profitable year in history in 2009. Notoriously, bankers raked in record bonuses" (2013) No wonder people were starting to lose faith in liberal capitalist democracy.

Other indicators pointed to an alarming hoarding of wealth — the offshore accumulation of hidden capital had increased enormously since it had begun in earnest in the 1980s, amounting to between $21 to $32trn (Henry, 2012). 672 brand-new private jets were sold the same year (Ewalt, 2013). Was there really no alternative to this? When German far-right party Alternative für Deutschland ("Alternative for Germany") was founded in the second week of April 2013, coincidentally the same week that Margaret Thatcher died of a stroke at London's Ritz Hotel, their name was an explicit answer to the "*alternativlos*" political language that had been deployed by chancellor Angela Merkel and the CDU. Unfortunately, their politics was not a viable or constructive alternative at all — it began as a simplistic, neoliberal party, opposed to public spending, before opportunistically embracing a deluded, xenophobic bigotry, angry at all the wrong people.

Meanwhile, in the five years between 2010 and 2015, the number of billionaires in the UK doubled, and the level of carbon dioxide in the Earth's atmosphere rose by 14ppm. Over the same period one hundred years earlier, 1910–1915, the rise was just 1.5ppm. In the United States, the Heritage Foundation could smell the possibility of a Republican victory after the Obama presidency they had so detested, and in 2014 had already begun preparing. According to one report:

> a year before Trump even declared his candidacy, the right-wing think tank [Heritage] had started assembling a 3,000-name searchable database of trusted movement conservatives from around the country who were eager to serve in a post-Obama government. (Mahler, 2018)

One of the other important hallmarks of this moment was an intense, if often unstated, inter-generational standoff that was described using a reductive language of "boomers" and "millennials" that obscured and exaggerated rather than assisted with the tension. The real problem was that, as part of the overall de-democratisation of the world over the course of the story given here, "boomers" had enjoyed the optimistic feeling of having a future and the prospect of genuine upward mobility, aided largely by the market value of their property increasing thanks to a deregulated housing market focused heavily on ownership. According to the *Financial Times*, those in the UK over sixty-five years old, as the owners of property, experienced a 96% increase in their overall wealth in the ten years from 2009–2019 (Asgari, 2019). The same was true in the US. *Vice News* reported in 2019 that:

> Back in 1989, when boomers were between 25 and 43, they already owned 20.9% of the country's wealth, according to data from the Federal Reserve [...]. In 2019, millennials are between 23 and 38, and they currently own a whopping 3.2% of wealth. That means boomers had more than six times as much wealth in 1989 as millennials do now. (Lubben, 2019)

Subsequent generations, who were less likely to own property than those older than them, experienced radically different conditions to their parents — not only as the looming prospect of irreversible environmental catastrophe became more apparent, but also in economic matters such as living conditions and employment. Meanwhile the relentless and increasingly untrue narrative that hard work produces upward mobility did not abate. The post-war boomers were telling their children and grandchildren to claim forms of prosperity that simply were no longer available.

The Dam Breaks

As far as our story is concerned, the first sign of rupture was the Greek debt crisis, which had been steadily worsening since 2010 and came to a head in 2015, when Greece was nearly forced to leave the Eurozone. This is also the year in which the Brexit and Trump campaigns were formally set in motion, with a Conservative victory in the UK and Trump's announcement of his candidacy. The following year, in June 2016, Britain voted by a narrow margin to leave the European Union, a result that was celebrated with vandalism of European-owned shops and EU citizens who had spent decades living in the UK being told to "make arrangements to leave" by the Home Office (O'Carroll, 2016). Repeated surveys of British voters show that departure from the European Union was much more popular with older age groups, indicating another dimension to the same inter-generational standoff discussed above. A 2020 survey by Ipsos MORI showed that only a quarter of those in the 18–34 and 35–54 age groups believed Brexit to be a good idea, whereas almost half of those over 55 did (Ipsos MORI, 2020). Amongst other factors, religion was also found to have played a significant role in voting for Brexit, in the sense that identifying as "Church of England" was "a major independent predictor of voting Brexit [that held] even when other factors are controlled for" (Smith and Woodhead, 2018: 208).

A leaked Government forecast later showed that leaving the EU would be economically damaging to the UK "in every scenario", particularly England's poorer northern and southwestern regions. A report from *BuzzFeed News* revealed that "Asked why the prime minister was not making the analysis public, a DExEU [department for exiting the European Union] source told *BuzzFeed News*: 'Because it's embarrassing'" (Nardelli, 2018).

The election of Donald Trump in the United States followed in November of 2016, with promises to put "America First", to lock up his opponent Hillary Clinton, and to build a wall to keep immigrants out — all cheered by millions of people. His campaign sounded like the National Front leaflet quoted earlier in this chapter, adapted into a US context. A lot has already been written about Britain's vote to leave the European Union, and Donald Trump's 2016 victory, so their extended discussion is not included here, but they are obviously amongst the most conspicuous signs of the overall crisis we are tracing.

In December 2016, Italy's resounding rejection of constitutional reforms put to referendum led centrist Prime Minister Matteo Renzi to resign. Then, in spring 2017, far-right candidate Marine Le Pen unexpectedly progressed to the second round of the French presidential election, in which she received around a third of the votes cast, against "hard centre" candidate Emmanuel Macron. In late 2018, neo-fascist ex-soldier Jair Bolsonaro, who had "openly praised the military dictatorship (in which he served as an army captain)" in prior years (Miranda, 2019), was elected President of Brazil.

In France, at the end of 2018 and in early 2019, an intriguing movement of "Yellow Vests" arose, that was ostensibly part of the same overall wave. What began as a protest against fuel price rises introduced by President Macron became a fascinatingly general protest. Rather than being issue-driven, or obviously left-wing or right-wing, to begin with it appeared simply to be a protest against the status quo. As it spread across the world, it was locally inflected. In Taiwan and Israel, it was a protest against specific taxes. In Germany, it was quickly taken up by Alternative für Deutschland and other far-right elements, whereas in Italy, where it became a protest *against* the right-wing Five-Star Movement's tough laws making it easier to expel new arrivals. In the end however, the movement was largely co-opted by far-right groups (May, 2019).

Britain continued along the trajectory set by Brexit in Boris Johnson's 2019 election win, including in post-industrial areas that had always voted for the Labour Party, and eventually left the EU in January 2020. The United States remained polarised and turbulent, stirred up by a stream of ever-more shocking tweets from Donald Trump, often posted in the middle of the night. Then the year 2020 saw the COVID-19 pandemic. Over a million people would eventually die, and the two countries that had spent the last forty years embracing the market-driven society most religiously — the United States and Britain — were amongst those with the highest total numbers of deaths, including hundreds of health workers who had not been provided the personal protective equipment (PPE) they needed to work safely. Despite a record wave in unemployment and a real strain for countless small businesses, the crisis also saw a wave of "coronacapitalism" that rose to exploit the disease. Amazon, which had paid an effective tax rate of 1.2% on more than $13bn in profit the previous year (Myers, 2020), saw income of $11,000 a second and a share price increase of as much as 36% due to all the people under lockdown buying things without being able to use brick-and-mortar retail outlets (Neate, 2020). This caused founder and CEO Jeff Bezos, already the world's richest man by this point, to increase his net worth by $24bn whilst the company fired and plotted to humiliate workers who had gone on strike to demand safe working conditions (Higgins, 2020). There was also a predictable degree of commercial exploitation of the crisis elsewhere in the economy. Although there was widespread outcry after the *New York Times* story of a man unashamedly hoarding over seven thousand bottles of hand sanitiser in his garage so that he could put his family "in a better position", hedge funds earned billions by making market bets during the crisis. One fund, run by UK investor Crispin Odey, reported it had made its "biggest monthly gain since the financial crisis" (Neate & Jolly, 2020). In another example, from the moment the US senate was briefed on the crisis in January, Georgia Republican Senator David Perdue and his wife began buying hundreds of thousands of dollars' worth of stock in a PPE company, hoping to capitalise on their rapid increase in value (Blest, 2020).

The Price of Fake Democracy

When we look at this story, the inevitable picture that emerges is of the development of a market-driven society in most of these countries, far beyond the free-markets envisioned in Mont Pèlerin as a "neoliberal" inoculation against totalitarianism — so far beyond that instead we see a society in which short-term profit is more important than the physical and mental health and security of its people, more important than genuine democracy, more important than the long-term health of the natural environment, more important than any notion of the truth, except as a commodified ideal. As Mark Fisher put it, "neoliberalism has sought to eliminate the very category of value in the ethical sense" (2009: 16-17). No wonder we have found ourselves *after the fact*. But the issue goes beyond the question of information, to the very foundation of what the fundamental principles of a democratic society even are.

As we have seen throughout this story, in much of the Euro-Atlantic world there has never really been a clear agreement as to the question of what its societies stand for. The divergent views of this collective existential quandary have often been given vague, simplistic labels such as "left" or "right", which date back to the French Revolution, but besides the strictly free market approach, most other worldviews have ultimately come into conflict with the overall move towards a market-driven society to some degree. For example, if the "left" means anything, it should refer to the way of thinking that places an emphasis on the idea of solidarity, and holds that we all have a degree of responsibility towards one another, even when we face very different struggles. Of course, there are divergent strands that emphasise its liberal or socialistic elements differently, but in this view, government exists not only for basic public safety such as police or firefighters, but to maintain this equality and provide a reasonable quality of life for all its people in a way that fairly shares the burden. The suffering of others is relevant to all, and healthcare, universities, public transport, legal representation and even public broadcasting are all considered important public services because they provide intrinsic value — not primarily for the economy but in the quality of a lived experience that exists outside of any market. The sick should be healed, the curious educated and ideally the hungry fed, because there is seen to be a moral obligation towards everyone in a society.

This was the underlying principle that drove the Attlee government when it remade Britain after World War II; it was also what informed Bernie Sanders' view of what the United States could and should be in 2016 and 2020, but it should already be obvious that this view of *what society is*, is essentially incompatible with the steady marketisation of society recounted on the previous pages, and which those who prefer this view of the world have tried to resist for decades. There have been protests, marches, petitions, even riots, which if anything only stopped the rapacious marketisation from being worse, but did little to actually prevent it.

Meanwhile, there have been those who saw the best possible society as one that was defined by hard work, upward economic mobility and ideally the accumulation of wealth. In this view, it is morally incumbent on everyone, rich or poor, to hustle as hard as they can, and it is their own fault if they encounter poverty or misfortune. The story above has been one of ambivalence for them — privatisation and free enterprise chimed with this moral imperative to work hard, stay independent from government and aim for economic security without help. Conservative communities that were oriented around a strongly moralised work ethic that assumed upward mobility and financial reward as goals saw this exciting, accelerated capitalism as their chance to be included in modernity itself. At least initially, they broadly supported the economic libertarianism and free-market capitalism touted by thinkers like Milton Friedman and Friedrich Hayek. And particularly during the Cold War, when the Euro-Atlantic world's bogeymen were said to be the communists, conservatism and free markets could be bent into alignment. But as Edward Luttwak wrote, there has been a growing contradiction in this alliance. Increasingly, the cold individualism of the market-driven society came into conflict with the moralised anchors conservative politics that exist outside the marketplace, such as family, nation, tradition and respect for regimented social structures, including patriarchal and racial ones. As with the left, this morally led relationship to politics is important, and psychologists have found evidence to suggest that different political worldviews are heavily informed by underlying conceptions of morality (e.g. Graham, Haidt and Nosek, 2009).

Looking across the world, it is not a surprise to find localised versions of this worldview — the rural US version of it looks different to the suburbia of the UK's Home Counties or the concrete blocks in what was formerly East Germany, but the moral table is more or less the same: there is nothing more sacred than hard work. Trump was appealing primarily because he represented a kind of straight-talking gung-ho entrepreneurial self that was distinct from the slick, Wall Street snob that has been so demonised in the form of the Clintons. His existing media persona, widely known from the NBC show *The Apprentice* as an arbiter of what constituted good entrepreneurship, combined with the simplistic, unforgiving harshness of his catchphrase, "you're fired", resonated with the reactionary middle classes Edward Luttwak and others had identified. It appealed to those who placed the moral value of hard work above the socially informed morality of not sexually abusing women or "screwing people over" that the left prioritised.

Of course, on closer inspection it was apparent that Trump was not a successful businessman — he was just able to evoke that theme because he and the people advising him knew it would be a persuasive message. But then comes the real kicker, and the source of much of the newer right-wing anger that exploded in the early twenty-first century — upward mobility had already disappeared. The illusion of Donald Trump's business acumen was dwarfed by a far greater deception: the promise of the "American dream", in which anybody could become CEO if they worked their way to the top, had been obliterated by the very people already at the top, who wanted to stay there, and were now pointing down at them, laughing.

The market-driven society has used whatever political language it can in order to legitimise itself. Sometimes this has been right-wing rhetoric, as for example in the ways that free-market politicians have spoken about immigration. Unfortunately, as we will see in chapter four, the sincere belief in the importance of equality, justice and environmentalism in the left-wing movements has also been imitated and worn superficially as camouflage by the most aggressive free-marketeers when it was more convenient to do so, meaning that those outside "the left" who see themselves has having been negatively affected by this marketisation and democratic decline, whether or not they explicitly make this attribution, often blame the left for their misfortune.

Drowning in some of the same forms of obfuscation and disinformation that those on the left had long-since identified in the ways that capitalism operates, the conservative right became angry. They realised their moralised anchors were no longer respected by the rapacious global expansion of markets that shipped their jobs overseas or replaced them with computers, and which saw no value in their traditions, families, patriarchy or patriotism beyond that which could generate value for shareholders, who were the only people whose voting rights still seemed to count.

As the sociologist Sivamohan Valluvan has argued, "There remain a multitude of conservative themes via which appeals to cultural meaning and national identity are popularly recalled independently of a neoliberal cost–benefit analysis that is economistic in type" (2019: 90). Indeed, as Max Weber also observed more than a hundred years earlier, "The most important opponent with which the spirit of capitalism [...] has had to struggle, was that type of attitude and reaction to new situations which we may designate as traditionalism." So it proved to be once the "neoliberalism" devised after the war slowly revealed how different it was from the ascetic godliness of hard work that Weber had identified in Protestantism, and made the only remaining values market values. The result? A violent reassertion of those traditional right-wing anchors that were deprioritised in this slow drift: nation, empire, patriarchy, white supremacy (hence "make America great again" or "blood and soil"). What better metaphor for this story can there be than the fact that many of Trump's "Keep America Great" banners, made in preparation for the 2020 election, were manufactured in China? (Lemon, 2018)

As we will see in following chapters, at the core of this development has been a variety of culturally enforced misinformation processes that initially enabled the free-market zealots to convince the traditional right that they were on their side, and then to slowly appropriate values associated with the left such as equality, while ultimately betraying both and exacerbating the already fundamental and bitter disagreements between them that stretch back centuries. And so we come to "fake news". Hopefully it should be clear that the problem is not so much fake news as *fake democracy*, in which everything has been put up for sale, any version of democracy has been hollowed out by corporate control over its institutions, and much of what those in power say is either spin or outright deceit. The market not only attacked the anchors of the left — social solidarity and the common good — it also attacked the anchors of the right — nation, family, and tradition — and tricked both in different ways into supporting exactly the process that has brought us to this point.

The Italian writer and philosopher Antonio Gramsci, who died a political prisoner of Mussolini in 1937, wrote of Italian fascism around 1930 that "The crisis consists precisely in the fact that the old is dying and the new cannot be born; in this interregnum a great variety of morbid symptoms appear." This "interregnum" has now lasted so long that Gramsci's quote has come to elicit an eye-roll in some left-wing circles, but almost a century later in the early twenty-first century, there were few more appropriate ways to describe the historical moment traced in this chapter. When Britain voted to leave the European Union, people on the right and left said it was the end of that market-driven society. When the US elected Trump in 2016, some feared it was the end of the world. When the COVID-19 pandemic gripped the world in 2020, bringing death and major disruption, people again speculated about what this would mean, and how the world would look afterwards. But those that speculated about "the end of" any part of that world that took so many decades, treaties, wars and propaganda campaigns to bring about, would have done well to consider that the liberal capitalist democracy that Francis Fukuyama extolled at the end of the Cold War had become a "zombie" democracy — a system which is already dead, but which refuses to die.

The argument is not that the left and the right as defined here will ever be friends or allies. Far from it — their moralised anchors around which to understand the world are simply too different. Neither is the argument that there is any moral equivalency in how these different positions assert themselves in the world, or in the consequences of their actions or policies. Racism, xenophobia and misogyny may *sometimes* only be irrational conduits for a deeper hatred of the system that has used egalitarian language as camouflage, but true substantive equality between all human beings is too important to be something about which we "agree to disagree".

However, rather than pointing at each other and crying "fake news", we would do well to respond to environmental destruction, declining standards of living, public health crises and other major issues by seeing them for what they are: pathologies of the free market. Although the left has a head start at this, it needs to become explicit to all political persuasions to constantly analyse and disarm the idea that everything is economic, and that nothing exists outside that market-driven society. In the chapters to follow, the development of this Euro-Atlantic "zombie" democracy will be analysed through the broad prism of misinformation and disinformation, and all their specific varieties: hoax, propaganda, myth, conspiracy theory, the deceptive qualities of liberalism, complacent, crappy journalism, and the digital platforms that have arisen to exploit them.

Chapter Two
The Disinformation Society

The challenge of modernity is to live without illusions and without becoming disillusioned.
— Antonio Gramsci

The further a society drifts from the truth, the more it will hate those that speak it.
— George Orwell

Just before Christmas 2018, I visited a branch of an up-market cosmetics chain, somewhere I never normally dare visit, to purchase a somewhat over-the-top stocking-filler for a loved one. The product I was looking for was not in stock, but a representative from the skincare brand whose product I was trying to buy was in the shop, and began to attempt to sell me something else instead. Catching me off-guard, her first question in order to narrow down our selection of the various creams that were in stock was "How old is she?" I replied that the recipient was "mid-thirties", and like clockwork, the sales assistant ventured something to the effect of: "Perhaps you should try this one, it's got anti-aging properties."

"She doesn't need that", I said with a cheeky smile, refusing the assumptions in the suggestion, but the meaning of my refusal was lost and interpreted as an insistence that the intended recipient didn't need that product because she looked so good without it. While it was true that the recipient looked young for her age, this was not what I meant.

"Well, she is mid-thirties, so she will be starting to age", the assistant responded earnestly, in a slight German accent.

Annoyed, but unable to articulate my frustration, I said after an uneasy pause "I think I'll just buy the one I'm looking for online", and thanked the assistant for her help with a forced smile before walking away. What I should at this point have clarified was: "No, I mean she doesn't need that because you are selling at least three complete lies here: first of all, that ageing is avoidable; secondly, that it is your moisturiser of all things that will arrest the ageing process; and thirdly, that ageing is even bad and that her value as a person will be in some way reduced by a natural ageing process, once it becomes discernible — which is the most malicious lie of all."

Of course, in a broader sense, the cosmetics companies are "winning" at the moment. Whatever clever response I may have been able to muster would not have changed the fact that as long as the idea that ageing is bad is commonplace enough in the cultural landscape, people will continue to buy products that promise to address the problem they believe it to be, and this type of culturally driven disinformation is extremely powerful.

Relaying this frustrating but instructive encounter to my sister later that day, I was scolded that I should have known better about what to expect before entering into that shop — the "Mecca" of such lies. Consider me told. But my sister is absolutely right. Venturing into the depths of the consumer society, I should have been expecting deceit from every direction. As the founder of another cosmetics corporation, Revlon, Charles Revson once reportedly said: "In our factory we make cosmetics. In the store we sell hope."

Against the backdrop of "fake news", we tend to talk about misinformation and disinformation as a very specific type of problem that certain people are responsible for: online extremists, "big tech", the Russians, or unreliable social media users who are apparently stuck in "echo chambers".

At the very least, any threats posed by these villains turn out to be more nuanced, but there is also the case to be made that this is an incredibly selective, exaggerated and at times disingenuous understanding of misinformation and disinformation that has arisen in response to the highly specific historical conditions outlined in the last chapter. If we are going to talk about misinformation and disinformation, there needs to be an honest engagement with the ways that power, and the shiny, appealing, market-driven forms it has assumed in the twentieth and early twenty-first centuries, wormed its way into our lives, invited us to participate, and guided what we know, believe and accept about the world we inhabit. Perhaps having our democracy taken away in the Euro-Atlantic world was actually quite fun for a while? As Alfie Bown has observed, we are after all being constantly encouraged to enjoy ourselves (2014).

Perhaps this is why my predictable encounter with the gleaming, LED-lit mendacity of luxury cosmetics, even if it may seem a bit silly, is as good a place as any to begin examining the ways that much more widespread patterns of misinformation and disinformation, such as hyperbole, propaganda, spin, illiteracy and myth, enabled the processes in the last chapter to play out. It at least provides us with the tip of an important iceberg: the market-driven society is invariably a *bullshit society*.

Perhaps a more palatable way to name this would be *disinformation society*. Not only are we fundamentally ill equipped by the information we do have, we are systematically denied the insights necessary to challenge and reverse the market-driven society. Political and economic power has long relied on obscuring our relationships to that power and to each other, and as we will see in the next chapter, this alienation-by-disinformation often drives the development of conspiracy theories as people try to make sense of those relationships. But one of the main outcomes of the process outlined in the last chapter — the hollowing out of democratic processes and ambitions and the marketisation of everything — is that this process of *obscuring* what is going on accelerated and became a lot more sophisticated as the free market took over after the Cold War. The "information society" that was discussed heavily around the end of the 1990s and early 2000s (e.g. Webster, 1995, or more critically, Gitlin, 2003) was already on the road to becoming a disinformation society.

Beneath the commercial hyperbole, slick logos and constant illusion of the free-market world, in which information is merely something you use to decide what to buy or sell, or which politician will make you better off financially, the crisis of belligerent incoherence and reactionary nationalism came about because of a variety of misdirection and disinformation that obscured the reorganisation and ethical unmooring that was happening beneath the surface.

As for the experience above, there are actually some pretty alarming connections to be discovered between the cosmetics industry, which attempts to derive profit from your insecurities about your skin and age, and the forms of reactionary politics to which this book is a kind of answer. For example, pseudo-French American cosmetics corporation Estée Lauder produces a "night serum" product that, like the products I was offered, is also supposedly "anti-aging". At the time of writing, it costs $72 per fluid ounce on Estée Lauder's US website, and £58 for just 30 ml in the UK. Anyone who has passed through an airport will have seen the product on display in the sterile, mirrored luxury retail section of the duty-free shopping area.

Less well known is the fact that Ronald Lauder, a former diplomat who is one of the heirs to the fortune generated by selling these products, and brother of the chairman of

Estée Lauder Corporation, used the funds at his disposal to support what can only be described as a propaganda outfit, called Secure America Now (SAN). Registered only to the offices of a Washington, DC law firm, SAN produces internet videos aimed at US Tea Party types, calling for resistance against the "Islamicisation" of America, and attacking the efforts of former President Barack Obama to find a diplomatic solution to stop Iran from enriching uranium. Allen Roth, the president of SAN, was Ronald Lauder's long-time personal advisor as well as having once been interviewed for *Breitbart News* by Raheem Kassam — later Nigel Farage's right-hand-man. Lauder, alongside major right-wing donor and former Cambridge Analytica owner Robert Mercer, has donated over $1m to SAN (Cortellessa, 2018).

This series of connections may seem highly specific, and certainly it entails a fascinatingly intertwined set of strands: luxury consumer brands selling false hope around a false idea of beauty, which in turn enables them to finance propaganda aimed at influencing US foreign policy or attacking a major world religion. But this is only one small corner of the complex, disinformation-fuelled world that we have built. Welcome to the disinformation society.

Power and Culture

As Michel Foucault and numerous others have shown, the nature and form of power is something that has changed considerably over the course of history. That discussion is not directly relevant here, but there are two things that must be born in mind in the context of how power relates to misinformation and disinformation.

Firstly, as we saw in Chapter One, power in a market-driven society is ultimately the private, commercial power of wealth. Think back to the trillions hoarded offshore, the proliferation of private jets, and stubborn refusal to address inequality. As we will see in Chapter Four, there is a tendency to overstate how democratic liberal capitalism is, and this tendency has been essential cover for the ongoing transfer of power into private, corporate forms whose voters are shareholders, not citizens. To say that true power is vested in the institutions of capital rather than of government is sometimes alleged to be a conspiracy theory, especially by people wedded to the idea that there is nothing wrong with market-driven society as we know it. As the next chapter will show, however, there is a huge difference between conspiracy theories and the actual partnership of government and capital that began to develop in the 1980s.

Secondly, as media scholar Manuel Castells and numerous others have observed, power need not be coercive in a violent sense, so much as exert its influence via media and culture, through the construction of shared meaning. The philosopher Byung-Chul Han echoes numerous thinkers of different traditions in reminding us that "the communicative *lead* of power is not necessarily repressive. Power does not [anymore] *rest* on repression. Rather, as a means of communication its effects are <u>constructive</u>" (2019: 6, underlined emphasis added; italics in original). Icons such as flags and parades are examples of this *constructive* power in that they invite you to participate in accepting that power on the terms it is presented.

In the context of slowly, quietly losing any substantive democracy and seeing it replaced by a market-driven society, what is central for the enquiry made here is how the quality of conversations about power, both governmental and corporate, deteriorated as that society was reconfigured. Tracing neoliberalism's arrival at what I have been calling the market-driven society, the political scientist Wendy Brown (who does not use this term) makes the important point that "democratic self-rule must be consciously valued, cultured, and tended by a people seeking to practice it and [...] must vigilantly resist myriad economic, social, and political forces threatening to deform or encroach upon it" (2015: 11). The importance of this principle cannot be overstated. Democracy does not just happen automatically. Any discussion of the rightly contested term "fake news" is pointless unless it takes account of what has happened to these conversations, and to the cultural and informational context in which they may or may not have been taking place as the market-driven society slowly took shape.

Belonging in the Same Conversation

The best place to start this enquiry is by examining the *public* conversations we have, since it is frequently when we encounter other members of our society that we do not already know that our ideas about what kind of society we should live in are tested, and we are forced to fall back on our assumptions about what we *think* we share by virtue of our belonging to that society. Standard media theory tends to assert a construct often known as the "public sphere", in which all the members of a society are, to a greater or lesser extent, part of the same conversation. As the sociologist Jürgen Habermas, who is credited with having developed the idea, put it, it is "the sphere of private people come together as a public" (1989: 27). To most people, this idea is intuitively familiar, but it is also obvious that this is a huge oversimplification of how public conversations take place. Habermas sought to limit his theory to the *bourgeois* public sphere, which he saw as distinct from what he called the *plebeian* public sphere because it was the "educated strata" of society (ibid. xviii), and was criticised for this exclusion, but the important thing about this theory is the idea of a number of people who are not otherwise known to each other coming together to affirm common values and discuss the material and political conditions that belong to them jointly, by virtue of their belonging.

As numerous critics of this theory have observed, there is not in fact any single public sphere in which everybody participates in the same conversation — especially not as equals within any social or economic hierarchy. As the philosopher Nancy Fraser and others have pointed out, social factors such as racism, sexism and class barriers tend to drastically shape who can participate and influence this public sphere and on what terms. The idea is more that as democracy developed and an industrialist bourgeoisie appeared, a *liberal* public sphere, in which people met to talk about the issues that affected their common interest, emerged in contrast to older, more repressive ways of organising and exercising power.

As a result of this contrast, and similar to the naïve understanding of neoliberalism envisaged in the late 1940s, the concept of the public sphere has frequently been coloured by a certain simplistic utopianism, and this limits its applicability. But the alternative to a single, equalising public sphere is not to do away with the idea altogether, so much as to recognise that a more complex arrangement of multiple, overlapping, fragmented spheres *does* exist. Obviously, this does not mean there is a total separation of society, however much the theory of "echo chambers" would have us believe. Even in the harshly polarised "culture wars" of which it has also become common to speak, the very fact that we get into pointless Twitter arguments and Facebook "comment wars" about the same issues, including the coverage of those issues on older media such as radio or newspapers, is an indication that there is a broader, shared political landscape that features common reference points.

The political scientist Benedict Anderson traced the history of these shared conversations and the potent ideas, reference points, and forms of belonging they could foster in the context the modern *nation* — potent enough that people are prepared to kill and die for them. Although he did not explicitly use the idea of a "public sphere", Anderson observed that even prior to the modern nation, shared signs and reference points fostered a degree of shared belonging through shared meaning, and internationally spread religions often provided these shared frames of reference, not least in their ability to "create a community out of signs" (2006: 13). A contemporary version of this, besides the saturation of consumerist imagery and brands that has spread around the world, might be the rich language of "memes" that has developed, which have been described as "a strand of creative play in *public conversation*" (Milner, 2016: 11, emphasis added). As we can see, public conversations are one of the most important means by which ideas about societies and their collective identity are spread, affirmed or challenged. And again, in the context of widespread polarisation, misinformation and disinformation, these processes cannot be allowed to pass unexamined. The next question is: whose ideas?

Particularly when we actually do look at the alarming state of the world, it should not be necessary to identify as left-wing in order to be receptive to frank conversations about power, capitalism, destruction and decline. Surely it is those who actually had power during the period when these crises developed who should be challenged and held responsible. Is this really the best they could do? Do these crises really amount to a situation to which there is "no alternative", or no alternative except fascism? As we saw in the last chapter, especially after the end of the Cold War, when it was declared victorious, capitalism has been the dominant form of power, with the market-driven society as the outcome. But even in the face of mounting evidence that it is not fit for purpose, the response to any criticism of the system phrased in terms of "capitalism" is an almost Pavlovian tendency toward defensiveness.

For example, I tried to show in my previous book that the lived experience of the market-driven society entails, amongst its innumerable CCTV surveillance cameras, junk food, high-visibility jackets, work emails read in bed when you can't sleep, sniffer dogs and long working hours, a kind of background malaise, as if almost everyone knows that something is wrong, but few are able to see what else our societies could look like or imagine a brighter future. One of the most stupid, predictable and numerous responses I received to that claim, even though the evidence is increasingly abundant, is that "communism was worse". Really? We should not examine our boring, dystopian insistence that everything is fine, because communism in the second half of the twentieth century was brutal and violent? The brutality of so-called communist and socialist regimes in the early to mid-twentieth century was utterly abhorrent, and just as horrifying to people actually familiar with the works of Karl Marx, who do not see these regimes as having been an accurate or proportionate implementation of his ideas at all, quite the contrary. But just because the republics calling themselves communist at that time were violent and repressive, is that really a reason not to draw attention to the flaws in the systems that have developed since then?

Historic invocations of Soviet gulags as though they were a contemporary threat — a phenomenon I call "cartoon communism" for its simplistic hyperbole — are illustrative of the observation attributed to Fredric Jameson and Slavoj Žižek that "it is easier to imagine the end of the world than it is to imagine the end of capitalism", about which Mark Fisher wrote so persuasively. They are a reminder that part of what has brought the world to such a state of crisis is not only a serious failure of political imagination in its inability to consider alternatives to the current political system, but a stubborn unwillingness to even acknowledge that there *are* flaws in the societies we have faithfully built according to the logic of the market. But these flaws require acknowledgement *before* the more imaginative conversations about how things could be different or better can get underway.

In the famous 1995 novel *Blindness,* by Portuguese writer José Saramago, it would not be a spoiler to say that all but one of the population go completely blind, and society breaks down into a chaotic, brutal, and at times fascistic nightmare. In a 2008 interview, Saramago made it clear that the novel was supposed to be about how such a widespread affliction would reveal aspects of "society as it is", which ironically, without literal blindness, we do not see. "With hunger, war, exploitation, we're already in hell", he said (Jaggi, 2008). What he might also have said is that while the blindness of the story had the strange effect of revealing aspects of our society, this is a convincing premise for a novel because on some level we recognise that that there is another form of blindness at work in our *seeing*, keeping that dysfunction beyond our attention. As a character in the novel says, "I think we are blind, Blind but seeing, Blind people who can see, but do not see."

There is frequently an outburst of indignation about any suggestion of "false consciousness" when culturally led accounts are given of irrational behaviour, including the widespread adoration of a system that is literally killing us. But what we need to be honest about is that we are all blinded in this way to some degree. Regardless of where we may identify ourselves in the political landscape, our language, tastes, aspirations, cultural familiarity and participation all underpin an understanding of the world that is, to varying degrees, self-detrimental, and more useful to capital than to us.

Capitalism and political power have long required forms of obfuscation to conceal the grim reality of inequality and uneven labour relations that they create. But it is crucial to understand that they also attack our means of learning about those systems, attribute the problems that they generate to other causes, and use cultural means to incorporate people into their invisibility or make themselves more appealing.

Despite common resistance from those committed to an individualist model of the world that assumes full agency and rational self-interest, this is not exclusively a left-wing idea. When the late right-wing founder of *Breitbart News*, Andrew Breitbart, said that "politics flows downstream from culture", he was only restating an idea that left-wing theorists had been articulating and exploring for more than a century. As we saw in the last chapter, the same is true of Friedrich Hayek's council to Antony Fisher that he should stay out of electoral politics: "If you want to change events, you must change ideas."

Even if the dominance of culture in shaping our understanding of power is not exclusively a left-wing idea, the left certainly does have a significant head-start in analysing the ability of political power and the institutions of capital to manipulate culture to their advantage — a body of analysis that the world can no longer afford to ignore. Some readers will already be aware of this analysis, and there are of course numerous scholarly texts where lengthy deconstructions of these concepts can be found, but it is important here at least to make a brief explanation of some of the more prominent and useful arguments and ideas about the relationship between power and culture. Some of the theories briefly outlined here belong to different traditions for exploring the overall idea of power's exercise via culture, but in the interests of space and the avoidance of tedium these have been somewhat rolled together around the central idea that political and economic relations are often legitimised and concealed in appealing cultural forms.

When Ideas Rule, from Karl Marx to Charles Koch (and back)

Besides economic ideas about commodities and value, there is a broad tradition for understanding how culture and power interoperate that originates with the work of Karl Marx. In 1846, Marx and his collaborator Friedrich Engels wrote that:

> The ideas of the ruling class are in every epoch the ruling ideas, i.e. the class which is the ruling material force of society, is at the same time its ruling intellectual force. [...] The ruling ideas are nothing more than the ideal expression of the dominant material relationships [...] grasped as ideas.

The effect of this, Marx and Engels wrote, was that metaphorically speaking "men and their circumstances appear upside-down as in a camera obscura", causing people to misconstrue their relationship to power. As we'll see in the following chapter, this illusion that conceals disempowerment is imperfect, and accompanied — perhaps increasingly so — by a sense that all is not as it seems. In any case, this was a crude expression of an idea in nineteenth-century terms that would later be elaborated by numerous other scholars and thinkers.

One of the mostly widely studied of these is Antonio Gramsci, who produced much of his best-known work whilst incarcerated in Mussolini's prisons, including the theory of *cultural hegemony* — "hegemon" meaning dominance or leadership in Ancient Greek. Although this concept is contested in its precise details, the important principle is that through partaking in common cultural activities, it is possible for large numbers of people to be incorporated into their own domination, even without realising it, and that this is what prevents the dominance of a ruling minority from being challenged. Again, this theory is often misunderstood as a patronising suggestion that "the masses" do not have any agency to challenge power, but this is a misreading of the idea at best. Rather, Gramsci wrote firmly on the side of the people he saw as dominated, whom he called the "subaltern". And it is important to bear in mind that the argument was written by somebody incarcerated by an incoherent, violent, fascist regime that was kept in place partly by enormous cultural participation, even if reinforced with the quiet promise of trouble for those who did not participate.

So Gramsci was not implying everyone was stupid or incapable of thinking for themselves, so much as making an important elaboration of Marx's theory about how the "ruling ideas" of a society actually function: to encode an *implicit* acceptance of the ideas that are most useful to power. These ideas have been expanded by numerous other later thinkers to explore different forms of power, whether it is our relationship to the state, a social relation such as gender, or to capital itself.

Another theory in the same vein as cultural hegemony is that of French theorist Louis Althusser, who divided power into a "repressive state apparatus" and an "ideological state apparatus" — the latter being a grouping of schools, the church, and similar organisations that, again, reinforce the dominant power in the ideas that they affirm in their normal operation.

In a parallel but distinct tradition of cultural critique, Theodor Adorno and Max Horkheimer, writing not long after World War II, famously saw the culture industries as "mass-deception" that was accommodating to power, and did not mince their words. "Even the aesthetic activities of political opposites", they wrote, "are one in their enthusiastic obedience to the rhythm of the iron system" (1989 [1947]: 120).

This is essentially an idea that Mark Fisher transposed into the much later reality of the early twenty-first century as part of his analysis of "capitalist realism", in which even the worst excesses of the market-driven society seem normalised, inevitable and even pleasurable; to recall the words quoted in the last chapter, they are an "invisible barrier constraining thought and action" (2009: 16). Fisher was the first to acknowledge the considerable influence on his work of the cultural theorist of "late capitalism", Fredric Jameson. One of the most important considerations for understanding the overall question of how culture sustained capitalism's hold on society, as Jameson also acknowledged, was the need for historical specificity, not only in the cultural forms that appear, but in the forms that power takes, and that is why this theory is useful here. The aim of all this is not to rehearse the history of capitalism's cultural dominance, although a brief account of these theories is hopefully helpful to some readers. Rather, the point is firstly that, although these conceptions are old, they periodically need to be tested and applied in new historical circumstances. What the relationship between power and culture looked like in the 1980s when Jameson wrote, or in the 2000s when Fisher wrote, is different to the moment in which you are reading this book, and the essential inquiry into how this process takes place needs to be constantly re-examined. Secondly, any discussion of "fake news" or "post-truth" is exactly an occasion for the application of these ideas, not least because so much of the misinformation and disinformation that has brought about the moment of rupture examined in the last chapter has taken the self-reproducing cultural forms outlined here.

All statements of information are an invitation to believe — one that can be accepted too readily, or not readily enough, as will be examined in the chapters to follow. But as the unending proliferation of "Keep Calm and Carry On" posters, fridge magnets and other merchandise remind us, governments themselves have a long history of trying to influence our thinking and action with explicit invitations to think of government, nation, and our own position to both in a certain way. The history of political propaganda in a governmental sense is well known, and its later revival to evoke wartime stoicism is an interesting, if somewhat predictable occurrence given the failure to imagine anything new that has accompanied capitalism's "triumph" after the Cold War. The major conflicts of the first half of the twentieth century, however, rather exhausted the ability of governments to simply put up instructional posters and signs, or to make radio and TV broadcasts. Instead, governments have had to resort to increasingly subtle and manipulative means, usually involving hiring unscrupulous public relations "gurus" such as Dominic Cummings or Frank Luntz. The better the disguise, the more potent the propaganda, even if awkward images of politicians watching sports or participating in ridiculous online "challenges" seldom go over as planned. As the market-driven society developed, and the line between government and commercial enterprise thinned, the already sophisticated world of public relations saturated every pore of the resulting enclosure.

Probably the most helpful and notable voice in the examination of public relations is that of cultural historian Stuart Ewen, whose fascinating enquiry into the innovations of modern public relations, particularly in the work of Edward Bernays, is essential reading for those truly interested in misinformation and disinformation. Once again, Ewen also confirms the enduring relevance of the theories sketched out above:

> In a democratic society, the interests of power and the interests of the public are often at odds. The rise of public relations is testimony to the ways that institutions of vested power, over the course of the twentieth century, have been compelled to justify and package their interests in terms of the common good. (1996: 34)

A good example of this is the work of Frank Luntz, who has specialised in helping mostly Republican causes to express their ideology in language that has the best chance of convincing people and shaping public opinion. In 2003, Luntz was revealed to have urged Republicans to frame global warming in terms of "climate change", in a leaked memo to the party, in which he also said that "a compelling story, even if factually inaccurate, can be more emotionally compelling than a dry recitation of the truth" (Burke, 2003). Fake news indeed.

Alongside these alarming attempts to manipulate the US public, we see ever more eye-watering levels of cynical manipulation in Russia and the former Soviet Union. The writer Peter Pomerantsev provides a detailed insight into the development of "information warfare" as a tool of post-Cold War Russia:

> the notion of information war as defining history [...] replaces hypocrisy [...] with a world in which there are no values. In this vision all information becomes, as it is for military thinkers, merely a means to undermine an enemy, a tool to disrupt, delay, confuse, subvert. (2019)

Fake news indeed. In February 2002, then US Secretary of Defence Donald Rumsfeld made a now-famous observation about three categories of knowledge: known knowns, known unknowns, and unknown unknowns. That this formulation, which was actually coined by a group of NASA engineers, captured the public's imagination in the way it did, despite its numerous flaws, indicated a widespread fascination not only with what we know, but with what we do not. The concept of "unknown unknowns", particularly coming from a governmental source itself, invited us to consider what we as voters and citizens might not know that we didn't know. If you like, *known unknown unknowns.*

This is a subject explored in the next chapter, on conspiracy theories, but the strategic use of silence is also an interesting feature of our relationship to power in its own right — it is not only about commerce or free markets. In her analysis of "strategic ignorance", sociologist Linsey McGoey observes that Rumsfeld overlooked the idea of the "useful unknowns" that assist stakeholders in power, to the detriment of the public, even when these omissions are not deliberate (2019: 52). Immediately following her analysis of Rumsfeld's highly quoted observation, McGoey provides an example of how "useful unknowns" were used by bankers to avoid culpability for bringing about the global financial crisis in 2007–2008, in several different ways. Chief among these, she says, is that "it was more profitable to say nothing", and that this gave rise to socialised forms of silence about the risks of what was happening, which made it easier to later say that nobody had been aware of what was happening.

The mention of "ignorance" invites a charge of elitism, but as Robert Proctor has argued in his analysis of tobacco companies' attempts to manufacture uncertainty, covered more fully in the next chapter, ignorance need not be understood in an elitist or pejorative way, so much as being "the simple fact that there is a place where knowledge has not yet penetrated" (2008: 4). Indeed, as we can see, ignorance is often something that is cultivated.

The snapshot I provided at the beginning of this chapter about Estée Lauder's connections to Secure America Now is just once instance of the activities of a vast international network of organisations that has arisen somewhere between government, commerce, research, journalism, and lobbying — usually under the auspices of being a "think tank", or worse, a charity. The last chapter told the story of Antony Fisher's establishment of London-based think tank and self-described "educational charity" the Institute of Economic Affairs (IEA), in 1955 — the first in a series of similar organisations that Fisher set up across Europe and North America. As above, despite being encouraged by Friedrich Hayek not to go into politics, Fisher was said by Chicago economist Milton Friedman to have had more influence on the policies of Margaret Thatcher than anybody else. More recently, the IEA was shown to be distributing a magazine to sixteen- to eighteen-year-olds in the UK that contained articles that argued against tobacco taxation and the science of climate change and promoting NHS privatisation, without disclosing that they received significant funding from oil giant BP, British American Tobacco, and US-American organisations pushing for privatisation of the National Health Service (Ramsay and Geoghegan, 2018).

Another of these organisations, also mentioned in the opening chapter, is the Heritage Foundation, which was founded in 1973. Behind the networks of which the IEA and Heritage are one small part, stands a very important factor that facilitates these institutions' very deliberate attempts to shape policy and public perception of major issues: money. As we saw in Chapter One, the development of the market-driven society has been accompanied by a hoarding of wealth by a very small proportion of people, including an assortment of billionaires that would rather undertake minimal philanthropy and send private rockets into space than actually pay their taxes. In 2017, a study by Oxfam found that just eight people, all men, held half the world's wealth. One of them was Jeff Bezos, and another was Mark Zuckerberg. But amongst more than five hundred billionaires in the US at the time of writing, there were and still are many others whose names are far less well known, and who funnel money into this network of ideologically driven institutions such as the IEA, often under the guise of philanthropy — a phenomenon often known as "dark money".

The journalist Jane Mayer has provided an invaluable and detailed examination of these organisations in her book *Dark Money*. One of the most important parts of her account of how US politics was transformed according to this process, is in her description of how the right-wing economist and businessman Richard Fink planned out a strategy for his boss, the oil billionaire Charles Koch — one of the central figures in the network described above — to take over US politics in the 1970s. Like Margaret Thatcher, Fink and Koch were greatly influenced by the "Austrian model" of free-market economics that was the brainchild of none other than Friedrich Hayek (2016: 142). Firstly, Mayer recounts, Fink told Koch to invest in individual intellectuals who would develop ideas that would serve as the "raw products" for this takeover — note the petroleum metaphor. Secondly, Koch was instructed to fund think tanks and other similar "research" organisations that would make these ideas palatable to the public. A petroleum way of saying it might be "refinement". Finally, Fink told Koch that he should sponsor citizens' groups to put pressure on elected officials to adopt and implement these policies.

Over time, the model, which became known as the "Kochtopus" for the network of think tanks and other organisations it financed, was streamlined, but hopefully it is clear what was happening: whether they knew it or not, Fink and Koch were not only plotting to put into practice Hayek's ideas, but confirming and directly applying exactly the idea of Karl Marx and Friedrich Engels quoted earlier in this chapter: "The ideas of the ruling class are in every epoch the ruling ideas". Here was what the late-twentieth-century oil-financed US version of that principle might look like.

Literacy and the Lack Thereof

Protesters against the COVID-19 lockdowns in the US, Germany and Brazil all displayed a basic failure to understand what a pandemic is, how a virus spreads, or what the dangers of such a situation actually are. Frequently appearing from the far-right, they were typically incoherent in their reasoning and basic grasp of the problems about which they were so angry — something that often exacerbates the destructive vitriol with which their positions are expressed. But as this chapter hopefully shows, there are a lot of forces at work to ensure that as many people as possible are unable to make sense of their political circumstances, and it would be a dangerously elitist and positivist fiction to point the finger at them and say that they are simply the stupid ones. All the same, it is important to consider the role of public literacy alongside these other forces.

To speak about the literacy — or illiteracy — of fellow human beings is always to invite a charge of elitism, but what I hope to show here is that while certain forms of literacy and illiteracy may vary according to proximity to power and prestige, the presence of some form of illiteracy wholly transcends those boundaries. Not only can misinformation and disinformation come just as easily "from the top", but the problem of literacy can and must be addressed in a way that is instead built on an ethic of solidarity rather than elitism, by wanting the greatest literacy for all. Literacy is a collective, social accomplishment, not something for which individual members of the public can or should be held accountable.

The idea of literacy can function helpfully in both in the literal sense — the ability to read and write easily — and the more helpful metaphorical sense: a familiarity with the accepted analytical systems and mechanisms of how the world works in a way that makes it more difficult to believe disinformation and misinformation that are at odds with this knowledge. Literacy is a perfect metaphor precisely because the skills referred to by its literal meaning have suffered the same fate, and for similar reasons, as the broader sense of "familiarity" which I will outline below.

As far as actual literacy, in the basic sense of reading and writing, it is important that this emphasis too should not degrade into a snobby reason to correct people's grammar instead of listening to what they have to say. But there is something telling about the fact that so-called "developed" countries that claim literacy rates near 100% feature growing levels of functional illiteracy. Aficionados of 1990s US politics will recall the controversy that arose when Dan Quayle, Vice President during the single-term presidency of George H.W. Bush, misspelled "potatoe", miscorrecting a twelve-year-old who had in fact spelled it correctly. Images abound on the internet of mostly right-wing Americans and Brits holding misspelled signs such as "RESPECT ARE COUNTRY - SPEAK ENGLISH", so much so that extensive collections of them have been collated for amusement (Tstotsis, 2010). When these reactionaries are unable to spell the most basic of words in a political context or articulate their beliefs with coherency, it is very easy for the critique that arises to meet them to constitute ridicule on account of their seeming lack of education. The same was true when a group of far right protesters from the "English Defence League" held a March in the English town of Luton in 2011, seemingly in protest against Islam. One young man, interviewed by a journalist about why he was there, launched into a baffling explanation of how "muslamic infidels" want to impose "Iraqi law" on the UK and have already done so in London. The footage was later turned into an "anthem", with the man's voice auto-tuned to "sing" his words. But however absurd people may sound, ridicule seldom if ever wins this kind of argument, and only deepens the resentment felt by those are sneered at, ridiculed and excluded. The man's extreme prejudice is abhorrent, but it is also clear he does not know anything about the people and systems he claims to hate. There is something extremely tragic about his ignorance, and the way it has allowed him to develop opinions that not only have no basis in reality, but also evidence his profound exclusion from any relevant debates about Islam, immigration, or multiculturalism in Britain.

In the UK, the 2006 government-commissioned report Leitch Review of Skills found that "more than one third of adults do not hold the equivalent of a basic school-leaving qualification. Almost one half of UK adults (17 million) have difficulty with numbers and one seventh (5 million) are not functionally literate" (2006: 1). This situation has not improved. More recently, it has been reported that as many as nine million adults in the UK are functionally illiterate — 13% of the population (Sherwood, 2019). Similarly, data from the OECD in 2013 showed that more than 17% of the US population were at or below Level 1 — the most basic level of literacy skills (OECD, 2013). Unlike the broader forms of literacy and illiteracy that I'll outline below, research suggests that actual illiteracy not only has a profound socioeconomic impact on people, but is tied to other forms of social deprivation and exclusion, often running in families by limiting parents' ability to help their children learn (ibid.). Whatever one's politics, this should only underline the importance of universal access to quality education, and the only appropriate response should be to call for these measures to be widely adopted. But even the basic form of actual illiteracy outlined here is hardly a fringe issue.

Whether, as Marshall McLuhan famously warned, the "medium is the message" is still arguable either way, but the media we use and the ways we use them certainly can be indicative of the broader changes to public literacy. The digital mediation of reading and writing may be particularly problematic, especially in so far as it indicates the potential for an even more widespread problem that is generationally demarcated, rather than economically. In March 2020, when the COVID-19 pandemic hit Britain, hashtags containing misspelled words relating to the crisis appeared in Twitter's trending topics bar, on two separate occasions: #Convid19uk and #Panickbuying. Meanwhile, the Ukrainian-American internet startup Grammarly, whose product uses so-called "artificial intelligence" to correct people's spelling and grammar, and whose long-standing YouTube ad campaign regularly reminded people in a cute voice as they were about to watch a video that "writing's not that easy" before they had a chance to skip the ad, had gained almost seven million daily active users, and their free plugin for Google's web browser Chrome had been downloaded over ten million times. Though possibly a useful tool, the issue with something like Grammarly is that rather than ameliorate the problem it addresses, except for an individual at the moment of actually writing, it profits from that deficit in the individual's writing skills. The last thing Grammarly would want is that the individual's writing skills actually improve — meanwhile, as of October 2019, the company was worth more than $1bn and had received millions of dollars in venture capital funding (Lunden, 2019).

In *The Shallows*, Nicholas Carr described how the reduction in size and depth of media distributed over the internet and accessed under the severe pressures on our attention that had already become common were "remapping the neural circuitry" of our brains in a way that made it more difficult and less pleasurable to engage with longer or more detailed texts (2010). One does not need to adopt such a technologically determinist position to be alarmed at the ways that our relationship to digital communications technologies may be exacerbating a crisis of actual literacy, more in relation to reading than writing, that serves to obscure our relationship to crucial information relating to matters of collective wellbeing.

Our relationship to numeracy is not much better. During the 2020 race to be the Democratic Party presidential nominee, journalist Mekita Rivas claimed that since billionaire candidate Michael Bloomberg had spent over $500m of his own money on political advertising, this was enough to give everybody in the United States $1m. Rivas was way off — the actual amount that Bloomberg would have been able to give every member of the US population was less than two dollars. It's bad mathematics, as Rivas later freely admitted, but an innocent mistake, and it's easy to understand how one rushed journalist under pressure to command the attention and clicks of ever more fickle audiences might get momentarily confused. Much more concerning was the way that this claim was amplified by several other journalists without any attempt to use their own basic numeracy to verify it. The veteran US news anchor Brian Williams, for example, while hosting his own show on network MSNBC, actually read Rivas's tweet out loud to viewers after it was mentioned uncritically on his show by fellow journalist Maya Gray, appearing to do the "calculation" and playfully saying to the audiences at home "don't tell us if you're ahead of us on the math" (Taylor Rogers, 2020). When journalist Dan Gillmor said of the audiences he wrote for that "my readers know more than I do" (2004: xiv), this was probably not the dystopian state of affairs he had in mind.

Similarly, in the run-up to the 2019 UK general election, the Labour Party announced a policy whereby those earning more than £80,000 per annum or more — roughly the top 5% of earners — would be taxed slightly more. During an airing of the BBC question-and-answer current affairs programme *Question Time*, one member of the audience challenged the MP representing of Labour Party, Richard Burgon, by saying that the Labour Party were "liars" for saying that those earning over that figure were in the top 5%, also accusing them of conspiring to "go after" salary earners instead of billionaires because they were "easy money".

The data in this case are easily obtained from official sources: the threshold at which one would have entered Britain's top 5% of earners was actually slightly below the figure named by Labour, at £76,800 per annum. Whatever you think of the policy itself, the numbers are completely unambiguous — this was at that time the annual income at which a person would move into the top 5% of earners, so assuming the man in question was telling the truth about his income, he was comfortably in the top 5%. Percentages are taught early in secondary schooling. But nothing Burgon could say made any difference, and his attempts to politely correct the man only met with groans from the audience. Worst of all, nothing about this exchange was enough to prompt the BBC anchor chairing the so-called "debate",

Fiona Bruce, from putting the matter to rest and ensuring the accuracy of the programme. In fact, the BBC later distributed a clip of this exchange on the Twitter account connected to that programme with no accompanying caveat or fact-checking whatsoever, as a result of which it received more than 2,000 retweets and nearly 10,000 "likes". Serious lapses of editorial judgment like this that encourage widespread misunderstanding and ideologically led acrimony will be discussed more in Chapter Five, but the utter dominance in this encounter of poor numeracy skills shouted angrily over reasoned argument, and the way that these likely harmed the public's comprehension of an important policy debate, are also essential to understanding the persistence of misinformation and disinformation that should theoretically be easy to disprove.

Literacy About the World Around Us

It should already be clear that the problem of literacy goes much further than basic reading, writing and a rudimentary grasp of numbers. The failure of literacy also manifests in much thicker, more politically important ways, as a kind of ignorance — again, not in a pejorative sense. Whereas ignorance is the absence of knowledge or information, this sense of illiteracy is a specific kind of ignorance that relates not to information or facts, but to a deeper understanding (or lack thereof) of *how the world works*. Texts do not just allow us to see snapshots of the world as they are or were, but provide us with an insight as to tendencies, directions and plausibility. A person who is highly literate in the works of Shakespeare is not just familiar with the *content* of those works, but is also familiar with the *ways* Shakespeare wrote and constructed the world. A person who is literate with the social network Instagram similarly has a deeper understanding of how it functions, and is fluently able to navigate it in a nuanced and instinctive way. The same idea can be applied to how we understand the world around us, whether scientifically, politically, economically or in some other sense.

Once again, as with basic literacy, the lack of this form of literacy is a problem that affects everyone and cannot be individualised. To do so is exactly what the market-driven society wants: not only so that we will compete with each other, but because individualised and fragmented understandings of the world are at least part of what hinders our emancipation of it. We all need as richly developed an understanding of the world around us as possible — a world, let us remember, that contains burning forests, nationalist leaders, pandemics, oceans full of plastic, and in which one in ten human beings does not have access to clean drinking water (WaterAid, 2019). We need literacy both for successful navigation of that world, and for escaping it and replacing it with something better. The structural denial of this literacy to one person is a deprivation to everyone, because we are dependent on each other to understand the world and respond appropriately.

As in the case of the audience member on *Question Time*, even when we are just talking about writing and numerical skills, these skills facilitate and support our understanding of the social and political — the words and numbers we use support a broader understanding of the world that we need in order to function and make decisions — an understanding that is sorely lacking, and seems to have deteriorated as part of the post-war story that we encountered in the first chapter. Indeed, the US political scientist Thomas E. Patterson tells us that:

In the period after World War II, studies showed an upward trend in citizens' awareness of public affairs. The trend line is no longer rising. Today's citizens have a poorer understanding of some topics than even their counterparts of six decades ago, when the typical adult had only a grade-school education. (2010: 15)

This decline in the standards of understanding is almost certainly related directly to the capacity for any form of disinformation to spread. The world in which 7% of US adults believe that chocolate milk comes from brown cows (nbc4i.com, 2017) is the same world in which we are able to convince ourselves that anti-aging cream works. It is the same world where those who criticise "cultural Marxists" have not read even a line of Karl Marx; where those who attack Islam do not know what is actually in the *Qur'an* or what prayers are said by Muslims; where those who assemble to "protect" a statue of Winston Churchill perform Nazi salutes while doing so; where the majority of those who attack the European Union cannot name or describe a single one of its institutions; where those who posit a flat Earth do not know (or care) what gravity is; where those who avoid vaccines or stockpile antibacterial supplies during a viral pandemic do not actually know what a virus is.

These kinds of illiteracy can manifest in incredibly serious and dangerous ways, one example being the measles outbreaks around the world that have arisen because of anti-vaccination conspiracy theories (Gregory, 2019), or another being the fact that the night the United Kingdom voted to leave the European Union in 2016, thousands of people were googling "what is the EU?" and "what is Brexit?" (Selyukh, 2016). During the COVID-19 pandemic, those people who attacked 5G equipment and innocent broadband engineers going about their jobs in the belief that 5G was the underlying cause were largely unaware of the difference between ionising and non-ionising radiation — something that may sound highly technical, but is taught in the physics curriculum of most secondary schools. Yet when it comes to actually protecting public health, this knowledge fails to make itself useful. Anti-5G agitators recycle a lot of the same paranoia about electro-magnetic radiation from mobile phones that greeted previous generations of cellular data technology. The difference with 5G is that the antennae are much more visible in public space because the technology uses a much shorter range than previous cellular technologies, inviting more attention. The people who pushed cocaine, hydroxychloroquine, nanosilver particle toothpaste, and other false cures for COVID-19 not only obscured the harms that some of these substances could do to the body — they frequently also did so because of an aversion to vaccines that was not based on any understanding of how vaccines work.

Lest it seem like these observations are a rebuke to the unempowered majority, to which those who have been most deprived of formal education opportunities generally belong, it should be stressed that these forms of illiteracy are also common *within* the institutions of power. For example, in February 2015, Oklahoma Senator James Inhofe brought a snowball to the floor of the US senate in a bid to try to refute the fact that 2014 had at that time been the warmest year on record. Probably the most prominent example of this is Donald Trump, who has also frequently made this claim. In January 2019, for example, as the US was battered by snowstorms and plunging temperatures, Trump even tweeted "What the hell is going on with Global Warming? Please come back fast, we need you!" For anyone familiar with even the basics of what climate change involves, the existence of extreme cold weather does not refute the science of climate change for even a second. If anything, it adds weight to the conclusion of many climate scientists that climate change involves a more extreme climate, not just an overall warming of a few degrees. "Even in a warming climate, you still expect to get extreme and sometimes record lows occurring — they'll just be occurring less frequently", Andrew Dessler, a professor of atmospheric sciences at Texas A&M University, told the *Washington Post* (Mooney and Dennis, 2019).

These displays of staggering ignorance and illiteracy are examples of a theory that has come to be known as the Dunning-Kruger Effect — according to which, we tend to be unaware of the limitations of our own comprehension (Dunning, 2011). Though this theory is quite specific in the scientific literature, it suggests a more general principle that the more limited our understanding of the world, the more likely we are to assume we have understood everything. Anyone who has ever taught in higher education will also have observed the obverse effect: those students who are most able and most thorough in their work are frequently the ones who are most likely to question themselves. Part of what good teachers try to instil is the balance between having confidence in one's ideas and critical distance from them. But this struggle takes place against a backdrop outside the classroom in which everything is always being simplified and reduced.

Indeed, the French philosopher Jean Baudrillard called this tendency to simplify everything as we try and make meaning out of it "negentropy" (short for "negative entropy"), a concept borrowed from physics (1994: 86). Whereas "entropy" is the tendency for a system to degrade into chaotic randomness, "negentropy" is the tendency for a noisy, chaotic system to reduce into increasingly simple terms. For information, this means reductive either-or arguments, lost nuance, fixed systems of unworkable categories, and false causality.

In some ways, this tendency is a response to the ironic fact that despite all the distortions of what we can collectively know about the world, we are awash with useless information. There is an additional irony in the fact that while low literacy about complex issues and systems may lead us to struggle to understand them due a deficit, it also negatively impacts our ability to deal with a *large* amount of conflicting information, as the Italian chemist Ugo Bardi has argued, calling the strategic use of this dysfunction "unpropaganda" (2015).

There is also an urgent issue with the actual availability of the kinds of information that could otherwise help publics to be more informed: the eye-watering price tags and aggressive paywalls that accompany even temporary access to a single peer-reviewed academic journal article. To access a single, standard article in the academic journal *Cyberpsychology, Behavior, and Social Networking*, for example, costs $59 at the time of writing. Enough to feed several people. The journalist George Monbiot wrote in 2011 of the ways that, as he put it, academic publishers "make Rupert Murdoch look like a socialist". Scientific and other professionally produced knowledge, where it has not been produced by a think tank, often takes place at universities, which are publicly funded, particularly in Europe. But publishers often charge those same universities, and that same public, exorbitant amounts to actually access research for which they have already paid once. Monbiot gives the figure of nearly $21,000 as the price of accessing a single journal published by Elsevier, the world's largest publisher of academic research. But in 2019 the University of California decided not to renew a subscription worth $10m with the same company (Resnick, 2019). Academic research as it is currently practised has numerous problems — not least the primacy of these journals and the competitive overproduction of articles to fill them, many of which will have very few readers, but if there is any shred of intellectual value in the work that scientists and other academics publish in journals — and to be clear, there absolutely is — should this not be available to everyone, instead of being enclosed and privatised by a small minority? As we'll see in Chapter Five, this is similar to the debates that are happening about journalism, the difference being that the public has not already subsidised the production of that journalism.

Overall, illiteracy is a complex and multifaceted problem and it is simplistic at best to make firm cause/effect statements about exactly which kinds of illiteracy are most productive of the overall crisis of politically useful information and knowledge analysed here. But over the last few decades, as our society has been reconfigured around the priorities of markets, our literacy has undeniably changed too, and as populations make collective mistakes that are critical to their collective wellbeing, such as the inability to address climate change, or the embrace of nationalism in response to global capital flows, the question has to be raised as to whether a public would espouse the same ideas and political outcomes if formalised knowledge about the basics of physics or chemistry in the first case, or European history in the second, were made a higher priority.

Quantitative studies that have examined the relationship between levels of education tend to find that more educated individuals are less Eurosceptic (Hakhverdian et al., 2013). In the context of Brexit however, this was not quite so clear cut, and individuals from a wide range of educational backgrounds showed support for leaving the European Union (Kunst, Kuhn & van de Werfhorst, 2019), probably because the leave vote was made up of a confluence of voters with different reasons for wanting the same outcome. This should be a reminder that no matter how badly we want to point at our political opponents and produce a world of right and wrong, correct and incorrect, public conversations take place in a much more slippery environment in which there may well be concrete facts or formalised knowledge, but there are also an inordinate number of other factors complicating the assumptions and references on which those conversations depend.

As far as how literacy in the sense I've outlined here relates to the market-driven society, my argument is not that the market-driven society deliberately produces illiteracy in this broader, non-literal sense. Rather, it is more along the lines of the distinction that bell hooks articulates in the context of education, which can be thought of as a difference between "education as the practice of freedom and education that merely strives to reinforce domination" (1994). This distinction can be applied not only to pedagogy but to the broader way we think about what knowledge is supposed to be. Knowledge can be passive or active; dead or alive; hold you back, or set you free.

For decades, we heard encomia to the "knowledge economy" and the "information society", but literacy in the substantive sense that is discussed here is not particularly valuable in the marketplace, as evident in the devaluing of humanities or arts education at the expense of MBAs and STEM subjects, and the focus on buzzwords like "enterprise" and "innovation" in universities, rather than on fostering a deep or emancipatory understanding of the world. In a society in which education and knowledge are only valued for narrow, market purposes and the broader value in understanding the world is regarded pejoratively, the market-driven society benefits from the forms of illiteracy I have outlined above far too much to make their alleviation a priority. Such literacy would only lead to the market-driven society being challenged more openly and more often! It also benefits from widespread illiteracy *about capital* which the market is of course disincentivised from ameliorating or reversing.

Ultimately, as far as misinformation and disinformation, the point about illiteracy in both its literal and figurative sense is not that it is necessarily a driver, but that it represents a serious vulnerability for the societies where it exists. Firstly, those societies are left wholly unprepared to deal with the vast amount of misinformation and disinformation to which they are exposed, often by the market-driven society, and secondly, they are less able to challenge and fix that society itself. The remarkable creativity and ingenuity of human beings need not decline for our ability to comprehend and challenge the systems that govern how we live to deteriorate.

Emotion, Attachment, Sociality, Knowledge

Away from the somewhat aloof structures of formalised knowledge, our understanding of our world and our societies is also conditioned and disrupted by something else extremely important: emotion. Indeed, it is essential not to underestimate the capacity that emotion, and the many aspects of life that produce strong emotions, such as family, friends, aspirations, loss, nostalgia or anxiety, have to shape the ways that we understand the world.

As the early sociologist Émile Durkheim wrote, our emotional condition is often linked with the form that society takes. More recently, as a number of authors have noted, there something distinctive about the emotional dynamics of the market-driven societies of the early twenty-first century. Elsewhere, I have written in detail about how a combination of social features of the market-driven society determine its emotional character. Intolerable boredom, loneliness, precariousness and the disappearance of the future that is endemic to postmodernism, combined with a heavy emphasis on aspiration reduced to increasingly economistic terms, all produce widespread malaise that is hard to describe in specific terms for those that suffer it, but is often demotivating or debilitating. The result is that we try to compensate, through the trappings of consumerism that have arisen to sell compensatory pleasure itself — the most obvious being the soaring popularity of delivery food, the seeming addictiveness of social media or gaming, or the quiet success of the sugar industry.

Much of this work was of course inspired by the links drawn by Mark Fisher between the principle of "capitalist realism", outlined earlier, and the epidemic of depression in what I'm calling market-driven societies, which he argued often led to a "depressive hedonia" — that is, pleasure-seeking — rather than the standard "anhedonia" of conventional depression — the inability to feel pleasure (or anything, for that matter).

The philosopher Byung-Chul Han is another insistent voice that has reminded us of the numerous ways that the market-driven society can affect feeling and emotion, whether by disrupting the selfless processes of love, or producing widespread self-exploitation leading to burnout (2015). Han makes a careful distinction between *feeling*, which is specific and directional, which he calls "constative" — you can have a feeling *that* something is true, or has happened — and *emotion*, which is both more transient, and is not constative (2017). Arguably, both come into play as far as how our conscious and unconscious understandings of the world are shaped. In fact, as we'll see below and as a number of people such as Will Davies (2018) have pointed out, *feeling* has increasingly come to dominate the approaches that we bring to public conversations about our world.

For example, the communication scholar Zizi Papacharissi reminds us that intense emotion can "dominate expression and distract from factuality, as is the case with the [emotional] structures that support the growth of the Tea Party movement in the United States", and that raised emotions "do not inherently enhance understanding of a problem, deepen one's level of knowledge on a particular issue, or lead to thick forms of civic engagement with public affairs" (2015: 120).

Emotion can even determine what we are prepared to accept as truth. Will Davies draws attention to the *Gerasimov Doctrine*, named after Russian General Valery Gerasimov — essentially the deliberate blurring of the line between war and peace — arguing that this has implications not only for war, but also in the sense that it makes peace more combative too (2018: 123). While this is no doubt true in the geopolitical context where Davies subsequently applies it, the idea of a *combative peace* also serves a more general argument about the nature of our public conversations. It is widely observed that, particularly in our encounters online with contrasting opinions, we seem to have progressively lost the ability to disagree bilaterally and respectfully. In some cases, this is fair enough, since as we'll see from the debate-positivism covered in Chapter Four and Five, not everything can be easily reduced to a debate with "two equal sides". But even within broadly aligned political camps, the tendency to argue or fall out over differences in approach or even language are increasingly conspicuous, to the point at which nuance is best attempted face-to-face with friends and family, or other trusted communities.

Interesting dimensions of how community and identity affect our understanding of the world were illustrated in a behavioural study by the legal scholar Dan Kahan and colleagues in 2013. Respondents were given a political questionnaire to determine how right-wing they were — a crass, reductive idea perhaps, but necessary for the good of the experiment overall. Their overall numeracy was also assessed. Next, half the respondents were given a tableau of four made-up numbers, showing people who had a rash, divided into half between those who applied a skin cream to treat the rash, and those who didn't apply it, and of each, how many improved and how many didn't. The goal of showing respondents these numbers was simply to provide a control condition that simply assessed if there was a correlation between how numerate the respondents were and whether they could accurately ascertain from the numbers whether or not the skin cream was effective. The numbers, being fictitious, were arranged both ways round, so as to indicate in some cases that the cream was effective, and in others that it was not, and made matters worse. The other half of the respondents were shown the exact same tableaux of data, but the labels were changed. Now, instead of a skin cream leading to a deterioration or amelioration of a rash, it was gun control — a highly polarising issue in the United States — leading either to an increase or a decrease in crime.

Interestingly, the results were completely different with a politically polarising issue such as gun control than with the more neutral one. In the case of the skin cream respondents, the more numerate they were, the more they were able to determine the efficacy of the cream. In the case of the gun control respondents, the more numerate they were, the better they were at twisting their interpretation of the numbers to support their existing political views, which of course had been measured beforehand. The authors of this study called this "motivated numeracy", which they explained with what they called the *Identity-Protective Cognition Thesis*:

> when a policy-relevant fact does become suffused with culturally divisive meanings, the pressure to form group-congruent beliefs will often dominate whatever incentives individuals have to "get the right answer" from an empirical standpoint. (2013: 3)

In other words, the anchors of our social community are so strong, they are frequently able to distort what we are willing to believe is true or not. Given the widespread social alienation I referred to earlier, it is perhaps not that much of a surprise that social factors have so much weight: lose your people in a market-driven society, and you really do have nothing. And when we do diverge from our communities on major issues, the consequences can be tragic, as evidenced by the families torn apart over Brexit and Donald Trump. But as the authors of the study point out, where people do think *along social lines*, the impact of this pattern on public conversations also has the potential for disastrous consequences in terms of the public conversations that take place under this pressure:

> At a collective level, of course, this style of engaging decision-relevant science can be disastrous. If all individuals follow it at the same time, it will impede a democratic society from converging, or at least converging as quick as it otherwise would, on understandings of fact consistent with the best available evidence on matters that affect their common welfare. (2013: 3)

Think for a moment about how the social and cultural factors of the Identity Protection Cognition Thesis from this research might combine with the Dunning-Kruger effect that makes us unaware of our own ignorance. Imagine people who are not only so blissfully unaware of the inconsistencies in their worldview that they do not have the impulse to question themselves at all, but who are also so bound by their identity-protective impulses that even when they are challenged, they will interpret any evidence that they are wrong as an affirmation of their beliefs. We have all met these people, and they can almost certainly be found amongst people from every socio-economic background, every ethnicity, and in every country in the world.

Behavioural economist Daniel Kahneman offers a simple metaphor for understanding the ways that our thinking can also be conditioned by emotion, a construct that is frequently misunderstood as physiological or neurological fact. Thinking can be roughly divided into two types: System 1 and System 2. Whereas System 2 is the detached, rational, analytical form of thinking that Kahneman calls "slow" thinking, System 1 is faster and more emotive; it is also dominant. "In the picture that emerges from recent research, the intuitive System 1 is more influential than your experience tells you, and it is the secret author of many of the choices and judgments you make." (2011: 13) This is perhaps why, as is often remarked, misinformation and disinformation travel so much faster over digital networks than the hefty, nuanced, more boring truth (Vosoughi, Roy & Aral, 2018).

Dan Kahan and his colleagues also used this idea of System 1 and System 2 thinking in the study mentioned earlier, and framed their research as a refutation of System 2 thinking altogether, which they called the *Science Comprehension Thesis*. It is true that their findings show that science comprehension is not enough on its own — remember, their more numerate participants were the most likely to distort their interpretation of the numbers. But it is also possible to see how the fast, intuitive thinking of System 1 may itself be constrained by identity-protective thinking and Dunning-Kruger-protected misunderstanding of an issue subject to discussion. Our reactionary impulses in response to culturally divisive issues like nationalism, immigration, religion, abortion, global warming, military activities or even the free market seem most often to start off with socially and intellectually habituated positions. In the profoundly lonely, anxious and illiterate context of the market-driven society, perhaps these studies at least offer some further indication that besides everything I've said above, *the truth isn't always relevant*.

In the first chapter, I used the metaphor of "anchors" to indicate our attachment to various ways of understanding and making sense of the world, and that is an idea I return to here in greater depth. Hopefully it should be possible to see how social structures themselves in some sense anchor the way we look at the world by tying ideas to the social relations we so desperately crave in the market-driven society. But as we will see again and again throughout this book, ideas can also be emotionally resonant even when they are not tied to the ones we love, simply because they provide us with a firm means of looking at the world. Unfortunately, people often cling to ideas such as nationalism, racism and misogyny that have become foundational to how they understand the world, to the point that no amount of "truth", argument or formal education will shift them. Worse still, these anchors frequently distort the issues they are intended to help understand, and the "free market" is one of the more prevalent examples. The next two chapters, in totally different ways, are explorations of exactly this idea: the story with which we attempt to understand some aspect of the world can take us further away from, rather than closer to understanding it. Both chapters also make use of the concept of "cruel optimism", developed by the sociologist Lauren Berlant — an emotional attachment in which "the object that draws your attachment actively impedes the aim that you brought to it initially" (2011: 1).

The Mythology of "Elites"

Hopefully it is already clear from these indications that any conception of "fake news", misinformation or disinformation is not some kind of phantom menace that reared its head in November 2016, but is instead built into the very thing most people were calling democracy until the seemingly unthinkable started to happen. The writer Nesrine Malik has persuasively argued that our societies are founded on a variety of dysfunctional myths, which she refers to as "perversions in our collective storytelling" (2019). This chapter will close with a brief exploration of one of the most pervasive and damaging myths, happily accepted and repeated by a surprisingly broad range of people: the slippery concept of "elites".

One particularly perverse feat of political and semiotic gymnastics is the way that most of the nationalist or neo-fascist campaigns of the historical period addressed here have been able to attack "elites" or imply sympathy with those who feel excluded from an often conspicuously international form of liberal capitalist power, without mentioning capitalism, or alienating that other essential part of the same overall political confluence — the actual elites. As we'll see, this rhetoric was only feasible because of several overlapping forms of misinformation and disinformation.

In July 2016, before he was elected president, Donald Trump used his speech at the Republican National Convention to try to appeal to potential voters. The language he used was instructive:

It is finally time for a straightforward assessment of the state of our nation.
I will present the facts plainly and honestly. We cannot afford to be so politically correct anymore.
So if you want to hear the corporate spin, the carefully crafted lies, and the media myths, the Democrats are holding their convention next week.
But here, at our convention, there will be no lies. We will honor the American people with the truth, and nothing else.

[...]

I have visited the laid-off factory workers, and the communities crushed by our horrible and unfair trade deals. These are the forgotten men and women of our country. People who work hard but no longer have a voice. I AM YOUR VOICE.

This was the moment when it should have become clear to everyone that Donald Trump was likely to win the election — not because it was an especially good speech, but because it was exactly the "product-improved Fascist party, dedicated to the enhancement of the personal economic security" that Edward Luttwak had predicted back in 1994. Fascism has long appealed by promising to give a voice to the voiceless. If the Democratic Party had selected Bernie Sanders, who was actually quoted favourably in this particular speech, the whole spectacle of the election would have looked very different, and Trump would have had to give a very different speech. But against the banal restatement of a moderate but increasingly unworkable political-economic status quo that Hillary Clinton represented, Donald Trump was cryptically appealing to those fed up with certain aspects of the market-driven society, even though they did not consciously realise that this was what the problem actually was. Even if it is now obvious as to why this was a winning strategy, more important is that it was an entirely artificial, disingenuous and cynical spectacle of a speech, utterly reliant on misinformation and disinformation.

For a start, there is the fact that it is framed in the standard language of the snake-oil salesman: "I'm going to give you the truth". Whenever you hear this from somebody seeking election, you can almost always expect a whopping great lie. This trick has also been used by Nigel Farage, and is just one of countless ways that a wholly uncritical relationship to the "truth" can help to obscure what is actually happening. Note also the moral evocation of "honesty", and even the reference to spin. What followed was a series of powerfully framed lies.

The most pervasive lie, one that was later used in some spheres to try to blame the poor for Trump's victory, was the insinuation that it is the working classes and the poorest economically — the victims of liberal, capitalist society — who would be championed and rescued by a saviour in the form of Trump. Again, Nigel Farage repeatedly played a similar game.

But victimhood is partly about who *feels* they are the victim. Indeed, the left-behind narrative did not work particularly well to convince actual poor people to vote for Trump, nor for Britain's vote to leave the European Union. As journalist Adam Ramsay has pointed out, the narrative that working-class or low-earning people independently or even primarily caused Brexit or voted for Trump, is not only empirically false, but is part of a long-term tendency in which "ruling classes have always sought to blame bigotry on the working classes" (2019). Dissatisfaction with social and material conditions certainly did have a role to play, and many less well-off people did vote for Brexit and Trump, but not as many as we were encouraged to believe, and for many more reasons than simply being at the bottom of the socio-economic ladder. Dissatisfaction with the status quo in the case of Brexit was more a case of a "squeezed middle" (Antonucci et al., 2017), while "Clinton led by 11% among voters who earn less than $50,000 [and] Trump secured his victory by winning among those who earn $50–200,000" (Ramsay, 2019).

In an interview for *Vice News* in 2017, Steve Bannon, a former Goldman Sachs banker who was the architect of Trump's 2016 electoral success, including the speech above, categorically refused to accept that Trump was an elite, while insisting that Hillary Clinton was. This was not only a strange claim; it represented an interesting development, because, as the sociologist Jo Littler has argued, "Whilst the existence of elites is hardly new, what is to some degree more historically novel is the extent to which large sections of today's plutocracy feels the need to pretend they are not an elite at all." (2018: 115). It may have been strategy, or it may have been blind denial, but it is certainly reminiscent of fellow sociologist Imogen Tyler's concept of "classificatory struggles" around class. Riffing on the work of French sociologist Pierre Bourdieu, Tyler argued that part of the struggle inherent in class is at least partly over how it is *classified*. It should barely need pointing out that one of the more effective obfuscations achieved by the market-driven society is in how we actually understand what our socio-economic position actually is or means, and this is no accident. Terms such as "middle class" or "working class" are woefully inadequate, as a variety of sociologists have shown. In the pejorative naming of vague "elites", we see the same principle not simply applied to how people classify or think about themselves, but externally, in how they think about and classify their imagined adversary or oppressor *above them* in the socio-economic order.

As Umberto Eco has argued, there is also the sense that fascism "appeals to a frustrated middle class" and often involves a resentment that looks upwards, as well as hatred that looks down. It entails a sense of insurgency against an enemy who is considered in some way superior. Eco put it that followers of fascist regimes "must feel humiliated by the ostentatious wealth and force of their enemies" (1995). In her analysis of the spread of these movements across the world, the author Ece Temelkuran has written that:

Academics, journalists and the well-educated found

themselves included in the enemy of the people camp, part of the corrupt establishment, and their criticism of, or even their carefully constructed comments on, this political phenomenon were considered to be oppressive by the real people and the movement's spin doctors. (2019)

In the case of Trump, and of the other nationalist movements associated with the same political moment, this is exactly the role that the "elites" play. Umberto Eco reminds us however, that "the followers must [also] be convinced that they can overwhelm the enemies. Thus, by a continuous shifting of rhetorical focus, the enemies are at the same time too strong and too weak", and here too, we can see how "elites" play this role.

The vagueness around the word "elites" helps to facilitate multiple, carefully deployed meanings whose continual switching is made easier without a widespread understanding of capital or of the market-driven society, and which facilitates this simultaneous weakness and superiority. The distinct ideas of *internationalism* — a borderless form of labour solidarity, *cosmopolitanism*, a cultural phenomenon — and *globalisation* — the forms of unaccountable cross-border commerce that arose in the 1980s — could be merged into a single signifier, and anger that was appropriate in respect of the owners and beneficiaries of the market-driven society could be tacitly redirected at the cosmopolitans and their *Lonely Planet* travel guides — despite their not having very much power. In other words, the bizarre confluence of seemingly anti-elite feeling and the wealthier rentier classes is possible because while one audience is cryptically spoken to as workers who have been deprived in economic terms, the actual elites are expected to assume these jibes are directed at cultural elitism, or simply be in on the ruse and vote according to aloof self-interest.

And sure enough, like Brexit, Trump was an elite-friendly outcome, and the first thing he did was pass a historic tax cut for the very richest people in the US, all made possible by the lie that he would stand up for those left behind. This billionaire-friendly allegiance was also discernible in the Brazilian elections in October 2018 that saw Jair Bolsonaro, who has openly expressed a desire to return to military dictatorship, elected president. Bolsonaro won in 98% of the richest cities, while his opponent Fernando Haddad won in 97% of the poorest, and the lower the Human Development Index of a municipality in Brazil, the higher the share of the vote for Haddad (Fernando Toledo, do Lago and Sueiro, 2018). Italy follows a similar pattern, roughly across a north-south divide, and the richer north has historically supported the reactionary right wing far more than the south.

Like most of the other reactionary movements in the world, Trump was pushed, campaigned for or indirectly financed by wealthy, conservative businesspeople such as Robert Mercer, Charles Koch and his brother David, and Arron Banks, who knew that transnational co-operation and consumer and environmental protections and worker's rights were bad for business. As we'll see in the next chapter, these economic elites are often the people who quietly *want*, or at least benefit from, baseless conspiracy theories about the Rothschilds, the Illuminati, the New World Order, and imaginary "elites", because the more people who preoccupy themselves with these vile, often anti-Semitic lies, the less they will pay attention to the more boring, if no less outrageous story of what the real elites are up to. George Soros and Bill Gates frequently appear in conspiracy theories precisely because they tend to focus on philanthropy that assists less elite-friendly causes.

As this chapter has hopefully shown, in certain contexts, if the term "fake news" means anything, it has essentially become a shorthand for the abundant misinformation and disinformation that is built into the market-driven society, and which we are *all* aware of to some degree. Throughout the numerous examples given above, it should be clear from this chapter that any simplistic notion of the "truth" is a dangerously naïve proposition that should not be relied upon, except with extreme caution. This is not to say that there is no such thing as truth — which would be equally ill-advised. Rather, the important point is that it has become so difficult to find out what actually *is* true, that truth in public conversations might as well be considered a theoretical ideal at best.

This is not something for which convenient scapegoats such as Facebook or Russian disinformation campaigns can be simply and easily blamed, much as they may both be nefarious influences on the world. Even they are part of a far more pervasive global system that is designed to exchange commodities and maintain its stability, not to promote or facilitate the "truth", least of all about that system itself or the localised market-driven societies that comprise it.

Meanwhile, the more unequal and undemocratic a society becomes, the greater the pressure on the control of information about that society, in order to ensure that its inhabitants are not motivated or empowered to change it. And by far the best way to ensure the world does not become more democratic is to control information in such a way as to ensure that people believe it already is; the only way to prevent the world becoming more equal is to mask the public's understanding of economics with cruel individualism or meritocracy. A bit like the information war described earlier by Peter Pomerantsev, which adjusts to whatever ideology is necessary in order to bring about a specific outcome, power in the market-driven society shifts to whichever narrative will keep it intact: be it with red-herring conspiracy theories, as in the next chapter; with the banal positivism and shallow understanding of liberalism, as in Chapter Four; with bad journalism, as in Chapter Five; or the attention-driven data-harvesting merriment of digital platforms, as in Chapter Six. It will stoke up far right talking points one minute, and deploy left-associated language of identity and social justice the next. The market-driven society is not only awash with misinformation and disinformation; it is kept in place by them.

Chapter Three
Wake Up Sheeple! This Is All a Conspiracy!

What difference do it make if the thing you scared of is real or not?
— Toni Morrison

Many of what we call "conspiracies" are the ruling class showing class solidarity.
— Mark Fisher

People of the same trade seldom meet together, even for merriment and diversion, but the conversation ends in a conspiracy against the public, or in some contrivance to raise prices.
— Adam Smith

Where justice is denied, where poverty is enforced, where ignorance prevails, and where any one class is made to feel that society is an organized conspiracy to oppress, rob and degrade them, neither persons nor property will be safe.
— Frederick Douglass

"How's your book going?" said Z, a friend of mine who teaches at a university in the US, during a video call.

"Oh, it's OK, a bit slow." I replied. "At the moment I'm writing a chapter about conspiracy theories."

"Wow, really?" She replied.

"Yeah, well I think they're fascinating." I began to explain. "Even if I don't believe any of them, I think that they tell you a lot about the popular imagination, and how disempowered people feel. Like, the fact that people think 9/11 was an inside

job is in some ways as important as whether it actually was or not, especially since most people have no way of ever knowing for sure — they're just choosing what to believe based on what they think is likely. So it tells you what people feel are the likeliest ways they might be conspired against."

"Yeah totally. But what about things like Stevie Wonder?" Z replied.

"What do you mean, Stevie Wonder?" I said, confused.

"Oh my god, you haven't heard about this?" Z enthused. "Stevie Wonder isn't really blind. Ok, I'm going to send you some links. There's this clip, where a mic stand is falling over right in front of him, and he grabs it, and loads of other stuff. He can definitely see. Apparently it was something he did when he was a child star, and then he had to keep doing it."

Before clicking the link she had sent, I paused for a moment and considered the unexpected direction the conversation had taken. Z is someone I look up to greatly and whose intellect dwarfs my own. The YouTube clip had 1.3M views. Some smart ass had looped a three-second section in which the stand is knocked over, punctuating each loop of the footage with a stickman illustration of every step in the sequence. In the clip, Wonder did indeed appear to try and catch it, clumsily doing so with his forearm as opposed to his hand as a sighted person would. It is mysterious how he was able to do this, but a long way from conclusive. Amused, I thought of the Eddie Murphy stand-up sequence in which he says, pretending to be in the car with Stevie Wonder, "the piano and the singin', I told you how I feel about singin' — I ain't impressed. You wanna impress me, take the wheel for a little while." The crowd goes wild.

It seems everybody wants Stevie to see. There is no good reason to doubt that Stevie Wonder is blind. But in what kind of a world does a famous and universally acclaimed musician spend his entire career going to the extreme inconvenience, expense, and downright dishonesty of pretending to have a disability, never mind the reputational risk, should he be found out?

My encounter with the apparently well-known conspiracy theory that Stevie Wonder can actually see was an important reminder of how commonplace conspiracy theories are. A playful theory about a musician most people agree is one of the greatest of his generation, blind or not, is relatively harmless. But conspiracy theories in general are one of the most bizarre, interesting, and frequently harmful ways that misinformation and disinformation can spread.

The world was given an especially acute taste of this during the 2020 global COVID-19 pandemic, when much of the tidal surge of disinformation in that specific context, such as false cures or inaccurate claims about the causes of that illness, was driven by conspiracy theories that had long preceded the pandemic, especially those involving vaccination and 5G technology. In the United Kingdom, 5G apparatus was repeatedly subjected to arson attacks that were attributed to conspiracy theorists opposed to that technology, and employees of UK broadband provider OpenReach pleaded on the Facebook pages of anti-5G groups to be able to go about their work without being abused on the street (Waterson, 2020).

Other common conspiracy theories include: a belief that the surface of the Earth is actually a flat disc surrounded by an ice wall that, in some accounts, is protected 24/7 by the world's military forces; that the moon landing in 1969 was faked; and that 9/11 was carried out by the US government or some other state actor. Frequently, conspiracy theories can take on a racist or similarly bigoted character — for example, that the world's Jews are secretly controlling the exercise of power, that the Chinese government created the SARS-CoV-2 virus that caused the COVID-19 pandemic, or that unbeknownst to most people, Muslims are trying to establish Sharia Law and/or replace the white populations of Europe or the United States in a so-called "great replacement".

Some of these beliefs are dangerous and abhorrent, and others are just plain silly, but the presence and nature of conspiracy theories are very instructive features of the cultures and information ecosystems where they occur. They are also extremely common. A major Leverhulme-funded study of conspiracy theories carried out by Cambridge University and YouGov in 2018 found that in the US, 64% of people believed in at least one of the ten conspiracy theories listed by the study, as did 60% in the UK (Addley, 2018). This should only confirm that, while the details of some conspiracy theories may be bizarre or upsetting, we ignore the prevalence of these theories at our peril. Even if at times their examination might require that we hold our noses, the cultural and political phenomenon they represent needs to be taken seriously by anybody interested in our relationship to information, misinformation and disinformation. This chapter seeks to make that exploration.

What Do We Know About Conspiracy Theories?

It seems inconceivable that centuries after the Earth was known to be round, there might be people who not only seriously believe it to be flat, but who *decide* to start believing this, having previously agreed with most people that it was round. So ridiculous and bizarre are the often-elaborate claims that underpin this theory that one might be forgiven for thinking it is really a playful, ironic hoax played on the most earnest empiricists to make them look foolish — a conspiracy theory about a conspiracy theory, if you will. Indeed, the first question on the FAQ page of the Flat Earth Society website is "Are you serious?", which is answered with a simple "Yes". But however tongue-in-cheek the Flat Earth Society may seem, the theory itself is increasingly common, and a wide array of celebrities have publicly stated support for it, such as English cricketer Andrew Flintoff, rapper and Gossip Girl backing vocalist B.o.B. aka Bobby Ray Simmons Jr, and basketball player Kyrie Irving (Lawrence, 2018; Tiffany, 2017). A football team in Spain even changed its name to "Flat Earth FC" in homage to the theory.

Like other conspiracies about science, the flat Earth theory manages to avoid the distraction of an overt political orientation, at least as far as the well-known left-right continuum is concerned. This political inconspicuousness may be part of its success, but more interestingly still, the assertion it makes as far as the actual flatness of the Earth is largely pointless in itself. While racist conspiracy theories almost certainly amplify and exacerbate existing racism, flat Earth theory is a symbolic belief with no effect, and so-called Flat-Earthers will never be able to make the world flat. In other words, the thrust of the theory is simply one of contesting a centuries-old scientific conclusion on the basis of subjective experience and poor scientific understanding, but this contradiction does not actually serve any purpose for the person who believes it — or not until you think about what is actually being contradicted.

The emptiness of the theory itself is in fact the best clue for understanding the provenance and functioning of conspiracy theories. While the flat Earth theory may seem to be a physical claim about one of the celestial bodies in our solar system, the refusal of a round Earth is more of gesture related to the type of knowledge the Earth being round *is*, and the provenance of that knowledge. Rather than the actual importance of the flatness of the Earth, the primary message of the theory is really that simply by virtue of having originated from sources that are powerful or dominant in the culture, *established* knowledge itself — science in this case — should not be trusted. Indeed, although the Flat Earth Society is convinced that those who espouse the "hoax" of a round Earth are lying, the answer on their FAQ page about why this might be the case is broadly that "there is no way to know", but that it is likely that the powerful are trying to "maintain legitimacy," to "hide the truth of the Bible", and to "gain power and money" by "siphoning off the space budgets and denying the world the resources of the Antarctic". In other words, the flat Earth theory makes it clear that conspiracy theories are not necessarily about the *content* of the theory itself, so much as an expression of suspicion — usually about the mendacious greed of some powerful, organised, wealthy elite. It just happens to be encapsulated in the admittedly drastic view of the Earth as flat. But this *suspicion-first-facts-second* disposition is the key to understanding conspiracy theories.

This disposition is also present in anti-vaccination beliefs, which often entail conspiratorial elements. For example, in 2015 a theory spread around that the polio vaccine given to ninety-eight million people in the United States was causing cancer, and that the United States Centre for Disease Control had deleted pages from its website that had contained the CDC's "admission" of these findings (Lacapria, 2015). There was no truth to this claim whatsoever, but the implication of a conspiracy, at the very least, to cover up the information is clear. In this instance, in contrast with the flat Earth theory, science is trusted and a government body, the CDC, is the conspirator.

Outside of science, other conspiracy theories have a similar distrust, but bring this attitude into more familiar and contested political areas. So-called "9/11 truthers" tend to assert that planned, concealed operations on the part of the United States and other state actors such as Israel were behind 9/11, rather than militant Wahabbist group al-Qaeda; that civilian aircraft containing real passengers were not flown directly into the towers by on-board hijackers who were predominantly Saudi nationals working for al-Qaeda; that the Twin Towers did not collapse solely as a result of the impact of the airplanes and resulting fires. One common claim is that the buildings could not have simply collapsed, and must have been demolished, even if the reasons and motivation for such an action are not clear.

Whenever major, unprecedented global crises arise such as terrorist attacks and pandemics, there is clear historical precedent to suggest caution around the official narratives given by governments. The 9/11 attacks were not a conspiracy, but in the years that followed, their aftermath likely became one. The way that 9/11 was used as justification for the wars in Iraq and Afghanistan, which were highly lucrative for private contractors such as Halliburton (whose former CEO Dick Cheney was US Vice President at the time of those conflicts), certainly demonstrate that powerful interests in the US stood to gain from the foreign wars and mass surveillance that those fateful attacks led to. Nevertheless, the idea that this even comes close to proving that the United States government conspired either internally or with its allies to murder more than three thousand of its own citizens at great cost and risk, and has so far been successful in covering it up, is not only highly improbable but likely to be considered downright ridiculous by anyone familiar with the disorganisation and poor resourcing usually entailed in working for government. Just like with flat Earth theory, here too is a rejection of an official narrative, both from governmental sources and of the science or engineering accounts given, but in this case the political context is far clearer.

In the QAnon conspiracy theory, which grew in the early months of Donald Trump's first term, we see the US's external geopolitical reality evaporate and domestic political cynicism replace it, combined with the bizarre, repressed imagination of the Anglo-American right wing.

The theory is widely described and discussed elsewhere, but a brief summary for illustration purposes is useful here. According to the QAnon conspiracy theory, Trump's arrival in the White House was a moment of emancipatory potential, effectively the coming of a messiah who proceeded to engage in a "war" against a cabal of so-called liberals like Hillary Clinton (who are said to have their own "death squads"), the deep state and the global banking sector, in order to "free" the United States. This cabal is of course very similar to those imagined in other historical conspiracy theories — for example, about the Illuminati — and the theory, of course, overlaps with the anti-Semitic theory that Jews are controlling everything. The difference with QAnon is that for many believers in the theory, the conspirators are accused of involvement in a global paedophilia ring — an element that overlaps to a greater or lesser degree with the proven abuses and underage sex trafficking of the late US financier Jeffrey Epstein and his inner circle.

The QAnon theory began when cryptic clues called "crumbs" began to be posted anonymously online and signed "Q". Q is believed by those following the theory to be a member of a group within the Trump administration, and the name is thought possibly to be a reference to a top-level security clearance at the Department of Energy. The "crumbs", which frequently involve predictions, footage of Trump saying or doing otherwise inexplicable things, strange photos, and cryptic, almost poetic texts have spurred flurries of interpretation. Interestingly, one could argue that in some ways QAnon is also a "counterconspiracy theory" since although it involves the standard accusation of a powerful cabal as most conspiracy theories do, it also entails a mysterious conspiracy against that cabal, by the Trump administration. Worryingly, if perhaps unsurprisingly, the theory appears to have significant support *within* the institutions of US government. In 2018, a police sergeant in Florida was pictured in a photo with Vice President Mike Pence while wearing a SWAT vest bearing a red QAnon patch accompanied by the words "question the narrative." (Hay, 2019).

The plot appears to be thicker still, as there is some suggestion that the QAnon conspiracy theory started as a prank *against* the fervent Trump supporters who tend to believe it. In 1999, a collective of Italian artists, later known as Wu Ming, published a book titled *Q* under the name "Luther Blissett", a pseudonym commonly used by the Italian left, that featured many of the same ideas and themes that would later appear in the QAnon theory. "We can't say for sure that it's an homage [to our book]", Wu Ming artists Roberto Bui, Giovanni Cattabriga, and Federico Guglielmi told *BuzzFeed News*, "But one thing is almost certain: our book has something to do with it. It may have started as some sort of, er, 'fan fiction' inspired by our novel, and then quickly became something else" (Broderick, 2018).

Just as above I alluded to the idea that the flat Earth conspiracy theory was a joke — enough at least for it to be flatly denied by the organisation's official website — here it feels a little as though we may have what is in effect a conspiracy theory about a conspiracy theory. After all, as political scientist Michael Barkun points out, the beliefs that "everything is connected", that "nothing happens by accident" and "nothing is as it seems", all of which apply here, are hallmarks of the conspiracist mindset (2013: 3–4). But the deliberate creation of conspiracy theories is not new. As recounted in Adam Curtis's 2016 documentary *HyperNormalisation*, the theory that the US government was suppressing information about extra-terrestrials visiting Earth was deliberately cultivated, including an intentionally "leaked" document forgery providing conspiracists with "evidence" to "discover", so that the testing of top-secret weapons systems in the southwestern United States was not revealed during the Cold War.

If there was ever a "hall of fame" for the conspiracy theorists of the Euro-Atlantic world we have been examining, two names would be written in lights above all the others. The first would be that of prolific British conspiracist David Icke, whose vehement delivery of baffling, complicated yet incoherent theories has the air of a drunk uncle in a Wetherspoon's pub explaining Newton's third law of thermodynamics to a stranger outside the toilets with the seriousness of a TV detective who has uncovered your murder plot. In an April 2020 interview during the COVID-19 pandemic, he stated "there is no COVID-19. It doesn't exist", before launching into a pseudoscientific monologue into which his interviewer could barely get a word in edgeways. Icke, who was banned for life from the UK's Green Party (after leaving) for being a fascist, and counts much-loved US activist and poet Alice Walker amongst his fans (Grady, 2018), became known primarily for his belief that the world has been taken over by a race of lizards called Archons who feed on human fear, and who have produced shapeshifting genetically engineered hybrids of Archons and humans who are in fact the Illuminati. The complex world Icke imagines, and around which he has cultivated an extensive international following, is described in detail elsewhere, but it is not hard to see why he is both controversial and derided.

It is worse than simply being foolish, however. Although Icke strenuously denies being anti-Semitic, his work suggests otherwise. Many of the ideas in his book are reminiscent of those in anti-Semitic forgery *Protocols of the Elders of Zion*, and he frequently uses the word "Zionist" in a manner that has no direct relevance to the recent geopolitical interests of the modern state of Israel, the local forms that nationalism has frequently taken there, or the post-war project of establishing the country. And that is anti-Semitic whether he and his supporters admit it or not. The issue of racism and bigotry in conspiracy theories in general, including anti-Semitism, is discussed later in this chapter, but Icke has certainly made use of many of those tropes, alongside an eye-watering array of climate change denial, alternative "new-age" medicine, 5G suspicion, anti-vaccination theories, and many other peculiar and destructive positions.

In second place, the other name to be written — in slightly smaller lights — would be US conspiracy theorist Alex Jones, who besides his numerous angry TV interview meltdowns, is infamous for espousing the view that the mass shootings, including those at the Orlando Pulse nightclub in 2016 and Sandy Hook Elementary School in Connecticut in 2012, either did not happen, or were "false flag" events used by "the left" to argue for stricter gun laws. Jones was ordered to pay $100,000 in court costs and legal fees in 2019 after claiming that the tearful, traumatised relatives of those killed in Connecticut were "crisis actors" who were in on the plot, leading to repeated and distressing harassment of these families by his followers.

Until Donald Trump announced air strikes against Syria in 2018, Jones had been a vocal Trump supporter, and Trump even appeared once on Jones's show *InfoWars*, prior to being elected. Jones also appeared outside the Bilderberg Meetings in 2013, making claims to reporters about how those inside "steer the world", and has stated that "criminal elements in the military industrial complex" were behind 9/11 — telling the TV personality and former journalist Piers Morgan that it was "the same ones that staged [the 1964 skirmish that led to an escalation of US involvement in the Vietnam War,] Gulf of Tonkin".

Jones's trademarks, including shouting tirades both on his own show and in interviews with others, have always given the air of somebody who really is convinced that they are speaking the truth. But an examination of Jones's commercial operations casts suspicion on his loathing for the "deep state". In around 2013, *InfoWars* started increasingly generating its revenue from an assortment of pills, potions, supplements and other products with questionable and meaningless names like "nutraceuticals" that exploit the insecurities of its predominantly male audience (Brown, 2017). As this business model developed, *InfoWars*' shows, hosted by an array of other conspiracists alongside Jones, such as British conspiracist Paul Joseph Watson, became increasingly punctuated by ad breaks and product placement, in a way that one journalist described as like "the QVC for racist uncles" (Lamoureux, 2017).

Several of the recurrent products contain colloidal silver, the only known effect of which on the body at the time of writing is to turn parts of it blue. During the COVID-19 pandemic in 2020, Jones said of the colloidal silver toothpaste that he was selling as a false protection against the virus that "the patented Nano Silver we have, the Pentagon has come out and documented, and homeland security have said this stuff kills the whole SARS corona family, at point blank range". So while many of *InfoWars*' products, such as "tactical pens" have been claimed to offer some vague hope of preparation for when the "deep state" shows up at your door, unspecified government goons have also been wheeled out to offer reassuring, if entirely fake, endorsements of some of these products when that might help close a sale. This is reminiscent of the way that David Icke has made countless appeals to "mainstream science", when his understanding of whatever scientific theory it might be leads him to believe it may support his theory

— a pattern we could call *selective empiricism*, and which is discussed later in this chapter.

Conspiracy theories can develop gradually over a longer term, but particularly with the help of social media platforms and discussion sites like Reddit and 4chan, they can also spread extremely rapidly in response to acute situations such as man-made crises and natural disasters. Crisis informatics researcher Kate Starbird and colleagues at the University of Washington have documented how after virtually every man-made crisis such as mass-shootings or terrorist attacks, conspiracy theories that the attack is a hoax or has been secretly carried out by the government — similar to those encouraged by Alex Jones — tend to arise almost immediately (Starbird, 2017). After the Boston Marathon attacks in April 2013, for example, disinformation rapidly spread — including the conspiracy theory that the attacks were in fact the work of US Marines (Starbird et al., 2014).

Conspiracy theories are not always quite so grounded in specific historical events, however — sometimes they are just a general theory about the means by which nominal governments, which by definition rule by consent of the people, continue to hold power. The theory of so-called "chemtrails", for example, asserts that where white lines appear in the sky in the wake of an airplane, this is in fact a government programme to spray chemicals into the atmosphere, in order to effect a number of different outcomes such as climate control or widespread mind control.

Beyond the broader features of the prevalent misinformation and disinformation that underpin the market-driven society in the ways outlined in the previous chapter, such as widespread illiteracy or outright bullshit, there are some important lessons we can learn about the social and political origins of disinformation from the prevalence of these persistent, if bizarre, accounts of how the world works. The most important of these are the prevalence of actual conspiracy, the fact that conspiracy theories are a response to the conniving nature of actual power, and finally, the socially and culturally driven ways that these theories often entrench themselves in our thinking.

We're onto You: The Prevalence of Actual Conspiracies

It should not be a contentious claim that there is something in the lived experience of people who hold such views that makes them feel conspired against. Believing such theories usually demonstrates a broad conviction that the world, or some aspect of it, can be and is rigged against them — that behind a veneer of civil, democratic fairness, a polished, gleaming, meritocratic world of benevolent politicians and celebrities, an alternative system of manipulation exerts influence not only over what happens at a political or economic level, but also over what can be known about those processes.

According to a Cambridge/YouGov study, 38% of people in the US agreed with the statement that "Even though we live in what's called a democracy, a few people will always run things in this country anyway", while in the UK it was 44%. As was pointed out by numerous people at the time, this statement is scarcely a conspiracy theory, so much as a statement of disaffection with and alienation from the democratic process. It is essentially a *politics of suspicion* — an idea to which we will return below — which has an extremely strong basis in terms of how people feel about political processes.

As explored in the last chapter, however, the workings of nominally democratic processes are not the sum-total of how power is exercised in a world whose democracies have been subdued by corporate power. Taking the exercise of governmental and corporate power together as one machine, examined on a purely empirical basis, it is hard not to reach the conclusion that conspiracy itself might be at least as commonplace as we think, whether you allow it to be considered a conspiracy theory in the classic sense or not. Indeed, you don't exactly need to scour the history of capitalism to reach the conclusion that we have most certainly been conspired against, even if not in the fanciful ways that designated conspiracy theorists prefer, but some exploration of this history is instructive.

On 23 December 1924, representatives of many of the world's leading lightbulb-makers, including General Electrics, Osram and Phillips, gathered in Geneva. The outcome of their meeting became known as the Phoebus Cartel, which sought to take control of the growing lightbulb market, charge more for lightbulbs, and shorten their lifespan. Despite the lightbulbs they produced being slightly brighter, "all evidence points to the cartel's being motivated by profits and increased sales, not by what was best for the consumer" (Krajewski, 2014). This is merely an early example of a pattern that was to repeat and develop continuously up to the present.

Before we try to reassure ourselves that such examples are not common anymore, it would be prudent to at least look at a few more, although there are far more than can ever be recounted here. One example that is too important to omit is that of the tobacco industry, partly because the control of information and the creation of disinformation was so central to their connivance. Knowledge of the link between lung cancer and smoking tobacco had been growing since the late nineteenth century. Yet when faced with this evidence in the 1950s and 1960s, not only did the tobacco industry not accept publicly that there was any danger in what they were selling, they took active steps to discredit this research in whatever way they could. As Robert Proctor tells us:

> Responding to this evidence, the industry launched a multimillion-dollar campaign to reassure consumers that the hazard had not yet been 'proven.' [...] epidemiology was denounced as "mere statistics," animal experiments were said not to reflect the human condition, and lung pathologies revealed at autopsy were derided as anecdotes without "sound evidence" as backing. [...] We don't know what evil genius came up with the scheme to associate the continued manufacture of cigarettes with prudence, using the call for "more research" to slow the threat of regulation, but it must rank as one of the greatest triumphs of American corporate connivance. (2008: 11–12)

In case one should believe that this is not conspiratorial, or that this industry was simply trying to maintain a rational and empirical debate around the safety of their products, Proctor tells us that "Cigarette makers [...] in some instances actually [quantified] the impact of their denialist propaganda" (2012). Before the law explicitly forbade it in the 1950s, tobacco companies even deliberately pushed the idea that not only that smoking was not unhealthy, but in some cases even subtly suggested that it may be healthy. "L&M filters were offered as 'just what the doctor ordered' [and] Camels were said to be smoked by 'more doctors'" (Proctor, 2008: 11).

More recently, beyond its actual advertising and health-related propaganda efforts, the tobacco industry has played a recognisably duplicitous game. While attempting to change their image by appearing proactive in the fight against counterfeit cigarettes and smuggling, which disproportionately affect children and the poorest people in the world, they are reportedly also trying to control and benefit from those very same illicit activities they purport to be against (Gilmore and Rowell, 2018). The same is true of their supposed commitment not to sell or advertise their products to children via otherwise legal channels:

> the largest tobacco companies have continued to market cigarettes to children across the globe despite claiming not to do so, and often in places where advertising is banned. In the UK, where tobacco advertising is banned, Philip Morris International has effectively circumvented the ban with its recently launched "stop smoking" campaign which actually still promotes its tobacco products. (Branston, Gilmore and Hiscock, 2018)

Overall, it should be an uncontroversial claim that rather than mere disorganisation or basic greed, this is an industry that has long had a clear sense of the harm that it does the world, and takes whatever steps it can to continue profiting from that harm while constructing whatever misinformation and disinformation it can — it is conspiracy by the powerful, with control of information at its very centre. It is also a good reminder of the important principle that actual conspiracies are almost always to be found at different points in the world than the ones conspiracists like Icke and Jones suspect — there are surely plenty of Flat-Earthers who smoke tobacco, for example.

This pattern is very similar with the oil industry and its attempts to manipulate consumer demand for petroleum-based products, and limit public understanding of the science of global warming over the twentieth and twenty-first centuries at the same time. The oil industry has long known the impact of culture and discourse on their bottom line, and so they have relied on their own forms of classic propaganda. In the 1930s for example, in a bid to encourage people into their cars, petroleum company Shell produced a series of what it called *Shell Guides* to help people explore the country by road, as well as other marketing materials such as posters that aimed to evoke the beauty of the countryside — all in order to encourage car-based tourism, roadbuilding and ultimately petroleum use (Shirley, 2015: 50).

Save for those who insist on seeing the fact of man-made climate change as some kind of conspiracy in itself, the link between carbon dioxide and atmospheric change is now widely accepted, and by the late 1970s the scientific debate was more or less over (Oreskes and Conway, 2008: 55). Indeed, there is reliable scientific research on the ability of carbon dioxide to trap thermal energy going back as far as 1859 (Hulme, 2009). So when it came to the possibility that their very business posed a threat to the wellbeing and survival of humankind and the planet it calls home, classic propaganda was no longer enough.

Speaking to petrochemicals executives at the headquarters of petroleum corporation Exxon in 1977, for example, company scientist Jeff Black told a room full of executives that "In the first place, there is general scientific agreement that the most likely manner in which mankind is influencing the global climate is through carbon dioxide release from the burning of fossil fuels". The company responded to Black's research by hiring more scientists, and deepening its own private understanding of climate change until the end of the 1980s, when it "put its muscle behind efforts to manufacture doubt about the reality of global warming its own scientists had once confirmed" (Song, Banerjee and Hasermyer, 2015).

Exxon was not alone in its denial efforts. Oil companies across the industry responded to the likelihood that their business was a grave threat to life on Earth with "a comprehensive, international campaign to change public opinion on the climate crisis by casting doubt on the scientific research, presenting it as unreliable when the overwhelming majority of scientists had reached consensus" (Lawrence, Pegg and Evans, 2019). Interestingly, the denial of the harms of tobacco and the threat of global warming from fossil fuels are frequently linked. Journalist George Monbiot writes in his book on climate change denial that an organisation formerly called The Advancement of Sound Science Coalition (TASSC), now The Advancement of Sound Science Center, which was set up by tobacco giant Philip Morris in 1993, "was the first and most important of the corporate-funded organisations denying that climate change is taking place" (2006). Knowing that something is bad for the public and then promoting it, deliberately organising the suppression of this information or throwing doubt on it is the very definition of deceit, and yet, just like tobacco before it, but with even more disastrous consequences, the burning of fossil fuels has been pushed for decades by people who knew it was harmful but were worried about their bottom line. But the harmful misinformation and disinformation around oil and fossil fuels does not end there.

Almost equally as illuminating as organised climate change denial is the story of diesel in Europe. After the 1997 Kyoto protocols on climate change, European governments began subsidising the adoption of diesel cars, as well as the fuel itself, because diesel engines produce about 20% lower carbon dioxide than petrol engines over the same time and distance (Petzinger, 2018). In the UK, Tony Blair's Labour government, desperate for good "optics" around their green policies, introduced an ill-informed policy aimed at limiting damage to the environment by offering drivers lower tax rates as an incentive to buy diesel cars, despite health warnings about the chemicals released into the air by burning diesel (Embury-Dennis, 2017).

Foolish, if well-intentioned policies do not count as conspiracies, necessarily, but where the actual car companies themselves were examined, there is much more clarity about what they were trying to do. While actual "conspiracy theorists" were arguing with somewhat baffled friends and family members about the imaginary menace of "chemtrails", Volkswagen and other car companies were organising something far more familiar.

In 2013, a team of scientists at the International Council on Clean Transportation (ICCT) in the US, led by John German, discovered something strange. When testing the exhaust of a diesel-powered Volkswagen Jetta, and then also a Passat, they found the levels of harmful nitrogen oxide emissions were up to thirty-five and twenty times higher respectively than they should be, compared to the published manufacturer standards. The team tested again and again, but produced the same results every time, and began to suspect something was amiss. The team were nervous about making accusations against such a large corporation, and moved ahead with their research. When German's boss later asked him why he hadn't said anything, he reportedly replied "We're an $8m organisation. VW could have squashed us like a bug" (Gardiner, 2019). Eventually, Volkswagen were tipped off about this anomaly, and said that it was a technical malfunction on their part. It was only when they were forced to turn over the code for the software running in their cars as a condition for being able to sell them in the US that the truth became clear: they had deliberately written the software to respond differently when it could sense that the car was being measured, and limit the emissions of the engine, removing the limitations once the testing was no longer detected.

But why? Hybrid and fully electric cars are developing quickly and provide enormous environmental and driver benefits, meanwhile car companies were investing in covering up diesel instead of developing those newer technologies further. One clue may be in a *Quartz* report in which BMW CEO Harald Krüger reportedly said "Electric cars in general won't be as profitable as cars with combustion engines" (Petzinger, 2018). This may be a natural consequence of what happens in a market-driven society in which, lest we need reminding, "all conduct is economic conduct; all spheres of existence are framed and measured by economic terms and metrics, even when those spheres are not directly monetized", as political scientist Wendy Brown puts it (2015: 10). The inevitable consequence of this logic is a conflict between public benefit and private capital, and this conflict *produces* secrecy, lies and conspiratorial activity as a means of resolution.

A similar pattern can also be found in other industries, particularly with regard to human health and the environment. Investigative journalist Sharon Lerner has uncovered how the plastics industry, which includes a lot of the same petroleum companies mentioned above or their subsidiaries, such as Exxon Mobil, Chevron Phillips and Shell Polymers, have pushed plastic recycling, including in schools, as a means to legitimise the continued use of plastics, despite full knowledge of the ecological dangers this represents. Put very simply, it is organised lying on a broad scale. Meanwhile, despite the fact that only 9% of plastics in the US were recycled in 2015, with 79% sent to landfill, these companies have lobbied hard against policies that would actually limit our use of plastics altogether, applying "a green veneer to its increasingly bitter and desperate fight to keep profiting from a product that is polluting the world" (Lerner, 2019).

Probably one of the most insidious examples of this pattern is that of drug company Purdue Pharma. Since 1995, Purdue has produced the highly addictive pain relief drug OxyContin, the only active ingredient of which is oxycodone, an "opioid" chemical related to heroin which is up to twice as powerful as morphine. Writing for the *New Yorker* in 2017, journalist Patrick Keefe reported that:

> In the past, doctors had been reluctant to prescribe strong opioids [...] except for acute cancer pain and end-of-life palliative care, because of a long-standing, and well-founded, fear about the addictive properties of these drugs. "Few drugs are as dangerous as the opioids," David Kessler, the former commissioner of the Food and Drug Administration, told me.
>
> Purdue launched OxyContin [in 1995] with a marketing campaign that attempted to counter this attitude and change the prescribing habits of doctors. The company funded research and paid doctors to make the case that concerns about opioid addiction were overblown, and that OxyContin could safely treat an ever-wider range of maladies.

After the other examples reported above, this story should sound familiar, but it gets worse. By 2000, OxyContin sales had reached over a $1bn a year, and in 2003, Keefe reports, "the Drug Enforcement Administration had found that Purdue's 'aggressive methods' had 'very much exacerbated OxyContin's widespread abuse'". By 2016, there were over fourteen million OxyContin prescriptions in the United States, making it the fifty-fourth most prescribed drug that year. Meanwhile, the Sackler family who own Purdue Pharma, the drug's maker, were the United States' nineteenth richest family, with an estimated fortune of $13bn (*Forbes Magazine*, 2016). By the same year, more than 400,000 people had died of opioid addictions (McGreal, 2019), and by 2018 the US Department of Health and Human Services estimated that two million people had opioid use disorder, two million more misused opioids for the first time, and 130 people were dying per day from opioid overdoses (United States Department of Health and Human Services, 2018). The crisis was estimated to have cost the United States roughly $1trn since 2001 (Glenza, 2018). Although the company did try to produce newer versions of its products that were designed to be harder to abuse, "By the time the company came out with an 'abuse-deterrent formulation' (which, ultimately, didn't completely deter abuse), and states slowly began to pressure doctors (and pharmacies) to decrease prescriptions, many users had already turned to heroin" (Halpern and Blistein, 2019).

In 2019, a massive lawsuit was brought against Purdue and other makers of opioids such as Teva Pharmaceuticals, for the epidemic of addictions that had swept across the United States — they agreed to a multimillion-dollar settlement before the case reached trial (McGreal, 2019). After settling a $10bn claim and avoiding the admission of any wrongdoing in respect of the thousands of lawsuits brought against them, OxyContin's makers Purdue Pharma declared Chapter 11 bankruptcy in September 2019, in the hope that it would shield them from further liability. If profiting directly from producing a public health crisis wasn't enough, Richard Sackler, one of the family who own Purdue Pharma, also invented and patented a drug for treating *addiction* to opiates, with the *Financial Times* reporting that: "The new formulation as described in Dr Sackler's patent could end up proving lucrative thanks to a steady increase in the number of addicts being treated with buprenorphine [which his drug is a new form of]." If this were merely an attempt to remedy the harms caused by the drugs that were the source of his family's wealth, he would not have patented it. Rather, this demonstrates an intention to profit from the very crisis that his family business is highly implicated in creating.

For all the examples here, OxyContin is one of the worst, but there are dozens more that have not been included, because the point has been made: in example after example, companies are making money from knowingly producing and selling products, from cars to packaging to medicines, that they know are bad for the people who buy them, bad for the environment, and often responsible for major ecological or public health crises. When challenged, despite knowing exactly what they have done, they either insist they were mistaken or come out on the front foot, disingenuously attacking the evidence of the harm their products are causing, or having the gall to say that this is "regulation gone too far".

In case this chapter seems to be disproportionately harsh on private sector corporations at the expense of letting governments off the hook, there are plenty of examples of governments, politicians and civil servants being equally conspiratorial against the public. On a broader scale, even if the wholly deceitful process of the US and UK governments setting in motion the 2003 invasion or Iraq cannot in itself be definitively called a "conspiracy", the ways in which the British and US governments sought to cover up their use of torture and extraordinary rendition after 9/11, for example, in clear breach of the Geneva Conventions, is most definitely conspiratorial. In order to pave the way for a "deal in the desert" with Libyan ruler Muammar Gaddafi that would allow petroleum corporations such as BP to make deals with the country, Britain's foreign spying agency the Secret Intelligence Service, commonly known as MI6, provided intelligence to assist the CIA kidnapping or "rendition" in 2004 of two Libyan rebel leaders — Abdul-Hakim Belhaj and Sami Al-Saadi — and handing them to Gaddafi, whose officials subsequently tortured them. This role was initially refuted by then Foreign Secretary Jack Straw, who categorically denied the claims in parliament and called them a "conspiracy theory". But evidence subsequently came to light when the office of Gaddafi's intelligence chief Moussa Koussa was destroyed by bombs in the 2011 NATO air strikes on Tripoli, and journalists found amongst the ruins a 2004 letter from MI6's counterterrorism chief Mark Allen to Koussa that congratulated him on Belhaj's "safe arrival" in Libya, a chilling euphemism, and added "This was the least we could do for you and for Libya to demonstrate the remarkable relationship we have built over the years" (Norton-Taylor, 2020). Even the head of Britain's domestic intelligence agency MI5, Eliza Manningham-Buller, was outraged when she discovered MI6's role in the renditions, and banned a number of MI6 operatives from working in MI5 headquarters (Hopkins & Norton-Taylor, 2016). The whole affair is like something out of a James Bond film, except that MI6 are shown to be the bad guys. Later, while Al-Saadi and his family sought compensation from the UK government, UK intelligence agency GCHQ spied on his communications with his lawyer, and were later forced to surrender these intercepted communications. A press release from an NGO supporting the families of both men reports that: "GCHQ and MI5 had for years advised staff that they could 'target the communications of lawyers,' and use legally privileged material 'just like any other item of intelligence.'" After years of fighting, the courts eventually awarded Belhaj and Al-Saadi payouts from the UK government for its role in facilitating their torture and kidnapping, the government having already spent £11m of public money fighting Belhaj's case alone (Bowcott, 2019).

What we see in many of the examples above is not corporate *or* governmental misdeed and information control, but the combination of *both* at the same time, which is typical of the market-driven society. Indeed, as Colin Leys (2008) and others have analysed, governments are not only mendacious, but their policymaking has increasingly been reorganised around market forces and a worship of big business, meaning their use of evidence in policymaking has decreased, and that their need for "economy with the truth" has increased. What all of these examples show is that conspiracies, both of the actual and imaginary kind, are by definition informational phenomena. While the exercise of power also consists of plenty of blatant wrongdoing against innocent members of the public, such as the killing of innocent civilians or the destruction of the natural environment, these acts become *conspiratorial* once the disclosure of their occurrence is restricted in a way that permits them to be carried out in the first place, to be continued, or to avoid consequence for their having taken place.

Michael Barkun tells us that a conspiracy belief is the belief that "an organization made up of individuals or groups was or is acting covertly to achieve some malevolent end" (2013: 3). When one considers the proven accounts of corporate and government malevolence told on these preceding pages, it is hard not to ask: What are these, if not examples of conspiracy of the highest order? Does that mean that the many painstakingly researched investigative reports on which these accounts are based should be considered "conspiracy theories", even with reliable proof? Some readers may think that the answer is yes, but the more sensible conclusion to reach is that whatever the details of the bizarre, unproven theories to which some people subscribe, this form of *actual* conspiracy is everywhere, and its careful control over information is built into the very fabric of market-driven societies.

Besides the relative disorganisation, resourcing issues, whistleblowers and other real-world complications, to make these historical examples into "conspiracies" also raises the important issue of *intent*. In Volkswagen's emissions scandal, we saw a good old-fashioned conspiracy of the most deliberate kind. But there are alternative ways that the partnership of capitalism and government that comprises the market-driven society can have the *effect* of being conspiratorial. Sometimes, people naively believe that the specific responsibilities they fulfil are part of an overall positive impact on the world — for example, the people working for Facebook who, however deluded they might be, may genuinely think that their employer really makes the world "more open and connected". That does not mean that their work is not part of an organised operation to exploit vulnerable people. The way that Facebook exploits its users' loneliness, vanity, boredom, and need for distraction in order turn a profit by selling those users' attention to advertisers using vast quantities of personal data to precisely target them, all while facilitating astonishingly poor user privacy, widespread government surveillance and the spread of disinformation, is ethically dubious, to put it mildly. But is there necessarily some "chief villain" at that corporation — stroking a white cat —who has a complete map of this "ingenious plan" in their head, including a realistic appraisal of all of the downsides for users, and remains determined to proceed, critics be damned (or smeared)?

The answer may still be "yes", but only if we understand the conspiracy in such cases a bit differently. However conspiratorial (or not) the individual mindset of an individual may be, the conspiracy may also be in the *structure* rather than in the conscious intentionality of any one person involved. Indeed, as Mark Fisher argued:

> There are certainly conspiracies in capitalism, but the problem is that they are themselves only possible because of deeper level structures that allow them to function. Does anyone really think, for instance, that things would

improve if we replaced the whole managerial and banking class with a whole new set of ("better") people? Surely, on the contrary, it is evident that the vices are engendered by the structure, and that while the structure remains, the vices will reproduce themselves. (2009: 68)

When the philosopher Hannah Arendt explored these ideas in relation to the Nazi Holocaust in her coverage of the trial of SS officer Adolf Eichmann (1963), who was responsible for putting Jewish people in extermination camps, she was accused of letting Eichmann off the hook. Regardless of whether this is a fair accusation or not, it represents a false choice. As far as the examples given above in the overall context of a society rife with people who feel conspired against, it is important to underscore that to draw attention to the conspiratorial *shape* of governmental and corporate structures should not mean that individuals are not also deliberately involved in conspiring against the public interest in some cases. Rather, the fact that it is also possible for organisations to be *institutionally conspiratorial* should only add to the sense we have that conspiracy theories exist because market-driven society itself is prone to conspiracy. You cannot expect people to trust institutions or even to trust each other, when the very premise of the capitalism on which Western society is predicated involves a profit motive: deriving the most possible benefit from any communication or interaction.

Lastly, when we examine any actual conspiracy — the types of cover-ups, insider-trading, corruption, or profiting from the sale of dangerous products that we have seen here — we tend to focus on the behaviour and morality of those *with* the information: the smooth operators, the spin doctors, the liars and the conspirators. At least as important, however, is to take into account those people on the other side: that majority of people that are, or feel, conspired against. This lack of information that derives from our alienation from various forms of power is something we could call *informational disempowerment*. Are your groceries mislabelled in a way that obscures harmful additives, your government ministers "being economical with the truth" about the effects their policies will have, or your bosses telling you your job is safe while planning redundancies? All of these are examples of informational disempowerment. The next two sections approach the phenomenon of conspiracy theories from the perspective of those who experience their political alienation through informational disempowerment, taking the irrefutably conspiratorial world established here as the context in which to do so.

The Toxic Effects of Alienation and Suspicion

Alex Jones may be abhorrent, racist, deceitful and rude, but the fact that, when questioned by reporters outside the Bilderberg Meetings in 2013, he said more or less correctly that "there are powerful corporate groups above government manipulating things [...] they set a lot of policies", suggests there was slightly more going on than the old adage that "even a broken clock is right twice a day". Conspiracy theories inherently involve an element of power, in the sense that you cannot conspire against anyone unless you have some kind power over them, whether it is sheer numbers, fancy weapons, celebrity influence, something they need, or some infrastructural advantage like control over their water pipes or their access to information. Social theorist Manuel Castells says that wherever you see the exercise of power, whether by coercion and violence or by the construction of shared meaning through discourse, you are also likely to see counterpower — a challenge to the exercise of that power (2011). Whether or not this is necessarily true, conspiracy theories should be seen as a form of counterpower at their core, even if a rather toothless variety; a unilateral response, albeit feeble, to the exercise of power by means of controlling information.

Michael Barkun writes that the "classic" view of conspiracy theories "implies a universe governed by design, rather than randomness" (2013: 5), such that those who plan and design the world (in a structural, rather than a visual or technical sense) are the ones who are usually considered to be in a position to control it and understand it. Many conspiracy theories are built on an association between power of various kinds, such as politicians, governments, corporations or celebrities, and a claim to knowledge of this plan — of how the world "really" works. Above all else, these theories are a response to the feeling that there is something, or many things, that those who believe them have not been told about that carefully managed, controlled world, which would help them to understand their own circumstances in relation to whatever forms of power they are able to identify. Alex Jones's and other conspiracists' obsession with the "deep state", for example, demonstrates the centrality of power in a recognisable, if demonised form, as does the fact that in April 2020, three in ten US Americans believed COVID-19 had been developed deliberately in a lab (Pew Research Center, 2020). Belying the flat Earth or anti-vaccination conspiracy theories is also a distrust for the sources from which scientific knowledge originates, or at least those sources deemed untrustworthy by their association with power and establishment. In some sense it is a selective articulation of Jean-François Lyotard's observation that "science seems more completely subordinated to the prevailing powers than ever before and, along with the new technologies, is in danger of becoming a major stake in their conflicts" (1984: 8). Even the "Stevie can see" theory is a minor version of this same principle of conspiracy as counterpower. Besides being a gifted musical talent, Stevie Wonder is a celebrity, loved by the establishment, which is the only reason that that the theory has any weight — were Stevie Wonder an obscure, struggling artist instead of a star and international treasure, the absurd theory that he is lying about his blindness would likely not be appealing or interesting to anyone.

The fact that the real conspiracies in the world (like those described in the previous section) *have* been reported extensively in the news should remind us that what we are talking about is not the perfectly concealed exercise of power, or the completely indistinguishable lie, but the *imperfect* restriction of information about the exercise of power in ways that still allow it to be discovered and communicated. In sections of the world that enjoy press freedom, reports of actual conspiratorial activity comprise a continuous feature of the media landscape in their own right — a constant reconfirmation that powerful people, somewhere, have conspired against the public in some way.

Certainly there is nothing wrong with this presence in itself — it is essential that people have access to this information. But the situation is not helped by the fact that these disclosures do not always provide a complete account of exactly what has happened. The restrictions of the reporting medium, the cursory nature of scrolling-heavy timeline media, the extreme complexity of the story, the tendency towards oversimplification or sensationalism on the part of some journalists, and the disruptive pressures of the attention economy all mean that these accounts may merely allow us to see that some wrongdoing has both occurred (or is occurring or being planned) and that it has been concealed.

The constant, if simplified, incomplete, misunderstood or hastily read news of wrongdoing has the effect of confirming our sense that everybody powerful is up to something, inviting us to informational counterpower without necessarily being as informative as it should. This sense of continually being excluded from the "full story" about what is "really" going on, at least until it is disclosed later, means that *we know there is something wrong with what we know* about the exercise of power. Over time, disinformation's often-central place in our disempowerment is both made conspicuous and normalised. Beyond the politics or ethics of actual conspiracies, it is also important to consider what the *symbolic* and *cultural* effect of this ongoing disclosure is: the vague sense that people in power are "probably up to no good" even where this is untrue, or not (yet) proven.

But it is important to be cautious here. The argument is not solely that people in power do bad things, we find out about it in imperfect ways, and consequently normalise the reality that we are conspired against by those in power, leading to conspiracy theories. To leave it at that would be to make the media inappropriately central, which is a myth that pervades the study of media all too often. As we will see in Chapter Five, the news media certainly have had an important role to play in how informed (or misinformed) we are, and as psychologist Daniel Kahneman (2011) has quipped, it is likely that we think of politicians as being more adulterous than doctors or lawyers simply because we hear about it more often. But it is not so much the media that drive conspiracy theories as the power they mediate, and our alienation from it, that is the ultimate driver of "classic" conspiracy theories. Coverage of the "actual" conspiracies of the market-driven society simply amplifies the feeling of suspicion and cynicism about the systems around which that society is oriented. The more cynical the actual exercise of power, the more jaded and cynical a population will be. To the extent that this suspicion colours our view of and participation in a nominally democratic society and provides the necessary conditions for conspiracy belief, we could go so far as to call this a *politics of suspicion*.

But there is more to be said about the ways that the highly capitalistic societies of the Euro-Atlantic world produce widespread suspicion. Accounts in the media of "real" conspiracy may in some cases be telling us what we already know: we are always in danger of being "fucked over" under capitalism, and this is celebrated as a strength, rather than being considered a weakness. Long before he became president, for example, Donald Trump bragged on TV about how he had "screwed" then Libyan leader Muammar Gaddafi when he came to New York and wanted to lease some space.

The original neoliberals in 1947 might have extolled the virtues of the free market, and thought that it would prevent totalitarianism from happening again, but they assumed the trading it involved would take place according to a certain moral and ethical standard, which was forgotten during the "greed is good" phase of the 1980s. As the market-driven society took shape during this period, the system of "you scratch my back, I scratch yours", became "even if you scratch my back a lot, I will only scratch your back to the minimum possible threshold I can get away with", and the burden of responsibility shifted from an honest seller to a cautious buyer, whose goal was not to get "screwed". To normalise a perverse game in which everybody is expected to try to extract the best possible result for themselves from every co-operative interaction outside their immediate family, be it a profit margin or some other outcome, makes a degree of suspicion virtually guaranteed. How serious Milton Friedman really was in the suggestion that the free market would "foster harmony and peace among the peoples of the world" we will never know, but capitalism's widely felt adversarial transactionalism is a key part of the politics of suspicion because it means swimming in waters that you *know* for a fact contain sharks.

Finally, as we saw in the last chapter, power is often exercised not only by informational control in a secretive sense, but by the construction of shared meaning. As such, while the analytical detail may often be lacking, it is common for already fringe beliefs and communities to regard any mainstream media or cultural figures with suspicion simply by virtue of their having expressed a view that is associated with an imagined conspirator. For example, Beyoncé Knowles's support of the Black Lives Matter movement in the United States brought her into Alex Jones's crosshairs, and he suggested that her sixth album *Lemonade* — which was critically acclaimed as an exploration of the struggles of Black women — was paid for by the CIA.

In all cases, conspiracy theories tend to occur in the "gaps". These gaps can arise because of the ways that information is restricted in the exercise of power, and be experienced together as what the sociologist Linsey McGoey calls a "loud unknown" — distinct but not unrelated to her concept of "strategic unknowns" mentioned in Chapter Two. But, as explored in the previous chapter, they can also exist in the thinking or understanding of an individual as a result of that individual's own uneven understanding of the world. Gaps are simply where either no definitive explanation has been provided (yet), or, as in the case of David Icke and Alex Jones, because there is enough suspicion towards official sources of information that any official not supporting the suspicions of the conspiracist is not regarded or represented as credible because of their position.

Knowledge Agency

The response to informational disempowerment, to suspicion and to these "gaps" may well be passive: a cynical shrug of "yeah, of course they're crooked", or an agnostic "we'll never know the full story". But as Aristotle said, "all men, by nature, desire to know", and the need to have some story, even if wildly inaccurate, about why their world is the way it is, seems very human.

If informational disempowerment is the subjective sense that power is being exercised and wrongdoing perpetrated by means of secrecy and manufactured ignorance, the first step to regaining control, and hopefully justice, is surely to lay claim to this previously unavailable or hidden insight into what is "really" going on by filling in the gaps and feeling that, unlike the masses, *we* have the answer! This unilateral reclaiming of control in respect of information about the world you inhabit in a way that empowers us is something that we could call *knowledge agency*, and it is an important part of what gives conspiracy theories wind in their sails.

Knowledge agency tends to be exercised using a varying combination of two major ingredients: on the one hand, conspiracists negate some widely accepted narrative or explanation as false, and that they stopped believing it — a process sometimes called taking the "red pill" in reference to the 1999 film *The Matrix*; on the other, they postulate a narrative or explanation that *does* account for the world in a way that they find more satisfactory. A conspiracy belief may attempt its counterpower by doing only one — for example, the flat Earth conspiracy is sometimes more focused on negating that the Earth is round, and sometimes entails a more complete imagination of how a flat Earth might actually look and function, complete with drawings and diagrams. Filling in a gap left by others, creating the gap yourself by negating the accepted explanation, or a combination of both are all different ways to exercise knowledge agency.

With the 2020 COVID-19 pandemic, for example, as with any global health challenge, the two most conspicuous and obvious questions initially were "how and why did this come about?" and "how can we make it go away?", but initially scientists weren't exactly sure from what source the virus had first been transmitted to humans, and there weren't any medicines or vaccines that could help since reliable scientific and medical knowledge tends to be produced slowly.

In the meantime, along came the conspiracy theorists, who had long had theories about 5G, vaccines, the "great replacement" and the "global elites", to fill in these gaps for us, and an abundance of theories arose that tied together people's desperation for answers to these questions with their pre-existing suspicions of technology companies and the pharmaceutical industry, prejudices against certain demographic groups such as those of Chinese descent or distrust of apparent geopolitical adversary countries, which in the case of the United States were China (where the virus was, after all, discovered) and Iran.

As should be clear from some of these examples, a major caveat to the idea of knowledge agency is that, despite superficially being a process or set of activities with an informational goal or goals in mind, knowledge-agency is above all a *feeling* about a person's knowledge of the world — it does not necessarily lead to any useful conclusions or new information whatsoever. The more suspicion and uncertainty felt by a conspiracy theorist, the greater the tendency to cling to anything that does feel like knowledge, regardless of its actual value or detriment.

It is not hard to see how the politics of extreme suspicion and the appeal of knowledge agency combine in a way that is simultaneously understandable and that produces harmful consequences. For example, there is ultimately no justification whatsoever for not vaccinating your children, but in a context of widespread suspicion and distrust directed towards those we identify, however incorrectly, as being responsible for our disempowerment, for example, it is at least comprehensible as to why people view vaccinations with suspicion: the drug industry is often a profiteering, greedy industry that can demonstrably be shown to have put profits ahead of the safety of its patients, and governments really have put their own ideologies and retention of power ahead of the health or human rights of society itself. So for the government to tell you to give your child injections manufactured by drug companies is hardly a thrilling prospect to those who view the world both suspiciously and heuristically. Add to that the amplification effects of user-generated content and social media platforms, which can potentially increase exposure to a variety of conspiracism and disinformation exponentially — especially in the ways that their content selection algorithms function — and the general transfer of authority in healthcare from doctor to patient that occurred in the late twentieth and early twenty-first centuries, then a reluctance to vaccinate is at least understandable, however misguided it is.

In other words, our response to informational disempowerment may sometimes be subjectively motivated by merely *feeling* empowered again, rather than becoming informed in any objective sense, and this distinguishes it from the actual synthesis of knowledge that we might encounter with other forms of theorising or investigation. While there are obviously points of comparison with an investigative journalist, academic or scientist, who all undertake the production of new knowledge, the motivation in these other cases is different, and much more detached. Instead, we might think of it more as a kind of attempted "sense-making", in the same way that some researchers have understood the related phenomenon of *rumour* (DiFonzo and Bordia, 2007).

To the extent that conspiracy theories are counterpower, to participate in them by elaboration and translation from one social setting to another is at least an attempt to undertake unalienated work that belongs to us and is pleasurable. Herbert Marcuse argued that the personality and its creative and productive impulses could be totally absorbed into the processes of capitalist production, and to take ownership of disruptive knowledge-making about that power is to challenge it. As we'll see, this feeling of ownership of the narrative is essential for understanding conspiracism, but brings with it a whole host of psychological, cultural and social considerations. The next section examines the forms of over-investment that drive our informational disempowerment, natural curiosity, and suspicion towards outright conspiracy theory in the flat Earth sense.

Emotion, Culture and Knowledge Synthesis

Police "whodunnit" dramas are popular on some level because of the reassuring piece-by-piece assembly process involved in discovering who the criminal is, which encourages us to think of the world as being wholly understandable by a similar process. The idea that if only we can discover the right pieces of information or follow the right trail, we too can have the complete picture of what has "really" happened is powerful utopian fantasy, and this is an appeal that it shares with conspiracy theories. In *The Principle of Hope*, the philosopher Ernst Bloch saw the possibility of utopia reinforced by the pleasing minutiae of everyday life. Here we see the promise of utopia in the idea that with the right forms of understanding and discovery, our alienated relationship to power can be ameliorated. On some level, this need for an entirely understandable, re-constructible world is a response to what Zygmunt Bauman called the *liquidity* of modernity — its ceaseless, confusing shapeshifting. We look at a complex world in which most people have no power, and hope not just for a better understanding of it, but hope that it even can be pieced together in this way.

In the first series of hit Danish crime drama *The Killing*, detective inspector Sarah Lund goes rogue as she tries to uncover who the murderer is. Possessed by an increasingly personal anger towards the perpetrator of this violent sexual crime on a young woman and frustrated by the institutional limitations of her job, such as constant bureaucracy, the need for evidence at every step of the way, and a need for political sensitivity against the backdrop of an electoral process, Lund starts to disobey her boss and outrage her colleagues, choosing instead to follow her instinct in risks that grow with every episode. That she is totally vindicated in the end, identifying the murderer when no one else has been able to, despite suspension from duty and eventual punishment, is also utopian and is exactly what made her a perfect heroine for the late-capitalist era. Whereas more conventional characters such as Poirot or Sherlock Holmes arrive at their conclusions by a devastating command of detail and rationality, what is most interesting about *The Killing* and some of the other shows in this genre is that it is the *criminal* who is a logical, calculating, rational and highly intelligent individual, whilst an instinctive, obsessive process of gut-driven investigation is what eventually results in their capture and the cathartic resolution that viewers crave. To hell with reason, institutions, or due process — she got there by following her gut instinct, and her emotions.

The conspiracist worldview that presumes a wholly designed universe is similar, and with a conspiracy theory, the holder of the belief in some ways imagines themselves as the detective or investigator, exercising their knowledge agency by following whatever "evidence" they can find. The only problem is that the information that conspiracists rely on and the process they follow is highly distorted and selective. Obviously, one of the sources of such distortions is the widespread illiteracy discussed in Chapter Two — for example, the complete failure to understand the theory of gravity in flat Earth theory or the difference between ionising and non-ionising radiation in the case of 5G conspiracy theories, but this broad feature of the disinformation society is not enough on its own.

Just as with these instinctively driven TV characters who cannot let go of their suspicions, to defend and hold "classic" conspiracy beliefs against a barrage of continual contradiction and even ridicule is not possible without a significant level of commitment and investment. There are reports of people being shunned or falling out with partners, family or friends over their adherence to flat Earth conspiracies, and the experience of many Flat-Earthers is one of "going it alone" against a sea of ridicule and ostracisation (Moshakis, 2018). It is important to understand what might motivate people to see the world in such an extreme way that they could invest so heavily in the unreliable forms of knowledge such as pseudoscience that support their diagnosis of the world that they would be willing to fall out with partners and family members.

Sociality is also an important reminder from the last chapter of how feeling and emotion have conditioned our relationship to what facts we are prepared to accept about the world, according to who else in our lives believes them, and how they make us feel. Investing our emotions in a particular narrative or speculative account of the world is a common way to try to make sense of the complexities of that world, as well as the kinds of "gaps" that appear in our encounters with power, and such beliefs can often provide an important anchor amidst a sea of uncertainty. Just as religions offer meaningful explanations of the world into which we invest a lot of emotion and meaning, so too do lesser forms of more profane anchors such as horoscopes. Analysing the horoscopes of the *Los Angeles Times* in the early 1950s, the cultural theorist Theodor Adorno suggested a concept of "pseudorationality" that, rather than being an abandonment of rationality, was an exaggeration of it (1994: 49). The same could be said of conspiracy theories, with the important additional feature that we can create and change conspiracy theories ourselves, if we so choose.

The emotional dimension to conspiracy theories is also magnified by a sense of moral outrage, particularly over the way the various parties in the theory are said to have behaved deceitfully. Swedish philosopher Sissela Bok analysed in detail the moral culpability of lying to the public from positions of power, which she likened to a kind of theft.

Conspiracies and the Power of the Imagination

One key element in conditioning the form that conspiracy theory takes is the rich world of the imagination. I said in Chapter Two that what we already know about the world shapes what we can imagine about it, not least in the sense that our strong conviction that we are conspired against by those around us or in power by the control of information is what invites us to imagine and discover the "real story" of *how* we are conspired against. But imagination is powerful, and we also see the inverse: what we *imagine* about the world shapes what we can *know* about it. Once we have started to invest in imagining specific details about how, for example, the Earth is actually flat, it becomes harder to accept that it in fact may not be. The imaginative work that goes into believing or elaborating a conspiracy theory intensifies the investment we have in it.

Conspiracy theories tend to arise in relation to whichever people or institutions we *imagine* hold power over us, which may be quite likely different from those stuffy government offices or banks that may commission our police or hold our debts. If we are more aware of our alienation from democratic or governmental institutions, then the conspiracy theories we find most compelling may involve them — for example, 9/11 truthers, QAnon, or that familiar obsession with the "deep state". If we are more suspicious of the corporate world, then the conspiracy theories most compelling to us will involve them — for example, those against 5G technology or genetically modified crops, that Microsoft held a patent number 666 that involved implanting microchips in the body, or similarly that the theory that conglomerate Procter and Gamble was working in league with the Devil. If we are warier of other forms of "elite" and seemingly powerful entities such as scientists, the police or judges, our conspiracy theories will probably involve them. Some of the larger and more prominent conspiracy theories, such as climate change denial and flat Earth belief tend to involve all of these forms of imagined power simultaneously.

The imaginary aspect of this power is important. The accused conspirator does not actually have to hold the power they are imagined to have. As a mere five minutes listening to David Icke speak will confirm, imagined conspirators can be pretty strange. Like rumours and hoaxes, convincing conspiracy theories spread by providing the imagination with a picture that has the right mixture of being both believable and surprising, but what is believable or surprising is of course highly variable from person to person. Indeed, the choice of whom your conspiracy theories — if you hold any — are about is highly political, cultural, and related to your economic position as well. In a 1988 essay, the cultural theorist Fredric Jameson famously suggested that conspiracy theories were the "poor person's cognitive mapping" (1988: 356) — without authorising institutions — but it is wise to interpret "poor" here more structurally than in the economic sense of the word. If you are already rich and powerful in your own country, that does not mean you cannot be a conspiracist, so much as that what you bring to your own theorising will reflect that distinct lived reality — perhaps the fear that you will lose the power you have. Your conspiracy theories will likely involve some other kind of distant entity that you consider powerful — perhaps countries that you are wary of, such as China or Russia (depending on your other political leanings) for those in the Europe or North America, or the United States if you are in the Middle East or Latin America. Space aliens, being from entirely outside the structures of power on planet Earth, are another perceived threat. However, for those with a poor knowledge of the world outside their own country, this threat might instead be vast numbers of people from whom there is perceived to be cultural or geographical distance (or both) as in the case of "swarms" of immigrants, or religious and ethnic tropes such as Jews or Muslims — not in fact the homogenous or unified groups they are imagined to be, and not especially powerful either. As we have seen above, scores of men in online "red pill" forums suspect women of being duplicitous, calculating, deceitful, and driven by undisclosed materialist aspirations. The appropriation of simplistic feminist rhetoric in marketing campaigns only lends weight to the perception of being conspired against, despite this perception being utterly misguided. Is this misogynist fantasy not also an unwitting admission that these men on some level are terrified of the power they feel women have over them, or that mainstream capitalism's commodification of femininity has over them? No wonder, then, that when a woman tried to become US President in 2016 who demonstrably *had* changed her position on several issues, given a number of private, paid speeches beyond her responsibilities as a politician, including one to the National Multifamily Housing Council in which she said "You need both a public and a private position", that America's misogynist imagination had a field day imagining what Hillary Clinton might *really* be up to.

But just like the "gaps" themselves into which conspiracy theories can ooze, this capacity for imagination is not only a private, individualised quality. Like rumours, a related category of statement, there is both an individual and a collective social element to most conspiracy theories. An examination of conspiracist popular culture, as Michael Barkun, Jodi Dean, or Adam Curtis have all done in different forms, shows an abundance of cultural reference points that suggest or encourage conspiracist narratives in different ways. Dean playfully begins her book on conspiracy cultures with the assertion that aliens "have invaded the United States" (1998: 1), by which she means that the imagined form of the alien had saturated popular culture.

Popular TV shows and films, particularly from the years leading up to the new millennium in the late Nineties, encouraged a certain kind of paranoid style, chief among them being the hit TV show *X-Files*, which continually reminded viewers to "trust no one", and that "the truth is out there", almost as if it was urging them not to lose heart in their sense of having been kept in the dark by mysterious and highly organised forms of power.

The imagination of power as an all-seeing, all-controlling, perfectly organised and resourced organisation will likely amuse anyone working in government or the corporate world. The conspiracist understanding of the

Machiavellian, faceless "deep state" of *X-Files*'s Mulder and Scully, for example, is a far cry from the actual civil servants and government employees of the real world, who are often underpaid and overworked. At the same time, this fantasy of a hyper-competent state is particularly interesting in a North American context, where the only parts of the government that are so well-funded and well-resourced tend to be for the purpose of fighting foreign wars. For example, the 1998 film *Enemy of the State*, starring Gene Hackman and Will Smith, was praised for its predictive accuracy as far as state surveillance is concerned. But fifteen years later, when Edward Snowden leaked what the government was actually up to in June 2013, the capabilities of the state that the film displayed were well beyond what the actual state possessed at that time.

Investigation, Theory, Identity, Belonging

As any academic or professional researcher will confirm, to make sense of the world involves a combination of research and theory. Research ordinarily provides some kind of objective data points, and theory explains *why* those data are the way they are. Whether conspiracy beliefs are adopted through passive discovery, such as via word of mouth or YouTube, or the work of a more original process, they tend to be a *hyperactive* form of knowledge synthesis in which the process and the conspiracist's relationship to that process matters more than the actual veracity of any results. Indeed, David Icke's strange theories are full of claims of his having "researched" various aspects of the world like some sort of Enlightenment-era polymath, but as we'll see, to call it "research" is already to overstate it. Although it feels like it has the teleological approach of genuine research, it is driven by personal and social factors that make it considerably more difficult to let go of than genuine theory or research. There is a degree of selectiveness about empiricism when anything resembling it does emerge. When in 2017 South African entrepreneur and Silicon Valley billionaire Elon Musk asked the Flat Earth Society on Twitter why there was no "Flat Mars Society", their response was instructive: "Unlike the Earth, Mars has been observed to be round". Likewise, the sheer physical impossibility of a flat Earth, for example, is not an obstacle if the theory of gravity is simply not taken into account. Gravity, according to the Flat Earth Society, "is false", but is not replaced with an alternative theory. "Objects simply fall", they state. OK then!

Veracity in fact becomes completely irrelevant, and as Michael Barkun says, "Conspiracy theories are at their heart nonfalsifiable. No matter how much evidence their adherents accumulate, belief in a conspiracy theory becomes a matter of faith, rather than proof." But there is a difference between conspiracist sense-making and religious faith. With religious beliefs, people know they have no evidence, and in the case of Christianity, for example, the very believing of something for which you have no evidence is part of what is said to make such a faith meaningful — according to the New Testament, Jesus told the pesky empiricist known as "doubting Thomas" that "blessed [are] they that have not seen, and [yet] have believed" (John 20:29). Conspiracy theorists are the exact opposite of this — they have seen, and then have insisted on believing something different. Sometimes, as in the case of 5G conspiracists' misunderstanding of cellular technology or Flat-Earthers' loathing of pretty much anything official, this type of knowledge rejection is adversarial — it is not only a rejection of existing accounts, but an open hostility to what they represent, for example, when empirical evidence from anybody actually qualified enough to provide it is dismissed as part of the conspiracy.

Genuine disclosures of the misuse of power often occur in the context of what we could call "grey" information, that is neither entirely secret, nor explicitly disclosed by those who it concerns and made accessible to a broad audience for scrutiny. In other words, this type of information is only available to those who are willing to expend effort in looking for it, such as tax filings, some court filings, dense scientific papers, or excessively long documents running to thousands of pages that require real effort to read in their entirety.

Ready access to user-generated content (e.g. of the type on Quora, Twitter, Reddit and Wikipedia) allows conspiracist "researchers" to enjoy a similar feeling. Although these types of sources have proven invaluable to investigative journalists, and organisations such as Bellingcat and Tactical Tech have demonstrated their immense practical value in a variety of ways, what they also highlight are the ways that knowledge agency and so-called "citizen investigators" have been transposed into digital realms in which valuable, if time-consuming, sources of useful information exist alongside an essentially unlimited amount of less reliable information, spread for spurious reasons. While Bellingcat on the one hand might have been successful in revealing the lies of the Russian government on more than one occasion, this type of enquiry does not always assume the same productive or informative quality. It can be very tempting for people to invest time and energy to discover the "truth" about what is really in their groceries, or what the government or their employers are planning, but it is even more so when there is no possibility that you may be proven wrong at any time, especially when "researching" an area in which you have no training or background. If you have already decided that "official" sources are intrinsically to be regarded with suspicion or avoided completely, then the temptation may be too great to resist.

After the 2013 Boston Marathon attacks, for example, conspiracy theorist and reactionary Paul Joseph Watson assembled a long, speculative blog post for arch conspiracy theorist Alex Jones's media outlet *InfoWars* about the bombings, using grainy, close-up photos captured (somewhat ironically) from TV news footage to suggest that they had been carried out by the US Marines, who had inadvertently left their logo on the suspicious backpacks they were carrying.

The fact that, having created or adopted certain conspiracist beliefs about the world, they are so difficult for people to shake off or leave behind leads to the most important of questions: Why?

I've said above that the sheer fact of investment in unalienated labour brings about a type of commitment bias. The person you are in love with who does not love you is still more interesting, even if they treat you appallingly, than the person who invites you to love but to whom you have made no commitment. But beyond that, there are more things to say. Broadly, the answers to this question can be grouped into two main categories: social factors and individual, psychological factors.

Starting with the social, there are a number of important social dynamics to conspiracist beliefs that intensify them, particularly against the backdrop of widespread social isolation and loneliness that is a regular feature of the market-driven society. For one, their near complete disconnection from demanding forms of knowledge-production means that they can feel inclusive, since they allow participation in knowledge social exchange processes without the need for anything other than basic cultural literacy and some degree of imagination. They are often perfectly able to be what French sociologist Émile Durkheim called *organic solidarity*, since they do not require adherents to live similar lives or have much else in common. In the case of certain theories such as Flat-Earthers, entire communities can develop around adherence to a conspiracy theory, making it hard to relinquish later without significant social cost. Recall from the last chapter the phenomenon that Dan Kahan and colleagues called the *Identity-Protective Cognition Thesis*, in which "the pressure to form group-congruent beliefs will often dominate whatever incentives individuals have to 'get the right answer' from an empirical standpoint" (2013: 3).

Perhaps partly because of the in-group mentality, some conspiracy groups such as the Flat-Earthers also demonstrate a remarkably *open-source* and egalitarian co-operation, in which ownership and development of the theory is collective and co-creative. Individual investigation and "research" into conspiracist beliefs in some cases starts as little more than chance discovery and acceptance of conspiracy beliefs already shared and published by others that then leads down a "rabbit hole" of further discovery. As I have written elsewhere, digital attention is driven by emotional arousal, in which neither the consumer or the architecture by which that content is experienced are primarily oriented around veracity or sincere information seeking — a picture we will return to in Chapter Six. As we saw in Chapter Two, this combination of affective arousal and disinformation encounter leaves us at risk of over-relying on what Daniel Kahneman has called System 1 thinking, which in comparison to more deliberative System 2 thinking is faster and more impulsive, but is also the main driver behind many of the choices and judgments we make (2011: 13).

The social and the individual are, of course, not really separate, and along with other cultural forms of misinformation and disinformation, conspiracism is driven by a combination of social factors. Major conspiracy theorists such as Alex Jones, David Icke or Paul Joseph

Watson all cultivate and perform a "personal brand" of conspiracism that is typical of the culture of the market-driven society. For every famous conspiracy theorist there are millions of unknown conspiracists, for whom the feeling of uncovering and "research" is both individually satisfying and also constitutes some kind of social offering within the types of communities described above.

There are also ways that the individual experience within a social order can drive conspiracist thinking and action, and one of these is gender. There is no space here to make an exhaustive examination of the gender dynamics of conspiracist thinking, but only because its gendered overtones are so complex and interesting that they could take up pages. There are a few observations that can and should be made, however. A good place to start is with Rebecca Solnit's observation that "the out-and-out confrontational confidence of the totally ignorant" tends to be gendered (2014: 3–4). Indeed, there is certainly plausibility to the idea that the arrogance of believing that you know better than the majority of the world's experts and trained professionals is a delusion that is afforded more often to men. This in itself is not unique to conspiracy theories, and neither are conspiracy theories more easily believed by those identifying as men — any hypothesis that conspiracism itself is a male behaviour is easily disproven by examining any anti-5G or anti-vaccination Facebook page. But the gendered pattern identified by Solnit and others to the way that people may assume that they are in possession of important information and authority, and that others are not, certainly lends itself to the aggressive ways that conspiracy theories are both synthesised and communicated. As Solnit later elaborates, self-negation is something that women are frequently habituated to, not least as a result of being regularly patronised, ignored and contradicted despite later being shown to be correct. In her examination of the public sphere, Nancy Fraser argues similarly that "men tend to interrupt women more than women interrupt men; men also tend to speak more than women, taking more turns and longer turns; and women's interventions are more often ignored or not responded to than men's" (1990: 64).

But the possible *maleness* of conspiracism and its belligerent assertion of nonsense is not necessarily a case of women's absence from these forms of behaviour so much as a male propensity to them. Claims of a "crisis" of masculinity may be overblown, or a code for attacking feminist advances that attempted to leave behind traditional patriarchal masculinity, but certainly those who may be unable to imagine alternative, more egalitarian models of masculinity appear to have also been left clinging to a sense that they can and must assert their value by constituting themselves as a source of unlimited explanation of the world. Mix this with the forms of political and economic disempowerment — real and imagined — discussed above, that have accompanied the market-driven society's disregard for traditional male authority, and it is little wonder that the towering wall of conspiracist hypothesising and blind insistence might be mostly male.

Another factor may also be men's inability to cope with being or feeling vulnerable, which drives an absolutist, have-all-the-answers approach to understanding the world and a silencing of the more rational but less assertive "we don't know" or "let's not jump to conclusions" or "it's complicated" ways of thinking that those who inhabit vulnerability may be more accustomed to. In his discussion of the eternal qualities of fascism, Umberto Eco said that "thinking is a form of emasculation" (1995). The other side of this is that the thinking or analysis that might turn out to be an inoculation against some forms of conspiracist thinking is something that the unreconstructed male disdains.

Conspiracy Theories and Bigotry

The mention of fascism, both in terms of its loathing for deliberative thinking and its preference for traditional gender roles, leads us to the issue of conspiracy theory and racism. Why are conspiracy theories so often racist, misogynist, homophobic or otherwise bigoted? In a way, this is already an inversion of the proper question. Conspiracism does not precede racism so much as the other way around. Racism, misogyny and other forms of prejudice are widespread, and they colour most of the forms of belief and thinking that people exercise, even when these are subjectively rationalised. If a person is patriarchal or racist, any religious beliefs they hold will likely also be racist, and likewise, just as the example of Nazi science shows, supposedly scientific research can also be driven by racism. As a general rule, conspiracy theories are no different in that they reflect those that believe them — that is, racist conspiracy theories are the product of a racist imagination, and the conspiracist pattern that I have described above only gives their racism or other prejudice a specific form. Not only are Muslims said to be backwards, or gay people perverted, or women hypermaterialistic, as per the standard prejudiced tropes, but they are also said to be conspiring to dominate you into conforming to their wishes and behaviours.

To provide a real-world example: the fear in 2018 in Sri Lanka that Muslim restaurant owners were putting sterilisation pills in the food they served in order to enable the Muslim minority population to out-reproduce the country's Sinhalese Buddhist majority, which led to rioting and a number of deaths, was driven by an existing, rampant Islamophobia in the country that provided the foundation on which these more specific theories were formulated.

Where racism comes from is a question that can be answered by much more qualified writers, but what is worth saying here is that a bit like conspiracy theories, "race" is a way of thinking about the world that gives its adherents an appealingly simplistic way of looking at and manipulating the way they understand the world, which John Hartigan has called "explanatory power" (1999: 25–26). Race thinking is thus highly compatible with conspiracist thinking, particularly amongst those "angry white men" that Michael Kimmel (2013) has portrayed so convincingly.

There are, however, a number of qualifications and complexities to this overall characterisation of prejudice as content and conspiracism as form. The first is that certain forms of racism take a conspiracist form much more often than others, and do so in a way that goes to the heart of the racist ideas for which they would otherwise be a vessel. For example, one of the oldest and most prominent examples of a racist conspiracy theory is the anti-Semitic trope in which Jews secretly control and manipulate the world to their advantage, and in particular the world's financial resources and institutions. "Bogeyman" figures like George Soros or members of the scattered Rothschild family repeatedly reappear in the imagined role of mysterious, proprietorial puppet-masters of the world's elite institutions. On superficial level, the conspiratorial behaviour alleged in the theory appears to be a much more essential part of the racist caricature, and Jews are denigrated precisely for being, first among other things, conniving, aloof and disloyal to the profane, secular modernity against which they are pitted. This is different to a pre-existing racism merely being shaped haphazardly into a conspiracy theory. However, the anti-Semitic conspiracy theory is one of the oldest recognisable racist conspiracy theories, and in the past it functioned more as a specific form of a broader anti-Semitism, in the same way that conspiracy theories about Muslims developed in the early twenty-first century. Over time, this ossified into a specific view of Jews as conspirators, but there is also a historical context in the older fascisms of Europe. Umberto Eco linked the "obsession with a plot, possibly an international one" to fascism, and argued that its followers "must feel besieged". The easiest way to solve the plot, he said, was to appeal to xenophobia. The plot also needed "to come from the inside: Jews are usually the best target because they have the advantage of being at the same time inside and outside" (1995).

Another caveat to the general rule that racism precedes racist conspiracy theories is one that brings us face to face with the politics of suspicion. It has long been the case that the establishment — that is, those who actually do hold power and ownership — have resisted radical social movements that brought greater social and political freedoms. The abolition of the Atlantic slave trade, the beginning of women's suffrage, the civil rights movement and the gay rights movement all faced fierce opposition in a world where social conservatism and economic power were aligned. But as I have outlined throughout this book, traditional social conservatism and the increasingly neoliberalised engine of economic power have drifted apart, at least as far as their public allegiances to one another. Along the way, the neoliberal architects of the market-driven society, whose original intention — let us remember — had been to avoid totalitarianism, realised that, like all power that does not rest primarily on explicit promises of violent coercion, their vision of society needed to have cultural legitimacy. In Chapters One and Two, we saw how culture and "coolness" became essential parts of the full-colour, surround-sound consumerist market-driven society that developed, particularly from the 1990s onwards. Mark Fisher described the way that "'Alternative' and 'independent' don't designate something outside mainstream culture; rather, they are styles, in fact *the* dominant styles, within the mainstream." (2009: 9) Nobody exemplified this "deadlock" more than the Nineties grunge movement, with which the band Nirvana was associated. As the market-driven society continued its slow incorporation of everything in its bid for ongoing legitimacy and even invisibility, it also absorbed the very victories that its one-time conservative allies tried for so long to stop.

One reason why conspiracy theories are so often prejudiced is because the very power in relation to which they have arisen, in other words, has also appropriated the values of anti-racism, feminism and gay rights as a means of camouflaging and legitimising itself in the gleaming environs of that liberal capitalism imagined to be the "end of history" (as will be explored further in the following chapter). Correspondingly, their suspicion and antagonism of that power, their counterpower, falls for this disguise and frequently begins to antagonise those values more generally. They conflate the market-driven society with its mask. Michael Barkun calls the tendency of conspiracy theories to contravene or come into conflict with contemporary, orthodox or accepted accounts of the world as "stigmatized knowledge" (2013: 12). Although his schema of five sub-categories — forgotten knowledge (e.g. "ancient wisdom"), superseded knowledge (lost status over time), ignored knowledge (not taken seriously), rejected knowledge (false from the beginning) and suppressed knowledge — do not include a category for socially taboo ideas about the world, one could posit alongside them something like "socially unacceptable knowledge". The only problem of course is that these are not knowledge, so much as firmly held suspicions, but as Jodi Dean (1998) has observed, conspiracism entails a challenge to the status quo and its stigmatisation confers a political character on such beliefs in themselves. The appropriation of feminist and anti-racist discourse into the institutions of mainstream capitalism such as banks and junk food chains has seen conspiracy theories shift further into realms where these discourses are attacked. It is not that the holders of such views would not otherwise have been racist or sexist, but that their racist or misogynist views might not have been expressed according to the tropes of feeling *conspired* against by the dominant hegemony. Even the Remain elements of the Brexit discussion after the referendum have been voiced in these terms: people voted to leave, but the "elites" are *conspiring* to prevent the democratic choice of the people from being realised, etc.

The same pattern is also visible in yet another type of conspiracism that is often racist: the denial of major historical trauma such as the Nazi Holocaust or the genocides in Bosnia or Rwanda. Such denial is sadly widespread. For example, a poll in January 2019 found that more than 2.6 million Brits denied that the Holocaust ever happened (Baynes, 2019). As we saw in the last chapter, and will see again from a different perspective in the next, the teaching of history is often cleaned and polished into an advert for some set of values — whether it is teaching creationism in the most religious states in the US or in UK schools' convenient omission of the brutality of colonialism when the British Empire is discussed. As the writer Nesrine Malik (2019) has observed, there is no country that can be happy with its current self and simultaneously conscious of its past. Once again, the noxious combination of imagination, suspicion and resentment rises to meet these entrenched narratives and to challenge the powerful ideological order of which they can appear to be a part, leaving the families of Holocaust or genocide victims painfully caught in between.

From Bogus Theories to a Grounded Understanding of Capital

As we have seen, conspiracy theories are a misfiring of a healthy and justifiable political instinct: suspicion. What the prevalence of conspiracy theories can teach is that misinformation and disinformation do not come about magically, in some kind of vacuum. Frequently they are produced and sustained by political and economic factors the determine the reality of people's lived existence. When we fret about "fake news" or other disinformation, we need to remember that it can only truly be addressed by going to the source, and appraising people's political and economic conditions.

In an era of such catastrophic distrust in government and the media, to act in even a remotely conspiratorial way against the public interest, in any way that can be evidenced later, is to invite even more far-fetched and extreme explanations and theories. Abuse of power *begets* conspiracy allegations, and the men and women of conspiratorial capital at least partly have themselves to blame for the extreme and fictitious allegations made against them. Creating new detection technologies or ridiculing or ostracising the proponents of such theories not only fails to stamp out the existence of disinformation itself, but it distracts us away from the real solutions.

Those people working to address the shortcomings and injustices of that society, including the vast amount of misinformation and disinformation it generates, face two significant hurdles. The first extremely frustrating issue is in the way that grounded theorisation about the normalised inequality and connivance of the market-driven society is dismissed as "conspiracy theory", usually by those who are too naïve or materially invested in the status quo to allow any change, as if the charge of a deliberately prolonged inequality were the same as the unhinged theories of somebody who believes in "chemtrails" and space aliens. Throughout this chapter I have used the phrase "conspiracy theories" to refer to the imaginary, bigoted, or just plain weird explanations of the world that are usually associated with those two words. But I've used the word "conspiracies" in its literal meaning to demonstrate that alongside these accusations there is also the more realistic conspiratorial exercise of power that we can prove has taken place. It should not be contentious to say that we *are* conspired against, as long as the conscientious and difficult work of journalists, academics and honest citizens is allowed to guide that analysis. To dismiss this work as "conspiracy theory" is profoundly insulting to those who really are poisoned, stolen from, and exploited by the countless real conspiracies that are inseparable from the market-driven society.

This points to the second issue, which can and should be laid at the door of the proponents of fanciful and unhinged conspiracy theories in the classic sense. Accounts of the true nature of power's cruelty and recklessness with public safety often *are* available, but are displaced by the ravings of attention-hungry bigots and charlatans who thrive both psychologically and financially by providing a bogeyman "conspiracy theorist" that the most senior beneficiaries of the market-driven society use as evidence that the charges against them are unfounded. It is not only the famous conspiracy theorists who merit this critique, however. Theories are not fact, but they are also not an occasion to indulge in fanciful bigotry and lay biology or science fiction either. Although we are conspired against, we see that much of the narrative that comprises relevant and common conspiracy theory in the broader media ecosystem and popular imagination is unrepresentative of actual conspiratorial activity or intention by capital, which is far too disorganised to perpetrate the kinds of conspiracies imputed to it.

Climate change denial is one conspiracy theory that allows us to see this difference clearly. The idea that climate change is a giant cover-up by the world's scientists is rather at odds with the reality that there are few other matters on which such a strong scientific consensus exists, and no incentive at all for either private-sector or university-based researchers to collude with the very powers that they frequently accuse of producing the climate crisis to begin with. The neoliberal capitalism that has given us the market-driven society essentially relies on conspiracy; it's usually just a much more boring and dysfunctional one than online conspiracy theorists would like to imagine. As much as suspicion is a justifiable political instinct, the affirmation of wholly unfounded and possibly outlandish theories like the kind described at the beginning of this chapter serves exactly the opposite goal that those who believe them think it will do: it distracts from and discredits those who are working hard to expose actual conspiracies — a far more important, if far less glamorous and exciting form of work.

Chapter Four
When Liberals Aren't Actually That Liberal:
The Politics of Shallow Understanding

Never be deceived that the rich will allow you to vote away
their wealth.
— Lucy Parsons

The Enlightenment *must consider itself*, if men are not to be
wholly betrayed.
— Theodor Adorno and Max Horkheimer

We're capitalists.
— Nancy Pelosi, Democratic House Leader, speaking about
the Democrat Party

*One scorching hot August day in 2018, at the time the hottest
year on record, I strolled through Washington Square Park in
New York City. The park was full of its usual convivial mixture
of New Yorkers of all descriptions talking, eating, relaxing
and sheltering from the powerful sunshine. As I approached
the main fountain area to find a seat at which to eat my slice
of pizza, I came across a man selling badges or pins, bearing
various messages and slogans. Judging by the man's makeshift
wooden stall and overall appearance, I suspected he wasn't
just there to sell badges for commercial reasons, but because
he believed in a cause of some kind. Given the background of
heightened political tension in the US at that moment, I went
to have a closer look once I'd finished my slice, to see what they
said. Sure enough, many of the badges bore political slogans*

and messages: "I miss Obama!" read one. "Impeach!" read another. "Science: Peer reviewed, not politician approved", and "Facts" read two more. There were a few others shouting various concordant political positions in block capitals and bright colours, but it is these four that resonated with me. Superficially they were pretty harmless, and in the binary polarity of Trump's United States they articulated a defiant spirit that was unquestionably on the right side of history. But that was not all. The badges, and the hope that liberal America was clearly investing in their messages, also gave me a feeling of dread: a dull ache that this was not a sufficiently creative or reflective form of resistance, however vibrantly arranged. Criticising what is in effect your own side, at least in the sense that your enemy's enemy is your friend, is always much more difficult. But whether we are longing for and rehabilitating the politicians of the past, urging the use of powers of the state to remove politicians who were elected by tens of millions of people, or uncritically worshipping "facts" with no acknowledgement that facts are ever politicised, we need to ask ourselves if the things that look like defiance may actually be reflective of the patterns of thinking that helped bring us to that point in the first place.

In an era of major political polarisation, clichéd as that might sound, it is easy to look at the extremes — particularly the far-right — and assume these are the source of the political instability we see around us. It should not need saying that there is absolutely nothing redeemable in far-right politics and there are no words to sufficiently describe the abhorrence and foolishness of dehumanising other human beings and destroying the natural environment, whether out of pure anger or in mistaken belief that it will achieve anything. But hopefully it should already be clear that, as well as being a cause, these politics are a symptom of a far deeper and more complex set of problems. Any study of the self-reproducing ways of misunderstanding the world that have led it to such a point of crisis would be complicit in the misinformation and disinformation it sought to analyse if its emphases were only towards those extremes. Reactionary politics of the kinds I have described would not have been mainstreamed without help from those elements of the political conversation that are often concealed beneath a veneer of polite, respectable, live-and-let-live pleasantness and who think themselves the custodians of reason, liberty, Enlightenment and justice, but are almost as equally deluded and misguided, including about their enabling effect on the very people at whom they point the finger. This process is an extremely important part of the disinformation society, because any dysfunctional system can only be fixed if its problems can be correctly identified and diagnosed. If a major problem with a car engine was concealed, fixing that car would be much more difficult, and the same is true with the market-driven society. A number of labels have been applied to these habits of political thought, emphasising different aspects and sub-categories of them: "liberals", "moderates", "centrists" and so forth, but all are unfit for purpose. Avoiding these labels where possible, this chapter will first examine these habits of shallow political thought before returning to the challenge of what to call them in greater detail.

The difficult truth is that even when we believe we are helping to make the world better, or at least consider ourselves to be invested in ideas such as "progress" and "reason", we are not necessarily immune to profoundly damaging misinformation, nor do our actions necessarily lead to a more equitable world. Writing on the margins of a newspaper smuggled into his cell in Birmingham Jail in Alabama in 1963, Dr Martin Luther King Jr, who had been arrested for non-violent resistance, wrote:

I have almost reached the regrettable conclusion that the Negro's great stumbling block in his stride toward freedom is not the White Citizen's Councillor or the Ku Klux Klanner, but the white moderate, who is more devoted to "order" than to justice; who prefers a negative peace which is the absence of tension to a positive peace which is the presence of justice; who constantly says: "I agree with you in the goal you seek, but I cannot agree with your methods of direct action"; who paternalistically believes he can set the timetable for another man's freedom; who lives by a mythical concept of time and who constantly advises the Negro to wait for a "more convenient season." Shallow understanding from people of good will is more frustrating than absolute misunderstanding from people of ill will.

The problem King describes here illustrates precisely these habits of political thinking that continue to plague the early twenty-first century as part of the disinformation society, but go back centuries. A number of other thinkers have also addressed the disastrous effects that this "shallow understanding from people of good will" can have, and, before going further, it is appropriate to offer a short summary of these contributions. Written after World War II, the most prominent of these critiques is that of the theorists Theodor Adorno and Max Horkheimer, who posed these contradictions and hypocrisies in relation to the modernity that had produced the war as a "dialectic of enlightenment" (1989 [1947]). How could the Germans, who professed a love of many of the values of the Enlightenment, have allowed these values to culminate in the genocidal, imperial, corporate-branded form of the Third Reich? The philosopher Domenico Losurdo (2011) traces these same issues back even further, detailing how so-called "liberals" fought *against* the abolition of slavery and the end of colonialism on the basis of "freedom". This is similar to the hypocrisy identified by the writer Richard Seymour in the ways that supposed "liberals" later supported wars in Afghanistan and Iraq by making US military power "an ally of progress rather than its enemy" (2008). Writing before the financial crash or the mainstreaming of reactionary nationalism in the Euro-Atlantic world that followed, Ulrich Beck and Chantal Mouffe were amongst those who critically re-examined Fukuyama's claim of the "end of history". Beck called the idea of the "end of history" a "mad joke" (1992: 11) and, as we saw in Chapter Two, argued that society had in fact shifted from being one primarily concerned with resource allocation to being one which was primarily concerned with managing its own stability. Mouffe also challenged the claimed obsolescence of engaging with the overtly political character of society suggested by this post-political view, "Such a longing reveals a complete lack of understanding of what is at stake in democratic politics and [...] contributes to exacerbating the antagonistic potential existing in society." (2005: 2). This was developed further after Trump took office in 2017 by the writer and broadcaster Eliane Glaser, who traced the distinctly anti-political rhetoric of the post-Cold War governance in the Euro-Atlantic world in producing the later wave of anti-democratic reactionary politics of which Trump's election was part. What is missing, however, is a broader account of how the same "shallow understanding" and complacency as King's "white moderate", whether wittingly or not, has come to be amongst the most accommodating supporters of the market-driven society, and thus indirectly of the extremism that it has produced.

Business as Usual

One of the defining facets of this politics of "shallow understanding", addressed by nearly all the thinkers and writers above, is an insistence on preserving all or most of the status quo. Often this preservation is not out of ideological commitment to the actual politics of the moment, which may explicitly be criticised, so much as a gut reaction that dreads change itself, or an aversion to inconvenience. Any disruption, even if likely to produce a more just outcome, often came to represent a risk that too much may be lost in any transitional turbulence, particularly by those who already benefit, regardless of the injustice that may have to be borne by others who are less comfortable, until some other solution — often technology — can be found that pleases everybody and involves no sacrifice. Usually, this is not expressed explicitly, or even believed consciously. Rather, it is often an opaque aversion to "rocking the boat" in itself.

Far from providing a degree of valuable caution, or a voice of reason, this way of approaching political problems functions as something of a permanent handbrake on the project of building a more just world. As the urgency for radical change grows, so too does the need that this handbrake be released. When Extinction Rebellion peacefully block a road, even if in peaceful co-operation with the police, the same voices say: "I agree climate change is an issue, but disrupting people's lives will not help", ignoring the burning planet and rising seas as if inconvenience and belligerence were the group's primary goals, or the only legitimate disruption to people's lives was the unpredictable weather and flooding that protesters are trying to prevent or draw attention to. This was very well illustrated when Extinction Rebellion protests disrupted traffic in London in April 2019, and Mayor Sadiq Khan insisted that while he shared "the passion about tackling climate change of those protesting", and supported "the right to peaceful and lawful protest", Londoners needed to be able to return to "business as usual". It was almost a paraphrase of the "moderate" that Martin Luther King complained of, but coming from the mayor of a city whose lofty position in the global economy and spiralling addiction to the market-driven society, at least before Brexit, meant it increasingly came to represent exactly that complacent mindset.

On numerous occasions in the US, photos have surfaced of anti-Trump protesters bearing signs to the effect of, "If Hillary had won, we'd be at brunch right now". After the widespread shock of the ruptures of 2016, things have become so illiberal that the flaws of the past, if they were noticed or acknowledged at all, are entirely forgotten. Or maybe it's that the years that appeared "normal" because "Brexit" wasn't a word and Donald Trump was only known for developing tacky residential buildings or telling people they were fired on primetime TV, were only tolerable for the people who were not affected by declining public services, low wages or zero-hour contracts. The stability of that moment to which these people want to return was, save for the brunches themselves, an illusion. And our inability to see that we were making a crisis was a key element of the very making of that crisis. One study, published in *Socio-Economic Review* (Mijs, 2019), showed that people in already divided societies are more likely to accept inequality, which makes sense: if you are ignorant of the poverty required to make your own comfort possible, you are less likely to be concerned by it. Radical structural change? Why would we want that?

This is a mindset that deserves more critique than it receives: the unstated conviction that problems such as the suffering of others and the destruction of the environment either have no solution, have a technological solution, or can be largely ameliorated with individual-level choices such as using specific language and buying different products such as wristbands or LED lightbulbs.

As a sidenote, it is important to say here that adjusting our consumer habits or improving the language we use to address sensitive issues are not problems in themselves — but they are almost never the substantive change in the status quo that they are imagined to be either, especially when they are offered by the same market-driven society that they are supposed to address, and it is counterproductive to overstate their importance. Ultimately, there is no effective way of protesting climate change, racism, economic injustice or any other major issue that is supportive of a wider "business as usual" attitude, especially if the mechanics of business as usual are what is creating the problem. Mark Fisher famously identified the ways that that status quo conditioned the political imagination into a "capitalist realism" that was incapable of imagining anything radically beyond it. And this failure of imagination has often meant that the action that purports to address the problem tends to have the effect of defending the status quo, because genuinely effective remedies are deemed too radical or require too many people to wean themselves off the glossy, momentary pleasures of the market-driven society's dystopia.

Order Over Justice

Moving away from individualised, habitual defence of the status quo, change has also frequently been prevented in more explicit, if abstract terms. The reader may recall that one of the features of Dr King's "white moderates" was that they were "more devoted to 'order' than to justice". This inversion is in some ways an instance of the unquestioning faith in systems, technologies, processes, categories and ideas at the expense of substance, that scholars have tended to call "positivism". The late political scientist David Held explained positivism as a "'freezing' of the status quo" that works by repeating and affirming its explicit ways of thinking about and structuring the world without challenging them or interrogating their actual effects (2013: 169). Its tendency to emphasise theoretical positives or enforce simplistic categorisations without acknowledging their practical complexities has been a regular obstacle to justice as far back as the Enlightenment with which it is often associated. For example, French poet Anatole France mocked the injustice inherent in the legal positivist thinking of the Enlightenment when he quipped in 1894 that "The law, in its majestic equality, forbids the rich as well as the poor to sleep under bridges, to beg in the streets, and to steal bread."

Positivism is similar to the concept of *reification* used by Marxian scholars — quite literally, the "making into a thing" of certain concepts — but is distinct in that it goes much further. While reification is often entirely unconscious, positivism involves an explicit, repeated advocacy for a reified concept in the belief that it is an unqualified positive, and in a way that helps to obscure the harms its overemphasis or oversimplification produces.

As such, positivism is relevant here because it is a frequent and potent form of emotionally invested misinformation that prevents political action and stokes resentment — usually against the wrong targets, as we'll see later in the chapter. It is another element of the "shallow understanding" of "good will" of which Dr King complained. Particularly when amplified by the architectures of misinformation and disinformation of the market-driven society, it is a common means by which people invest heavily in the theoretical systems that help them understand the world, but then refuse to see the complexities and flaws of those systems in practice.

Technology Can Fix Everything!

One area in which this whole-hearted belief in systems became prevalent is that of technology, which was afforded a place in the market-driven society where it was assumed to be a net positive and had a history of facilitating the expansion of capitalism. The so-called "liberal" mindset at issue here has always been keen to emphasise the promise of technology, which frequently functioned as a symbol of "progress" — from the clocks and steam engines of the industrial revolution to the cohort of Silicon Valley companies that emerged over a century later.

The California senator and US presidential hopeful Kamala Harris was only one of a long tradition of Euro-Atlantic techno-positivists when she was heard telling two different supporters looking for advice to "learn to code" in October 2019 (Enjeti, 2019), something that had already become such a cliché in the context of the market-driven society's worsening Schumpeterian "creative destruction" of entire industries, especially journalism, that it ended up as an internet meme in itself.

Why use a pen and paper when there's an app for that? Why drive your own car badly when the car can do it for you? Whereas clocks and steam engines provided affordances that could be easily placed in the context of an industrial revolution that really wanted to go faster or be more efficient, technology later became something that was also implemented for its own sake, rather than the direct and obvious needs of capitalism, although this tendency also continued. As Jim McGuigan observed in 2009, headlines regularly praised Apple, Google or even Microsoft as "cool", according to the ascendant or declining popularity of their products. Apple's long-term self-description as "insanely great" was superseded only by its pioneering reframing of technology as a luxury lifestyle product, which was deliberate and accelerated after the company hired Burberry executive Angela Ahrents and other fashion executives in 2014.

Belarussian writer and scholar Evgeny Morozov, regularly an incisive and intelligent critic of the market-driven society's love of technology, noted the ways that technology is habitually deployed to address social problems, including those actually produced by the market-driven society itself:

> all too often, this never-ending quest to ameliorate [...] is shortsighted and only perfunctorily interested in the activity for which improvement is sought. Recasting all complex social situations either as neatly defined problems with definite, computable solutions or as transparent and self-evident processes that can be easily optimized [...] is likely to have unexpected consequences that could eventually cause more damage than the problems they seek to address. (2013: 5)

Technology scholar Meredith Broussard calls the belief that technology is always the solution "technochauvinism". One of its hallmarks, she says, is "abundant lack of caution about how new technologies will be used" (2018: 69) As part of this pattern, we could say there is a more specific blindness involved in believing that the market-driven society would provide us with technology that in any meaningful way mitigates or challenges that same market-driven society. As Broussard rightly observes, "Computer systems are proxies for the people who made them" (ibid.: 67), and as Virginia Eubanks (2018) and Safiya Noble (2018) have both addressed, technology is often a means for reinforcing injustice, or turning a blind eye to it, even when the reverse may have been imagined. Against the background of the market-driven society's intrinsic cruelty, one example is the "anti-homeless" surveillance robot in San Francisco — somebody really thought that would be a "totally awesome" idea. Only in San Francisco. Note how it is the injustices of the market-driven society that is actually causing the homelessness, as well as providing the technological "solution".

This illusion of technology as saviour is a pervasive one, however. As Yuval Noah Harari (2020) and others cautioned at the onset of the COVID-19 pandemic, the overly trusting adoption of technology to solve complex problems can often actually assist in regressive policies such as surveillance. While positivists may cast technology as "cool", the only other people cheering for it are those who have a much more specific and calculated agenda in mind. Indeed, Umberto Eco observed, a fetishisation of technology was one of the hallmarks of fascist thought in the twentieth century — not indicative of fascism by itself, but certainly one of the diagnostic criteria for identifying fascistic thought (1995).

One would think that a sincere belief in technology as a net positive would be quickly put to bed by an honest assessment of who actually benefits from its affordances and why. For example, in 2018, police in Norfolk, England, began using an algorithm to determine whether burglaries should be investigated or not, which ultimately helped neither the investigators nor those who had had their possessions stolen, but was surely useful to those wishing to cut back police services as a whole in the name of austerity. In 2017, a study was published by two scientists including Michal Kosinski (whose data and studies were also misappropriated by Cambridge Analytica), that claimed to be able to use artificial intelligence to determine from a person's photograph whether or not they were homosexual. Never mind the fact that when the experiment was repeated later by different scientists, its results were not replicated, what possible good reason is there for programmatic detection of a person's sexuality from their photo? The only people who would have found such a technology useful would surely have been those repressive governments in the market for a more "efficient" way of rounding up and harming gay people.

Technology positivism can also be harmful in the ways that it oversimplifies much more serious and complicated problems. Journalism will be considered more fully in the next chapter, but by way of an example, it is worth mentioning that the belief that technological measures can effectively counter "fake news" is also a part of this pro-technology faith. Not only is technology seldom the solution to problems that are not technological, it is often produced by those very same corporations who are most invested in the continuation of the broader status quo of the market-driven society. Technological innovation becomes a call to *inaction* in other more complicated spheres. And why might this be? Perhaps because in many cases, as Adorno and Horkheimer observed, "the basis on which technology acquires power over society is the power of those whose economic hold over society is greatest" (1989 [1947]: 121). One example of this may be the ways that as the number of smokers in the world slowly reduced, tobacco companies began to take over the "smoke free" and "stop smoking" campaigns, to help them sell vaping products (Branston, Gilmore and Hiscock, 2018).

This love of technology also involves an often-explicit, institutional alliance between supposedly liberal capitalist democracy and the world of technology. In January 2017, it was leaked that had Hillary Clinton won the 2016 US presidential election, she was planning to appoint

Facebook's Chief Operations Officer Sheryl Sandberg to her cabinet (Mathis-Lilley, 2017), and only a few months before the election, leaked emails also showed she was considering Apple CEO Tim Cook, who fundraised for her, for a cabinet position (Weintraub, 2016). British ex-politician Nick Clegg, who was a leader of the Liberal Democrats — a party that perfectly embodies the political habits that this chapter addresses — surprised some by moving to work as an executive at Facebook once he was ousted from that party after a humiliating election defeat brought about by breaking a promise to the electorate not to raise tuition fees. But like his betrayal of Britain's young voters, this new job should not have been a surprise at all, and not just for the positivist love of technology in a consumerist sense, although this was present in Clegg's case too, as he admitted in his book: "On the morning after I resigned as a party leader [...] I went to the nearest high street with my oldest son, determined to cheer myself up by going on a shopping spree for new gadgets" (2016: 13). Particularly as enormous corporations like Facebook have pioneered surveillance capitalism into the brightest hope of that embattled model of intellectually bankrupt pseudo-democracy so loved by Fukuyama, Giddens and others, digital platforms have become a popular choice for its cheerleaders to continue their work once they have been exiled from electoral politics, second only to hedge funds. The most prominent example heading in the other direction has probably been Eric Schmidt, who built Google into the giant company it became as its CEO. When he left Google's parent company Alphabet in May 2020, he became an "innovation advisor" to the US Department of Defense under the Trump administration — from surveillance capitalism to murder capitalism. Is there an emoji for laser-guided weapons systems yet?

Freedom and Liberty

In some ways, the most positivistic concepts of all are those of "freedom" or "liberty". Politics that emphasises "freedom" by itself is rarely precise or detailed enough to bring about genuine freedom. Announcing freedom for everyone only undermines the enduring struggle of freedom for some. One need only examine the vast range of campaigns and issues advanced in the name of freedom to spot the AAA-grade positivism taking place in its name. The ideologues of the market-driven society continue to rely heavily on the idea of "individual freedom" or "free trade" (which Marx and Engels called an "unconscionable freedom") to resist and reverse attempts at market regulation on the grounds of public health or environmental protection, as well as to push for privatisation.

As the political economist David Harvey observes, 9/11 was almost immediately cast as an attack on "America's freedom", without any explanation of what this meant, or acknowledgement of the complex ideological and geopolitical interplay between violent Saudi-backed Wahabbist groups in Afghanistan and Pakistan and decades of misguided US foreign policy that had at one point supported them. The same concept was then used to frame the rebuilding of Iraq's economy according to strict neoliberal principles.

As Harvey put it, "the word 'freedom' resonates so widely within the common-sense understanding of Americans that it becomes 'a button that elites can press to open the door to the masses to justify almost anything" (2005: 39). One of the more famous and troubling applications of "freedom" in recent years has been by an otherwise forgettable bakery in Colorado in the United States, whose owner Jack Phillips refused to prepare a wedding cake for a gay male couple on grounds of his Christian beliefs. After the bakery was referred to Colorado Civil Rights Commission, it was ordered to make cakes for gay couples in the future, but appealed on grounds of religious *freedom*, eventually winning in the United States Supreme Court.

In the realm of media and information, besides the wholly misleading positivism around "freedom" itself, one of the most pervasive applications of nineteenth-century freedom positivism is that of "freedom of speech" or the "free marketplace of ideas" it was later said to foster (note the additional sprinkling of subtle "free-market" positivism in this coinage). When Richard Spencer or Nigel Farage are invited to express their views in the mainstream media, these mistaken attempts at "debate" are often defended with the suggestion that not to have done so would have been to participate in "no-platforming" these figures in a way that ultimately hurts them by violating their right of freedom of expression. This claim is either naïve, disingenuous, or just plain stupid, but whatever it is, it is intensely positivistic — a belief in the functioning of a set of principles that have long since been revealed to be dysfunctional.

Freedom of expression tends to be associated primarily with nineteenth-century English philosopher John Stuart Mill, whose treatise *On Liberty* is most frequently reached for by freedom of expression positivists, although it did not mention any "free marketplace" of ideas. Mill argued that when all opinions were afforded the same platform and made to reason with each other, audiences would be able to make a rational decision about which was best. Nearly two hundred years later, in a world rife with bizarre conspiracy theories despite forms of information technology that would have amazed Mill and his contemporaries, some people still claim to believe in this principle. When the

New Yorker, the Oxford Union and the *Economist* all invited Steve Bannon for live debates, this was the rationale that was given. And up to a point, it is indeed important to hear and be familiar with what fascism sounds like. By suppressing it, we do not automatically drive it away after all. But giving it mainstream platforms that provide it with amplification and attention without labelling it as what it is or being prepared to challenge it properly, in a world where the market-driven society has already undermined the widespread literacy that would enable people to do this for themselves, is naïve at best and deluded at worst, and reveals a catastrophic failure to understand the cultural and political context in which such "debates" take place, or the dangers faced by those affected when such ideas are put into practice.

As we saw in the last chapter on conspiracy theories, profound alienation from power brought about by the de-democratisation of the market-driven society has combined with anger and imagination to the point where large numbers of people believe absurdities that actually *prevent* them from understanding the world. As the philosopher Jason Stanley has argued:

> Disagreement requires a shared set of presuppositions about the world. Even dueling requires agreement about the rules. You and I might disagree about whether President Obama's healthcare plan was a good policy. But if you suspect that President Obama was an undercover Muslim spy seeking to destroy the United States, and I do not, our discussion will not be productive. (2018: 69–70).

That's putting it politely.

As we can see, "freedom" is regularly a cover for oppression, and though this may in some cases be cynical and deliberate, even these cases are often aided by a background positivistic view that freedom is a sufficiently noble goal that no further analysis is needed. But the great irony here is that freedom is engendered most effectively not by positivism about liberty but by looking *past* freedom at the complex structures of the market-driven society or of the nationalism that has been put in place in its name. Liberty is of course important; the issue is more that the empty concept of "liberty" by itself is not enough. Capitalism loves the idea that we are free to purchase, participate and endorse. But it has also always relied upon the hidden unfreedom of others to secure those freedoms, be they domestic labour at home, or sweatshop labour in the factories of the developing world. Human rights are essential and non-negotiable, but they are frequently considered in a way that is untethered from material reality. In parts of the world where torture or violent suppression is a proximate danger, their immediate application is obvious, but in liberal capitalism, to couch everything in terms of *rights*, wilfully or otherwise, obscures, hinders and discredits the true struggle for liberty and often becomes a form of "do-nothingism".

This is one reason why the label "liberal" is ultimately so misleading in reference to the politics addressed in this chapter. Never mind its long history of dramatically different meanings, including the harsh vitriol with which it is directed at essential causes such as anti-racism and feminism in the United States, it also emphasises liberty in a way that utterly misunderstands and simplifies the issues that many who describe themselves with the term consider to be important in the first place, and undermines rather than promotes actual liberty.

Facts and Science

The near-religious dedication that can be seen in relation to positivist conceptions of technology and liberty also has interesting implications for the ways that knowledge itself is thought about. It should come as no surprise that one of the ways this blind belief in systems frustrates the essentially nuanced, deep understanding of power in the market-driven society is in the insistence on the superiority of certain kinds of knowledge over others. As Adorno and Horkheimer argued, the idea that the universe is entirely measurable and understandable solely according to scientific method was the Enlightenment's primary achievement. Positivism about "the facts" has been a recurrent part of discussions around journalism — addressed in the next chapter — but there is a broader way that this desperation for certainty in the realm of knowledge can both occlude and harm the very goals of "progress" that the Enlightenment supposedly represents.

One of the greatest current enablers of this *doubling down* on science is popular science author Steven Pinker. As well as being the author of a number of interesting linguistics-themed books within Pinker's actual realm of expertise, Pinker also specialises in taking what we could call "hyper-empiricist" positions — that is, positions that focus only on a narrow, quantitative claim about a sensitive political subject, often in a way that can be easily misinterpreted or used as a justification of the status quo. For example, in *Better Angels of our Nature*, Pinker argues that our concern about violence against civilians in post-invasion Iraq or the Democratic Republic of the Congo is ill-founded, because the numbers are frequently recorded with poor methodology, overstated and overly moralised (2011: 381–385). Empirically speaking, he argues, violence is declining, and we are living in the most peaceful time in the history of our species.

The problem with this argument is not the rigour with which it is made, nor the numbers on which it is based, or even the intentions with which it is offered: if, empirically speaking, violence has fallen, then this is something that should unquestionably be celebrated. Rather, the problem is that this relationship to the world, in which everything is a numerical, empirical matter, improved with methodological tweaking and a wait-and-see approach, allows for an interpretation according to which conflicts such as the war in Iraq, however unintentionally, can be justified or made more palatable in hindsight — something for which genocide deniers in East Africa and the Balkans (for example, in the works of Edward Herman and David Peterson), and the Nazi Holocaust (for example, David Irving) are quite grateful for, despite convincing eyewitness and survivor accounts that would have been impossible to fabricate.

As economic anthropologist Jason Hickel made clear in an open letter to Pinker in 2019, the claim that the data even support the conclusions Pinker draws about global poverty is tenuous in any case. In other words, the ideological intervention of Pinker's work, contrary to any implication that he is driven by data alone, is clear. Pinker is not alone in this form of hyper-empiricist reasoning and communication, however. Arch-hyper-empiricist Richard Dawkins, whose 1976 work *The Selfish Gene* was used, however erroneously, as a justification and naturalisation of the glorified "greed is good" selfishness of the early Thatcherites in the 1980s, provoked outcry on Twitter when he claimed in 2014, with no personal experience of rape, that "Date rape is bad. Stranger rape at knifepoint is worse. If you think that's an endorsement of date rape, go away and learn how to think." This was an unhelpful remark not only due to its eye-watering insensitivity in essentially suggesting that some forms of rape were *better* than others, but because it did not actually provide any useful information or insight whatsoever — that is, even on empirical grounds it had no value at all.

Dawkins is no stranger to the hyper-empiricist variety of controversy. In February 2020, after a contracted adviser to the UK government at 10 Downing Street was discovered to have made a number of questionable statements in the past, some of which were eugenic, a furore ensued when Dawkins insisted that human eugenics "would work". As far as Dawkins was concerned, people who were offended or angered by his statements were "determined to miss the point". But what Dawkins seemed unable to grasp was that affirming the scientific feasibility of human eugenics — or any other immoral practice — was about as productive and sensitive as discussing the technological feasibility of mass-murder. Bizarrely, Dawkins seemed determined to introduce irrelevant and unhelpful scientific reasoning into what was squarely an ethical issue, whilst saying "Let's fight it on moral grounds. Deny obvious scientific facts & we lose — or at best derail — the argument." Then why foreground science at all, unless your career is in the toilet because the world has worked out your views are not quite as conducive to "progress" as they once believed.

It seems that quite a few celebrity scientists have a penchant for hyper-empiricism. Six months earlier, in summer 2019, fellow popular science personality Neil deGrasse Tyson caused outcry when he tweeted that:

In the past 48hrs, the USA horrifically lost 34 people to mass shootings.
On average, across any 48hrs, we also lose...
500 to Medical errors
300 to the Flu

250 to Suicide
200 to Car Accidents
40 to Homicide via Handgun
Often our emotions respond more to spectacle than to data.

Again, the data here are not incorrect, nor even is the claim that Tyson makes. More at issue is firstly the expectation that emotion would *not* figure in how the public views an acutely dramatic and traumatic event such as a mass shooting, compared to largely accidental or individually premeditated losses of life, even though all of course are equally tragic. The same can be said of Dawkins' apparent incomprehension at people's sensitivity to his aloof, selective logic. Secondly, whether intended or not, both Tyson's and Dawkins' points do permit a degree of complacency about, for example, the United States' singular position amongst the world's developed nations in terms of the frequency of mass shootings, which are a daily occurrence (Younge, 2016), the NRA's continued lobbying to prevent the legislative steps that would reduce the frequency of such acts of violence, or the continued failure of the criminal justice system to take acts of sexual violence against women seriously.

Thus, the mistake of hyper-empiricists is not usually that they are incorrect or that their data or logic are faulty, but that they seem oblivious to the inevitable political and social reality of what they are saying, or the ways that it softens or normalises brutal social or political tendencies that its authors have never experienced, with no awareness that this is a likely misreading of their empirically true statement. That is to say, even if this type of argument does not explicitly value or defend these harsh social realities, what they communicate often permits the status quo, or aspects of it, to remain unexamined, be considered unsolvable, unworthy of continued amelioration, or forgiven altogether, even if this is not the intention or argument made by the hyper-empiricist.

To plead "what do the data say?" while people are dying, because less people are dying than before, becomes a call for *inaction*, or what Martin Luther King called "do-nothingism", that is useful to exactly the wrong people. Meanwhile, whether the environment, public health, or some other crisis, we race towards a series of disastrous crises. Reliable data can and should be used to inform an assessment of the world, but no data yet does not mean no truth. Data tell us that objects are pulled towards a centre of mass in mathematical relation to the size of that mass and our distance from it, but it is the *theory* of gravity that gives us a convincing reason why. And in a politically organised world, political theory has an important role to play too. The varied handling of the COVID-19 pandemic by the world's governments should have confirmed beyond any doubt, particularly to the most committed empiricists themselves, that data and science are not the only methods with which the world should be understood. An understanding of what Chantal Mouffe (2005) and others have called "the political" was always going to be essential in understanding any such crisis, and in making sense what was happening when governments insisted that they had "followed the science".

As with technology, even when it is not such an obviously deliberate attempt to avoid the political realities of a problem, hyper-empiricism often evolves into oversimplification and the unwitting removal of politics from complex problems. This reservation has been most usefully echoed by Emma Uprichard, a sociologist of "big data" who has repeatedly sounded the alarm about the overapplication of data science to complex political problems:

the big ugly nasty social problems [...] are difficult to change not because of lack of data, but because of the nature of the problems themselves. Poverty, for example, may be understood generally across the world, but to tackle particular poverty traps in particular neighborhoods for particular households, the local context needs to be taken into account; and poverty anywhere is often both a cause and a symptom of other problems, such as poor health or normalized racism. (2014)

Indeed, one of the most obvious ways in which data positivism has been expressed in recent decades has been the dominance of gross domestic product as a measure of economic wellbeing. As US economist Joseph Stiglitz told the World Economic Forum at Davos:

GDP in the US has gone up every year except 2009, but most Americans are worse off than they were a third of a century ago. The benefits have gone to the very top. At the bottom, real wages adjusted for today are lower than they were 60 years ago. So this is an economic system that is not working for most people. (Thomson, 2016)

As with the case of hyper-empiricism's assistance to genocide denial, there is also a way in which quantitative emphasis of complex issues, especially when repeated again and again, can spin out of control as disinformation that, even if later shown to be untrue, can do real harm when timing and action are everything. The same "Flu kills more people" line that Neil deGrasse Tyson somehow thought would be a helpful reflection on North American gun violence was also used by COVID-19 deniers who felt that the lockdowns and other widespread health measures were overkill. The genuine empiricists may have quickly adjusted their position as new information both about the virus and about the policies of various governments became available, but the line itself had already developed into a pervasive lie that was facilitated by a quantification-centric view of the world.

Science historian Alfred Crosby's meticulous history of quantification *The Measure of Reality* provides a perfect metaphor for the role of data positivism in conditioning thought. When Flemish cartographer Gerard Mercator drew his famous map of the world in 1569, he was merely trying to help the world be navigated more effectively, partly for the colonial contest that was getting underway amongst European powers. Crosby tells us that:

> The result was a map in which northern lands, Greenland, for instance, were enormously larger in proportion to the more southerly areas than in reality. But (a very useful but) sailors could plot compass courses as straight lines on maps drawn in accordance with Mercator's projection. [...] the consistency of a single characteristic was preserved, but at the expense of just about everything else. (1997: 236–237)

Data and quantification positivism are similar. They undoubtedly provide valuable affordances and insights within their own realm, but when they are applied beyond the questions where they are appropriate, they introduce distortions that while possibly useful to some, are profoundly misleading to others.

What has been explored so far is the strange pattern by which data, facts, technology and democracy, though all essential parts of building a better and more just world, are worshipped in a way that suggests, as Adorno and Horkheimer wrote, "Ruthlessly, in despite of itself, the Enlightenment has extinguished any trace of its own self-consciousness" (1989 [1947]: 4). Indeed, their arrogant overemphasis at the expense of political and structural consciousness has the effect of hurting that cause. But there are also newer forms of positivism that accompanied twentieth-century capitalist modernity rather than the originating in the Enlightenment.

Meritocracy

One of these newer social constructs that both co-occurs with and illustrates a positivistic belief that reinforces the market-driven society is meritocracy — the belief that upward mobility, wealth, fame, or other forms of success continue to be earned from hard work and ingenuity alone. Sociologist Jo Littler argues that "the idea of meritocracy has become a key means through which plutocracy — or government by a wealthy elite — perpetuates, reproduces and extends itself. Meritocracy has become the key means of cultural legitimation for contemporary capitalist culture" (2017: 2). It is important that we understand meritocracy as another positivistic *belief* that, like many of the beliefs in systems already described here, has the effect of preventing rather than bringing about the very benefit that it claims to support (upward mobility and success for everyone).

For a good example of meritocratic belief, we can turn to one of the high priests of idiotic meritocracy, Elon Musk. His statement on Twitter that "You get paid in direct proportion to the difficulty of problems you solve" perfectly illustrates this foolish and naïve worldview. Meanwhile, as the French economist Thomas Piketty famously showed in 2015, the primary means of producing wealth has ceased to be labour, but the possession of existing wealth. In meritocracy, as with other positivism, we see that certain economic and social factors are made invisible. But there is another way that the withering of "success" down to individual action that meritocracy involves can undermine the social benefits such as equality that it claims to support: the narratives it provides to the far-right who are antagonistic to those goals. We saw in Chapter Two that the language of "elites" is based on a wholly *meritocratic* understanding of identity that goes at least as far back as Margaret Thatcher's self-narrative as the daughter of a greengrocer who became Prime Minister, and connects to Donald Trump's fraudulent claim to be a "genius" but not to be an "elite" — in contrast to Hillary Clinton's more overtly bourgeois styling. What is also interesting about meritocracy is that its socially liberal proponents seem unaware of how useful it has been to attack them and the very individual liberties they espouse, which are coloured as bourgeois. Not only is meritocracy largely a myth, it helps to create other myths that assist in undermining those who see measures such as social welfare and affirmative action as undeserved. The narrative of the talented working-class hero (with an undisclosed inheritance) taking on the "elites" without any help from feminism or state handouts is a favourite of the far-right, who have long resented such measures.

Democracy and Capitalism

The area where positivism has probably been the most damaging of all is in conditioning how democracy was understood within the market-driven society. There are a number of examples of this, of which an obvious one might be the "free markets" glorified by Milton Friedman. Friedman's writings and interviews about the subject reveal a creepy fanaticism for the free market that is increasingly detached from reality.

The moment of rupture with which this book began was widely characterised by reliable scholars such as Wendy Brown as a turn towards *anti-democratic* sentiment, rather than a resentment towards the free market. Eliane

Glaser suggests the far-right "have managed to convince everyone that the problem we have is the political system itself" and in probably the most extreme example of this, Jair Bolsonaro, Brazil's reactionary far-right president, repeatedly praised the country's military dictatorship that ended in 1985, and during the country's COVID-19 lockdown attended explicitly anti-democracy rallies. But this is only the most belligerent manifestation of a much more widespread dissatisfaction with democratic function. In Britain, for example, 72% of people agreed that "the system of governing needs 'quite a lot' or 'a great deal' of improvement" (Hansard Society, 2019). Likewise, in North America, even as US Americans' faith in Congress rallied sharply in April 2020, a Gallup poll showed that between three and four times more people in the US disapproved of how the United States Congress was handling its job than approved (Gallup, 2020).

Barring the extremity of Brazil's far-right and some elements in the United States, most so-called populists have been subtler, but the anti-democratic feeling in countries such as the US or the UK had comparable roots to that of Brazil — a simulation of democracy that no longer served the majority of its citizens and which had lost the ability to control its markets.

After the Cold War, there was a tendency to be positivistic about capitalism itself. Capitalism had ostensibly "won" the argument. Anthony Giddens, the principal architect of Tony Blair's "third way" policies, articulated this misapprehension when he wrote in 1999 that "No one any longer has any alternatives to capitalism — the arguments that remain concern how far, and in what ways capitalism should be *governed* and *regulated*" (1999: 44, emphases added).

The obvious assumption here was that, ideologically, capitalism's logic would be dominant — it simply needed to be kept in check by government. Belying this quote, in other words, was a second positivism — a blind faith not about capitalism's triumph or features, but about democracy's ability to govern and regulate that capitalism. Here, positivism took the specific form of conflating liberal capitalist democracy, whose victory was announced by Fukuyama and Giddens among others, with the general principles of governance and regulation typical of the post-war era, without seeming to comprehend that governments' ability to regulate capital had already started melting away in the 1970s. Capitalism and government had been welded together, and markets were already running the show in a way that was profoundly undemocratic. As writer Tariq Ali put it, "The successors of Reagan and Thatcher were and remain confected politicians: Blair, Cameron, Obama, Renzi, Valls, and so on, share an authoritarianism that places capital above the needs of citizens and uphold a corporate power rubber-stamped by elected parliaments." Since there was "no alternative" to capitalism, there was apparently no alternative to *this* hollowed out capitalist-run implementation of democracy either.

Positivism about the workings of the market-driven society under the guise of democracy was increasingly a bourgeois affliction as this semblance of "democracy" was progressively hollowed out: to carry on affirming an arrangement that labels itself democracy but had put companies and profits above citizens, destroyed the welfare state, turned a blind eye to tax avoidance, weakened trade unions, and implemented cruel austerity policies, required one to either fail to notice these effects, to be unaffected by them, or to actively benefit from them. In effect, it was democracy-for-the-rich, at the expense of everybody else.

Given the misinformation and disinformation on which the market-driven society depends, it was not just the proponents of liberal capitalist democracy who so artfully made this conflation between ideal and implementation. Crucially, the anti-democratic tenor of 2016's resurgent nationalism suggested it also tended to have coloured the thinking of the critics — all democracy is bad, they concluded, because this democracy is bad. As Eliane Glaser pointed out, "legitimate critique of democracy in terms of its corruption [...] merges confusingly with a critique of the system of representation itself" (2017: 82). Lest it need repeating, this conflation between the reduction in the social contract and the social contract itself will only ever benefit those who are so rich that they have no need for the provisions of the social contract. As explored in Chapter Two, the fastest way to let the "elites" win is to attack democracy — this is what they have spent the last few decades doing, hoping nobody would notice!

As Fukuyama's claim about the end of history was increasingly discredited, especially after the financial crash in 2008, explicit defence of current implementations of capitalist democracy became less common. Instead, blind faith about liberal capitalist democracy tended to be voiced by point at the pantomime adversaries of the "populist" elements of the West, at Putin's Russia, at violent jihadism, or at historic invocations of "cartoon communism" (covered in Chapter Two). Once these seeming enemies had been identified, the proponents of this form of democracy could go back to simply wishing they would go away or celebrating their demise, so that they could sink back into the warm bath of the "end of history", a bath that had drained long ago.

As political scientist Benjamin Moffitt wrote of this mode of thought, "In this era of extreme partisanship, the argument goes, what we need is more unity and moderation to bring us together. And if there is one group of politicians who have been blamed for the sorry state we find ourselves in, it is populists" (2020). In this respect, they invoke the same Manichean world of "good" and "evil" that is favoured by conspiracy theorists, and simply insist that everybody be "good". Former leader of UK party the Liberal Democrats and later Facebook Global Policy Chief, Nick Clegg, for example, in his book *Politics Between the Extremes*, wrote confidently that "The present squall of angry populism will fade", and that "the politics of reason must fight back" (2016: 235). The implication being that once this naughty extremism has been vanquished, we can return to the happy, functional, clockwork world of liberal capitalist democracy and live happily ever after.

Despite Nick Clegg's highest hopes, the politics of "reason" alone tends to end up pretty far out of its depth if it is merely composed of a multi-layered assortment of depoliticised positivism. The longer you insist on the perfections of what is inevitably an imperfect system, or on downplaying or not seeing those imperfections, the greater the anger and the weaker your position when the accumulated tensions that those beliefs facilitated are released. There are two distinct ways that positivist habits contribute to the disinformation on which the market-driven society depends. Firstly, by overemphasising the enduring power and relevance of *other* systems outside of politics or economics — most of which date back to the Enlightenment, long before the market-driven society existed in the sense that developed in the late twentieth century — the economic blindness on which the market-driven society was founded is exacerbated. Why address economic injustice or the ruthless commodification of everything when you can apply positivist Enlightenment-sounding analyses you read about in the *Economist*?

Secondly, and even more deceptively, not only does positivism about other systems distract from and obfuscate the market-driven society, all of these causes outlined above — defending the democracy that we have, defending "facts" and science and empiricism, and advocating for upward mobility based on hard work — all *sound* like progressive causes that those invested in justice should embrace. Democratic institutions, technological innovation, empirical method and hard work all have a role to play in building a better world, but positivism about these approaches without an explicit acknowledgement of the missing component of political economy almost always has the opposite effect, making them a key part of the architecture of disinformation that serves the market-driven society and the forms of corporate and sovereign power that lie behind it. As Littler notes in her analysis of meritocracy (2017: 51), this type of positivistic "freezing" of the status quo is a good example of what sociologist Lauren Berlant has called "cruel optimism" (2011), in the sense that we place our hopes in something that frustrates the exact purpose for which we are using it. The longer we carry on hoping that meritocracy is true, or the free market efficient, the longer it will take to discover that these hopes will never be realised.

FBPE, Mueller and the Paradox of Liberal Authoritarianism

There is another, even more bitter contradiction in play, however. Few things may have confirmed capitalism's domination and capture of democracy more than its enclosure of the democratic imagination itself. Indeed, although positivism about democracy's ability to regulate capitalism continues to cloud the ways that the market-driven society is understood, those who are least questioning of capitalist democracy are also those who can convince themselves to ignore it when it does not provide a suitable result. Just as conspiracy theorists are selective in their love of science according to a highly irrational set of beliefs they can't shake, so is the politics of "shallow understanding" selective in its application of democracy.

The idea of the "centre" will be explored more fully later on, but it broadly overlaps with the politics of "shallow understanding" explored in this chapter, and as political writer David Adler has observed:

> Contrary to conventional wisdom — anti-democratic sentiment is strongest at the center. Respondents who identify as centrists are the most frequently critical of democracy and most likely to support authoritarianism. These patterns are generated, in part, by higher levels of apathy among self-identified centrists (Abramowitz 2011). However, even when I exclude politically apathetic respondents, the relationship between centrism and hostility to democracy remains robust. I refer to this surprising finding as the "centrist paradox." (2018)

This tendency was visible on both sides of the Atlantic to some degree, in the ways that some fixated their hopes on a second Brexit referendum or on the fantasy that Special Investigator Robert Mueller would remove and incarcerate the core team of Donald Trump.

Feint hopes of a second referendum or of a Robert Mueller-driven removal of Trump from office are more than just a desperate fantasy. As ideas, they also suggest something about how the people who believe in them really think about democracy — not as justice but as a means for managing and ideally avoiding instability, just as Ulrich Beck described. Unless grounded in the detail of the Trump and Leave campaigns' fraud and corruption, the Mueller and second referendum fantasies told us that once democracy is perceived to have gone awry, and "the people" start voting for illiberal policies and ideas, it is essentially invalid; it can be simply ignored, repeated, or replaced with something more pragmatic, even technocratic.

To be clear, the argument is not that there were not also legitimate reasons for calling into question the dubious means by which the Brexit referendum and Donald Trump's arrival in the White House were brought about. Whatever the actual problems with the EU's institutions, the British people *were* undoubtedly misled and had their latent traditionalism, class antagonisms, postcolonial melancholia, and unqualified xenophobia cynically whipped up in a way that was both deceitful and unlawful, becoming the subject of a number of criminal investigations. Likewise, although it is difficult to evidence that direct foreign interference in the US elections was actually what secured Donald Trump's victory — a position that overlooks the numerous other issues that also contributed to Trump's popularity and Hillary Clinton's weak campaign — there was definitely a concerted effort by Russia to interfere in the US election in 2016. At least theoretically, elections run periodically, but it probably would have been sensible for Britain to hold a confirmatory referendum, clearly distinguished from the first, with better regulations in place, and with the details of both remain and leave positions already negotiated — not because Brexit is bad (it is), or the EU an unqualified good (it's not), but because the first referendum was vague and rife with bare-faced deceit.

But the issue with both countries is that large numbers of people who were dismayed by these outcomes — Remainers and Democrats — did not care to try and understand them before pinning their hopes on the possibility that they simply be "walked back", as US secretary of State John Kerry said of Brexit, preserving the status quo, yet again. Indeed, in the case of Brexit, the campaign to cancel it out with a new vote, known as a "People's Vote", had a direct lineage back to the Blair governments, whose policies had been at least inspired by Giddens' triumphalist view of capitalism and democracy in perfect harmony. As British commentator Owen Jones put it, "People's Vote became a refuge and a means to regain relevance for those [Blairites] exiled from frontline politics by Jeremy Corbyn's assumption of the Labour leadership" (2019).

However disgusting it may be, and however much you may have to hold your nose, in the end the only way to beat these elements in our political culture is to have a profound and nuanced understanding of the forces that brought them about — of their grievances, however ridiculous or misplaced, their weak spots, their occasional discernments, and their motivations. This is the only way to fight a beast and win, particularly one that may be stronger and bigger. Instead, the politics of "shallow understanding" looks on, aghast at the way democracy appears to have been short-circuited — their surprise owing largely to the ways that they were oblivious to capital having taken over that democracy a long time ago, leaving it vulnerable to those who may divert it away from the genuine public interest for any other reason: fascists, nationalists, disaster capitalists, and so forth — all come as some sort of evil surprise. It also confirms the dubious character of that democracy itself — that it was not in a healthy enough state to withstand the questions asked of it by society's anti-democratic forces.

Ideological Drift and the Drifting Status Quo

Over time, the meaning of democracy, of capitalism, of socialism, and indeed of almost any political idea, is reconfigured and shifted. Legal scholar Jack Balkin (1993) offered a useful framing for this type of slow change in meaning that he called "ideological drift". The valence of different styles of argument and legal theories, he said "varies over time as they are applied and understood repeatedly in new contexts and situations".

A great example of this theory at work is its application by fellow law scholar David Pozen to the idea of transparency. In the last chapter, the dangers of mendacity and conspiracy within capital were highlighted, and transparency is an important means of avoiding corruption and protecting democratic functions, but as Pozen argues, transparency has undergone an ideological drift:

> the meaning of transparency has changed. Transparency is still celebrated as a tool to root out undesirable conduct, and transparency laws are still used for this purpose. But across many policy domains, the pursuit of transparency has become increasingly unmoored from broader "progressive" values such as egalitarianism, expertise, or social improvement through state action and increasingly tied to agendas that seek to reduce other forms of regulation and to enhance private choice. If legal guarantees of transparency were once thought to make government more participatory and public-spirited, they are now enlisted to make government leaner and less intrusive. (2018: 105)

As numerous commentators have analysed, the right, left, and neoliberalism have all experienced ideological drift over time. The centrists of the post-war period, for example, "defended state programs that the centrists of the 1990s would gut" (Leary, 2018).

Earlier in the chapter, I highlighted a somewhat irrational investment to maintaining the status quo, and always trying to restore "business as usual" in response to any disruption. The most serious problem with this attachment to the status quo and the forms of positivism outlined so far is that their blind resistance to change does not actually mean the status quo is indefinitely preserved. Rather, the status quo itself can also suffer from ideological drift, meaning negation of or blindness to any slow change that is occurring. If the naïve, arrogant, complacent positivism described in this chapter is a form of misinformation, it is surely that same delusion and political illiteracy that permits it to drift with the prevailing winds of the market-driven society — imperceptibly to its adherents. We are left with a paradox of what we could call the "drifting status quo" in which the political reality moves imperceptibly whilst being defended as though it were static. This is surely what political scientist Wendy Brown meant when she described neoliberalism's slow ascendancy over four decades as a "stealth revolution" (2015).

The drifting status quo is also what allowed tension to build under the market-driven society. As we saw at the end of Chapter One, the conservative impulses of right-wingers in a pre- neoliberal world that was still patriarchal, segregated and upwardly mobile became untenable in a market-driven society that came to involve rigid economic segregation and disingenuously fly the colours of the hard-won left-wing civil rights victories its conservative architects once opposed.

US writer Naomi Klein's work on disaster capitalism is helpful here too. Milton Friedman, she tells us, understood the day-to-day conservatism of liberal capitalist democracy, and felt that major shocks were the best time to impose radical new policies, before resuming the "tyranny of the status quo" (2007: 7). As we can see, the drifting status quo is actually something of a dialectic between the appearance of a reassuring status quo, and the slow modification of the machinery that stands behind it, sometimes in response to crisis — which both diverts attention away from the change and provides a superficial justification for it, but always in response to changing historical conditions.

"Goldilocks Politics" and the Myth of the Apolitical Centre

The drifting status quo is often facilitated by the claim of not having any ideology at all. As Eliane Glaser (2017) and the late political scientist Peter Mair (2013) have both shown, this refusal of conspicuous ideological allegiance is a political strategy, but not always one used by the same people, or for the same purposes. The delusional claim not to have any ideology has long provided cover for various kinds of nefarious politics, including the positivist, naïve complacency outlined earlier in this chapter. Wherever it comes from, and whoever makes it, a claim to not be ideological is almost always a camouflage. Just as in the old joke about one fish saying to the other "what's water?", in the market-driven society, the claim not to have any conscious ideological positions at all signifies at best that the person making such a claim has simply absorbed the dominant ideology without realising. It may not be a fixed, ideological commitment in the way that conservatives, anarchists, fascists or communists might demonstrate, however, but it is not a genuine absence of political beliefs either.

Both Glaser and Mair note the example of Lord Falconer, Lord Chancellor in the Tony Blair Labour governments, who said he favoured the "de-politicisation of decision-making" by government. Over a decade later, British far-right anti-Islam activist and provocateur Stephen Yaxley-Lennon, known publicly by his pseudonym "Tommy Robinson", has repeatedly denied that he is of the far-right, telling newspapers, "There's nothing far right about me" (Hope Not Hate, n.d.) and describing himself in a 2015 interview for *Union magazine* as "liberal in many senses", particularly with regard to gay rights, apparently. More recently, when "centrist" breakaway party "Change UK" fielded candidates in the 2019 European Parliament elections, one of their spokespeople told Channel 4 News of the new party that "We may not have any policies, but is that not exciting?" As Canadian writer Nick Srnicek quipped on Twitter, the group had "Mike 'pro-Iraq War' Gapes in charge of foreign affairs, Chris 'austerity is good' Leslie in charge of economics, Heidi '£12 billion in welfare cuts' Allen in charge of welfare, and Angela 'funded by water companies' Smith in charge of the environment".

As we saw with the examination of positivism earlier in the chapter, it is a common tendency in political thinking to rely heavily on systems of categories, which of course constantly need adjustment because, as any botanist, zoologist or linguist will confirm, all systems of categories are flawed. One of these taxonomies is that of "left-wing" and "right-wing" politics. A poll of UK voters in 2019 showed that a number of views, such as converting to green energy and allowing doctors to end the lives of people who are terminally and seriously incapacitated through illness are as popular with the so-called right-wing voter as they are with those who identified themselves as left-wing. And a significantly large number of people from the "wrong" side of the political spectrum supported views that they "shouldn't". For example, 59% of those considering themselves left-wing believed that school discipline should be stricter, 55% that the criminal justice system was too soft, and 47% that more controls were needed on immigration — all classic right-wing views. Meanwhile, 57% of people who identified themselves as right-wing thought that the government should play a more active role in managing the economy, and 48% thought that the minimum wage was too low — usually considered left-wing positions. Furthermore, individual views that might be associated with a quintessential left- or right-wing position often coincided far more than people who believe in this classic left vs right ideological arrangement would imagine. For example, 72% of those who want a greater redistribution of wealth (considered a left-wing view) also think the criminal justice system is too soft (considered a right-wing view) (Smith, 2019).

Even if it is specific to just one country, this research should only confirm that there is a danger in over-simplifying our political language with this kind of rhetorical shortcut. As we have already seen, doing so has the power to distort or occlude our understanding of the complex political world we inhabit, and hinder any chance of making that world better. And yet the idea of left vs right is incredibly persistent. Eliane Glaser, who makes frequent use of the terms "left-wing" and "right-wing", argues that "politicians and journalists routinely state that 'Right' and 'Left' are no longer meaningful categories. That removes a vital plank from any analysis. And it has enabled the rise of the populist Right". The thinking here — that eliminating "left" and "right" invalidates any analysis, or that refusing to speak about the "right" has enabled their rise — feels like an unnecessary absolutism. Rather, it is precisely the application of toothless phrases like "right-wing" to indicate both the architects of the market-driven society and the reactionary or socially conservative politics to which it normally corresponds, that means it has had little effect. The emergence of terms like "far-right" and "alt-right" is yet another clue as to the inadequacy of this political nomenclature. If we are to use language to describe the problems in any political ideology, surely we can do better than abstract spatial metaphors that date back to the French Revolution. The options are not to either keep using "left-wing" and "right-wing" or dispense with them entirely, but to find ways of talking about the important political ideas they encode without always reaching for the same simplistic metaphorical labels — by no means easy, but an important conversation.

Besides the fact that politics is simply not a linear continuum, however, the very idea of a political spectrum with something called "the left" towards one end and "the right" towards the other, encourages a relationship to politics that favours those claiming neither by portraying it as the most agreeable or reasonable option. As is well known, in the story of Goldilocks and the three bears, Goldilocks tries three bowls of porridge. The first is too hot, the second is too cold, but the third is just right. I call this spatial normalisation of the forms of politics outlined in this chapter, which frequently claim to have no ideology at all, *goldilocks politics* — particularly when it characterises itself as being at the "centre" of the political "spectrum". One way that the false continuum of left and right facilitates political misunderstanding is in the way it allows for those who present themselves either explicitly at the "centre" or as having no ideology at all as the "goldilocks" option — the reasonable, "objective" camp who see themselves as pragmatic, and above the impulsive, ideological, unfounded political logic of the left and right, which are represented as intrinsically unbalanced or extreme. This is of course similar to Antonio Gramsci's critique of "common sense", and later those of the American economist J.K. Galbraith, who made a similar observation about "conventional wisdom", but goldilocks politics more explicitly centres the "happy medium", "centre" or "moderate" connotation that claims a position in the middle, to varying degrees.

Rainbow Capitalism

Ironically, the claim to have no real political ideology pairs quite well with the explicit communication of certain values, if they can be pushed outside the political-economic realm. We saw in the last chapter how the incorporation of social issues into the cultural dominance of the market-driven society meant that they were regarded as suspicious by virtue of their seeming (but in fact illusory) proximity to power, and which made those very social issues into targets of vile, angry, bigoted theories. But it is also crucial to note the ways that these causes became distorted and co-opted into propaganda *for* that market-driven society. That does not mean that the underlying issues and causes ceased to be relevant or important — far from it. Rather, as these vital social and political causes had their names written in neon by the market-driven society, they were carefully de-radicalised or pointed at very specific contexts, and their original advocates frequently cast aside, sanitised or erased entirely.

The most galling example at the time of writing is the European Union's declaration that "Black Lives Matter" during the worldwide uprising in the name of that movement that began in June 2020. At face value, this is of course welcome, and European policing did not need to be as racist or violent at that of the United States for major reconstitution to be needed. But as the Black Lives Matter movement rightly and inevitably grew to be about more than the brutal racism of policing and criminal justice systems, the EU's statement began to appear rather tone-deaf and hypocritical given the number of black and brown people they had allowed to drown in the Mediterranean Sea as a matter of policy over the preceding years.

Another obvious example of how important social and political values can be cynically and insincerely appropriated is the way that Martin Luther King Jr, whose words opened this chapter, has been recast into a friendly if emotive man who made a lot of lovely poetic speeches and simply "had a dream" of racial equality in the United States. King's grace and eloquence were indeed remarkable, but as Gary Younge (2018) and bell hooks (2002) have both pointed out, the fact that King was fiercely anti-capitalist and anti-imperialist is omitted from the ways that he has been canonised. As hooks put it, his true political character has been *censored* in the process of his immortalisation. Above, Tariq Ali called Tony Blair and Bill Clinton "confected" politicians, and the same is also true here, in the way that King is retroactively confected. This is a microcosm of the same process of alignment with the market-driven society that was outlined earlier in the chapter: more sugar, less spice. King is not the only one who has been made more palatable in this way. Another example is how thirteenth-century Persian poet and mysticist Jalaluddin Rumi, described by the BBC as "The best-selling poet in the US" (Ciabattari, 2014), has been cleansed as he became mainstream material, enjoyed by celebrities such as Brad Pitt and Tilda Swinton. But as one writer put it, "Curiously, however, although he was a lifelong scholar of the Koran and Islam, he is less frequently described as a Muslim" (Ali, 2017). As we will see below, the phenomenon of "liberal Islamophobia" functions by insinuating that Muslims intrinsically do not conform to the values of the Enlightenment. Here we see a Muslim who is loved by the politics of "shallow understanding" and has had to be de-Islamicised as a result.

Besides the market-driven society's top-down incorporation of these figures, it also does the same with broader values — such as multiculturalism, feminism, gay rights or environmentalism – that originate in radical struggle. Obvious examples include the Gillette and Dove ads which ostensibly sought to convince consumers that they were actually serious about undoing the very same gender norms they had used to sell products for decades. You can't suddenly decide to go from a man in the mirror with high cheekbones and sculpted pecs talking about "the best a man can get" to problematising conventional masculinity and expect people to take you seriously. Historically, specific causes such as Black Lives Matter, which Facebook displayed on a large screen outside their headquarters in July 2016, or the UK's outpouring of gratitude for the country's health workers during the COVID-19 pandemic, have also been the targets of commercial incorporation in this way.

But it is important to distinguish here between this kind of incorporation as a top-down strategy of power by the market-driven society, and the people of "shallow understanding" whose liberal-minded enthusiasm it is intended to secure — the main subject of this chapter. It has become common for people to roll their eyes or use air quotes when they use the word "woke", and given the reductive way that that word has distilled complex and highly sensitive issues into a single "gets it" or "doesn't get it" quality, perhaps a degree of caution is indeed advisable. But what these meta-communicative cues might also indicate is a way in which adherence to specific values, important in themselves, is performed in a way that also participates in and amplifies this "cleaning" of radical struggle. The surprising and worrying thing about a major oil company that decorates its buildings and logo with rainbows every Pride and boasts about its investment in renewables, while continuing to pump out countless tons of carbon dioxide and support governments of oil-producing states that impose harsh repression on gay people, is not only its hypocrisy, but the fact that it works! Ideally, it is essential that companies are actually run in a way that puts people and the environment first, and makes their employees of all backgrounds and their customers feel welcomed. But the choice between a "greenwashed" or "pinkwashed" market-driven society and an outright repressive one is a false choice — we can and must demand something better than either of these options, but few people do. Perhaps this is because when these values are allied with consumerism and the institutions of the market driven society, they appear so much easier and friendlier, even if they are far less effective.

The problem is the way we make explicit allegiance to a meaningful and important cause into a meaningless, powerless gesture by accepting it in packaged form on the terms of the market-driven society and its subsystem — consumerism. As Paul Gilroy has noted: "Political institutions, even whole nations themselves, can be condensed into visual symbols. They are being seen and therefore experienced in novel ways. Summoned by icons, even they can be sold according to the same commercial science that sells all other products" (2000). The same is true of values that appear to challenge the system. What Mark Fisher called "capitalist realism" will constantly try to reconfigure any politically meaningful movements into an occasion to buy, whether now as in advertising, or later as in branding. The danger is that these packaged forms of social liberalism, wheeled out in support of major global brands, can actually hurt their cause or others. As Cora Gilroy-Ware has observed,

> Today, there is also a separate, more pervasive discourse around identity that is entangled with consumerism. Its end is visibility rather than emancipation. [...] Pirelli is set to release an edition of their pinup calendar featuring only black models, a move justified by the (white) photographer's assertion that "Any girl should... have their own fairytale". (2017)

The same has happened to environmentalism, for example in the ways that plastic drinking straws were quickly replaced — unquestionably a positive development, while the amount of plastic entering the oceans, and greenhouse gases entering the atmosphere, continued to rise. The words of Lauren Berlant, quoted above, are worth repeating here, too: "the object that draws your attachment actively impedes the aim that you brought to it initially". The mainstreaming of anti-racism, gay rights and environmentalism is essential to their success, but their appropriation by the uncaring institutions of the market-driven society, while possibly a momentary comfort, needs to be challenged at every turn if they are to retain their emancipatory potential.

Even food has been sanitised and repackaged in this way, heralding gentrification and obscuring the global dynamics of class, as Dan Hancox has written brilliantly on "street food":

> In buying a small slice of authenticity, customers are often choosing from quite a narrow list of cultural tropes: here's a stall that only does ramen, another that only does German wursts, another that only does fish and chips, another that only does sourdough pizza. In the place of a genuinely cosmopolitan and accessible civic cultural life, we have a sanitised smorgasbord of multiculturalism, available at an inflated price, with security guards on the door. It is the offer of a culinary grand tour, designed for a generation of yuppies who don't want to leave a converted tramshed in WC1. [...] in most parts of the world, street food exists specifically for time- and cash-poor workers on the move. (2020)

Once again, what we see here is the precise opposite of a conspiracist. Whereas a conspiracy theorist's suspicion of and alienation from power manifest in an overactive "discovery" of phantom forms of power at the expense of an accurate understanding of how it operates, the "shallow understanding" outlined here is content to let the powerful construct something that feels like a challenge to that power, but in a way that only fosters more consumerism and less chance of any actual challenge. Quite often, these are the people who point at every expression of political suspicion as a "conspiracy theory", and so we see a similar dialectic to the one that Adorno and Horkheimer described, transposed to its twenty-first-century form.

Besides the sanitisation and depoliticisation of important social issues and historical figures, the same pattern can function in reverse, rehabilitating those who worked against the interests of very issues that their fans would consider essential today, and this is equally damaging. One obvious example is Ellen DeGeneres's affectionate socialising with former US President George W. Bush at a Dallas Cowboys game, where they were both guests of the Jones family, who own the team. DeGeneres responded to the widespread criticism she received by saying "be kind to everybody", which is hard to disagree with, even if her own staff did not experience this kindness when working for her (Murphy, 2020), but suggested that George W. Bush simply had different political views to her — hardly a reason in itself not to be kind, to be sure. What she failed to mention in her response, however, was that George W. Bush was not only of a different political persuasion, but had presided over a military invasion that resulted in between 185,000 and 200,000 civilian deaths, surely something that can never be rehabilitated. The pattern is far more pervasive. Another example is ex-Liberal Democrat leader Jo Swinson's call for a statue of Margaret Thatcher, the primary enabler of the market-driven society and all its cruelty, or the way that the early suffragist Millicent Fawcett who supported brutal wars and colonial projects is celebrated with a statue in London's Parliament Square, while her fellow suffragists who took anti-war positions and were not such loyal advocates of the British Empire, such as Emily Hobhouse, are largely overlooked (Ware, 2019). It is hard as a man to write critically about any aspect of feminism without sounding like some kind of unbearable, boorish naysayer who thinks feminism to be a dirty word. But the argument is precisely the opposite: the permanent commemoration of feminism and normalisation of its principles are essential, but are also undermined by these forms of amnesia that overlook war, racism and empire. The same is true with the way any other important issue is centralised in our culture: the erasure of injustice in the name of justice only helps to facilitate more injustice in the future.

Ultimately, when organisations fly the colours of once-radical struggles or announce seemingly progressive values, and then consciously or unconsciously espouse a money-first, market-driven agenda that strips back public services in favour of the private sector, squeezing ordinary working people in the process, they undermine both democracy as a whole and those progressive values themselves. They also magnify their own power. Just as how Saudi Arabia's relaxation of the ban on women drivers provided a cover for them to harass or arrest the activists who had first attempted to fight the ban (Begum, 2018), when banks, military contractors, fast-food chains and real estate developers claim socially progressive values, whether they intend to or not, they are almost always creating cover for themselves to carry on working *against* the public interest, rather than on behalf of it.

Contrary to right-wing and alt-right naysayers, these challenges do not indicate that efforts to mainstream social justice are worthless or that the causes they address such as environmentalism and social justice are unimportant. Rather, they confirm that to fight those issues effectively, a literacy of the functioning of power and the market-driven forms it has assumed is sorely needed. Anti-racism will never be something you can buy on Amazon.

Symbiotic Complacency About Fascism

Ellen DeGeneres's apparent desire to overlook the small matter of an illegal war, waged on false premises, that caused hundreds of thousands of civilian deaths, like the Fawcett Society's commemoration of a suffragist who condoned women and children being placed in camps during the Boer War, also points at another issue. The market-driven society does not only facilitate or benefit from ignorance about itself: it also creates the noxious by-product of misinformation about other important issues, like war, fascism and economic injustice. Why would we need to learn about those, if we are all meant to be working to be the next Jeff Bezos or Elon Musk?

In reality, the erasure of an era-defining conflict in the Middle East or earlier exercises in organised mass-killing matches other ways in which those who do not see themselves as affected by a given injustice are seemingly quite happy to look past it. We have already seen hints of this complacency about racism, fascism or the cruelty of the market-driven society in the discussion of "freedom of speech" earlier in the chapter, where "shallow understanding" meant that it seemed like a great idea to invite Steve Bannon for a chat and then challenge him with simplified Enlightenment concepts from the eighteenth century. In another example, in 2019, the UK's Channel 4 — once intended as a more representative and politically aware presence in the UK's media ecosystem — aired a programme called *Sleeping with the Far-Right*, which involved living in the house of a far-right ideologue and his family and having breakfast with them every morning. And belying this naivety may also be a certain recklessness about the struggle of others that betrays a sort of passive racism or friendliness to tyranny in itself. What ultimately is the difference between not noticing the struggles of others or the cost of foreign wars, and not thinking that these issues are important? We can see other examples of the same unthinking friendliness to repressive, war-like and genocidal powers elsewhere, such as Twitter CEO Jack Dorsey's 2018 visit to Myanmar on a meditation retreat about which he bragged on Twitter, without mentioning the country's ongoing ethnic cleansing of the Rohingya Muslim population in the country's Rakhine state. One gets the sense that those Martin Luther King Jr described "constantly [advising] the Negro to wait for a 'more convenient season'" for their freedom maybe didn't really care much about that freedom either, and the "I agree with you in the goal you seek" part may have been a *noblesse oblige*.

If ignorant complacency about the struggles of others, particularly on the receiving end of extremist far-right violence that has been platformed or ignored, is not bad enough, however, the ways that these pathologies are called out is often little better. The sociologists Aurelien Mondon and Aaron Winter (2017) trace the ways that "liberal Islamophobia" allows and encourages a discriminatory attitude towards followers of Islam by highlighting (and greatly exaggerating) its ostensible failure to conform to positivist Enlightenment values like those outlined earlier in this chapter. They argue that this functions in symbiosis with "illiberal Islamophobia" — the kinds of hate crimes against Muslims that have become increasingly common in Euro-Atlantic world as nationalism has been increasingly emboldened after 2016. "Liberal Islamophobia" provides the far-right with a language of "reason" to make their hate more palatable to the mainstream, while "illiberal Islamophobia" gives the moderates with "shallow understanding" someone extreme to point the finger at, as if only the extremes were racist. Once again, we see a Manichean world not unlike that of conspiracists: you can be good or you can be evil.

This is a pattern that exists well beyond the debate about Islam. As we saw earlier, the same can be said about discussions of democracy, where each accuses the other of being undemocratic whilst the moderates enjoy the trappings of the market-driven society's ongoing destruction of the state and the extremists call for the end of democracy itself, or the environment, where the centre flies to Davos on a jet to have disingenuous conversations about climate change, while the far-right are increasingly using the same language of ecological preservation to justify acts of racist violence against immigrants. The "shallow understanding from people of good will" of which Martin Luther King Jr wrote has become an unwitting collaborator with the "absolute misunderstanding from people of ill will" that he described, all to the benefit of the market-driven society which exploits the alienation and disenfranchisement that this inevitably produces. The true left look on, virtually powerless to intervene.

It is one of the great ironies of our time that the ignorance and political illiteracy fostered by the market-driven society has enabled a thawing of relations with exactly the forms of totalitarianism that the original architects of neoliberalism hoped naively to prevent.

What's in a Name?

This chapter has explored a constellation of related habits of political thought that all *appear* to be guided by the desire for a better world. As with conspiracy theories, however, what these forms of thinking show us is that when a mostly well-intentioned desire to challenge power or wrongdoing is deceived by the obfuscations of the market-driven society, it often helps to produce or reiterate misinformation that is beneficial to the very power that is subject to challenge. As Lauren Berlant has observed, "all attachments are optimistic", and just as with an unrequited love, that optimism can blind us to our poor chances of success. As we've seen above, this group of political outlooks varies from at one extremity a naïve belief in nominal systems such as democracy, law, and technology, accepting them at face value without examination of their structural realities, to outright anti-democratic, authoritarian leanings at the other.

Throughout this chapter, the reader may have noticed my discomfort at using the words that normally indicate the different facets and varieties of these politics, especially "liberal", "moderate", "centrist" and "progressive". Admittedly, these are not synonyms, and not all of their meanings are equally encompassed in the analyses offered above. But all of them usually share some degree of this tendency to overlook the entrenched reality of the market-driven society, or be romanced by the simplified conceptual landscape that it offers.

The word "liberal" is the most widespread, and the most difficult to pin down. On the one hand, some of the uses of the word describe the politics analysed in this chapter fairly well, particularly in Britain where there is a political party that exemplifies the "politically apolitical" positions set out above — the Liberal Democrats. There are a number of problems that have prevented me from adopting this label, however. For a start, in the United States the word has a very different meaning: generally, it is a slur used by conservatives and reactionaries that refers to outsiders, from Hillary Clinton — a hawk in foreign policy terms who also sat on the board of Walmart but never said anything about the company's dubious labour practices — to everybody to the left of her, plus anybody else they don't like or understand — hardly a meaningful taxon. In this vitriolic US-American context, it is especially common to hear people complain about "liberals", to whinge about the "liberal media", or to speak of "owning the libs".

The US-American dictionary *Merriam Webster* defines a liberal in broad ideological terms: "a person who believes that government should be active in supporting social and political change". This is an interesting formulation. What are the other options? That somebody other than the government should? That nobody should? Like the politics it surely addresses, the definition omits any reference to markets or capital, and, as we saw above, it is precisely this blindness to the market-driven society that makes this politics conducive to less liberal outcomes, rather than more actual liberty. "Liberals", in this sense at least, are not actually very liberal.

"Progressive" is much better in so far as the people and organisations it refers to tend not to be quite as clueless, but "progress" is about as positivistic a concept as it is possible to muster, and again evokes the Enlightenment rather than later struggles against the oppression of global capital, even if some of its adherents are aware of the nature of this challenge.

"Moderate" is a less spatial version of "centrist", but as we saw above, both are a way of disowning any explicit ideological positions, whilst affirming the dominant ideology and resisting dramatic changes to the status quo. As we have seen, however, not only do these explicit claims tend to provide cover for materialism and fiscal conservatism, they also enable an "ideological drift" according to the prevailing winds of the market-driven society. Those that profess no ideology are simply unaware of their ideology, and are often the most useful collaborators for those looking to remake society to nefarious ends.

The objective of this chapter is not to be divisive, but to add to the analysis provided by previous chapters in outlining and revealing the troubling role of certain political habits that consider themselves benign in producing the crises of 2016 and beyond, whilst preventing solutions to the forms of injustice that have brought us to this rupture.

At the time of writing, most of the loudest and furthest-reaching critiques of liberalism come from right-wing elements in the political conversation. When your arrogance and positivism means that you fail to critique your own political beliefs, you leave yourself open to others formulating that criticism for you, usually with a lot more antagonism. It is hoped that the critique offered in this chapter provides insight that makes these nasty attacks from the US right, especially, more difficult rather than easier.

There is no moral equivalency between the hate crimes of the extremes and the seemingly mild-mannered hypocrisy of the kind described above. But the either-or is an illusion. To stop far-right political movements we also need to be loud and honest about the blindness and hypocrisy of its enablers. As we have now seen, the two are part of the same system, like two planets that orbit each other. The fight between these faux-Enlightenment positivist arguments that insist on not seeing the struggle of others or the arrogance and hypocrisy of the positions they take and the belligerence and hate that were so emboldened after 2016 is an indivisible whole. Where one brazenly ignores facts and systematised understandings of the world outright, the other insists on adherence to their simple adoption with an arrogance that invites their many complexities and unknowns to be cynically, almost gleefully exploited.

Chapter Five
Trouble in the Newsroom

Get your facts first, and then you can distort them as much as you please.
— Mark Twain

News can be faked and spun, and truth held hostage, not by the politics of knowledge but by the political machinery that assembles carefully-managed ignorance, a curated ignorance.
— Paul Gilroy

Attacked for a controversial presentation of "facts," newspapermen invoke their objectivity almost the way a Mediterranean peasant might wear a clove of garlic around his neck to ward off evil spirits.
— Gaye Tuchman

One of my most cherished colleagues at the university employing me while this book was written, a seasoned TV news journalist who later turned to teaching, has a fondness for asking students a provocative question at the beginning of our second-year media law, ethics and regulation lectures: What's the point of journalism? Given the lectures in question are part of a journalism course, the question is not a rhetorical way of suggesting that journalism is pointless, so much as an invitation to students to recall (after a long summer of distraction) the fundamentals they learned in the very first few weeks of their course a year earlier. Despite the early hour of the class, students venture most of the expected responses:
    "Hold power to account", says one.

226

"Expose wrongdoing", says another.

"Give people the information they need to make informed decisions in a democracy", says a third.

The answers continue, and my colleague smiles at each. It's clear that they have not forgotten. Their answers are knowingly a statement of what journalism should be, more than what it is, and their idealism is somewhat at odds with the depressing realities of the world beyond our classroom.

Looking out the window, I think to myself, "if only" as I listen. One of the best things about teaching is discussion with students. I've often felt that if they ran the world, it would be a fairer, more equal and more just society. Their answers in this case make a good springboard for the class. But they also make a good starting point for this chapter. Assuming mainstream journalism ever actually met these ideals, when and why and how did it move away from them?

The stories we tell ourselves about the world have the effect of conditioning how we understand it. Against the backdrop of the last chapters — the conversion of democracy into a market-driven society in Chapter One, the foundational position of misinformation, disinformation and misapprehension in liberal capitalism in Chapter Two, the role of disempowerment in driving misinformation and disinformation in the form of conspiracy theories in Chapter Three, and the misinformation and disinformation that originates in the arrogance and complacency of those at or near the top in Chapter Four — it is also imperative to examine the profession of providing the public with information: journalism. Any journalism scholars reading this chapter may roll their eyes in protest, but it is important at the outset to be clear about what the history and scholarship of journalism tell us our expectations for what journalism can and should be. When asked, journalists have tended to reveal an occupational ideology that characterises what they do as an important public service (Deuze, 2005). That is, most journalists at least believe that what they do is more than just producing information or "stories" or "content" — it has a context, a position in the overall order, a *raison d'être*. Journalism both as a professional activity and as a discernible layer of the media ecosystem has tended to claim its legitimacy in the context of a broader democratic system, having been a fundamental aspect of the development of modern citizenship itself, that was also rooted in the affordances of the industrial revolution (Anderson, 2006). If power is to be delegated to people who are elected to represent us, we ought to know what they are up to, and much of journalism's early claim to be a serious profession was justified on the basis of a claim to fulfilling a public responsibility to provide the truth about public affairs (Allan, 1999).

The root of journalism as an idea, in other words, is part of the aspiration to democracy itself — at least historically. And just like democracy, everyone should value good journalism, because we do need it. As with many professions or activities, however, there is a contrast between the idealised view of what journalism *should* be and what actually takes place in reality. Much of the world faces the problem that journalism is unable to do its job effectively because of outright violence against and repression of journalists. For every high-profile case such as the murders of Jamal Khashoggi or Lyra McKee, dozens more journalists are killed around the world for daring to challenge those in power, and hundreds more are imprisoned every year (Committee to Protect Journalists, 2019). These are complex cases for sure, but the vast number of these journalists encounter danger and violence precisely because they are trying to hold various politicians or corporations to account.

But elsewhere there is another problem, more directly tied to the issues covered in earlier chapters of this book: if you want to protect democracy, to defend it against the people who are constantly trying to undermine it or reorganise it in the interests of the market-driven society, you have to understand it, value it and be ready to fight for it. Strangely, in the Euro-Atlantic world where press freedom is not so much of an issue, despite the efforts of some extremely talented and motivated individual journalists, particularly in the area of investigative reporting, journalism on the whole has not actually done itself, or the ideals of democracy, many favours, as post-war democratic aspirations were hollowed out into the market-driven society. Is this simply a valiant effort that in the end just wasn't enough? If so, why are journalists now amongst the least trusted professions at the time of writing? A 2017 Ipsos MORI report placed journalists amongst those rated least likely to tell the truth, with only politicians and professional footballers trusted less (Skinner & Clemence, 2017). A 2019 survey by Gallup showed that only a third of US Americans trusted journalists, and this was after a ten-point increase (Brenan, 2019). Incidentally, nurses were by far the most trusted in both surveys. What these numbers reveal is that the off-hand dismissal of inconvenient journalism as "fake news", like the dismissive "liberal media" slur used mainly by US conservatives for years before that, indicates more than just a basic cover used by those in power trying to avoid being held to account for their mistakes by journalists, or a means of cognitive dissonance for people whose political views are contradicted by a news report. The crisis of integrity that professionalised journalism has experienced goes well beyond the typical political persuasions of these slurs. Such dismissal has a longer history, and the BBC was, for example, referred to pejoratively as the "British

Falsehoods Corporation" by radio listeners who saw the BBC's coverage of the general strikes of 1926 as one sided (Pegg, 1983, cited in Allan, 1999). When these reactionary invocations of "fake news" arise, they are exploiting an existing distrust for journalists that has been made easier since the development of the market-driven society by the fact that the world of journalism on the whole has not done its job particularly well in actually challenging power and standing up for the people it was supposed to represent. As we will see below, this meant effectively shooting themselves in the foot, since as the market-driven society developed, journalism essentially assisted in hollowing out the very thing that gave them their legitimacy: democracy. Democracy in its *ideal* form needs something that will do the job journalism has assumed, and journalism's very reason for existence is *ideally speaking* tied directly to the ideal functioning of democracy. Each is dependent on the other, and as we will see, this mutual dependency helps to understand the crises that have befallen both journalism and democracy itself.

In the latter decades of that same process, journalism also changed *as a product* in the overall economy, both in terms of its economic viability and its content, as it sought to cling to whatever kinds of value still existed in an increasingly marketised information economy that did not value or trust the claim to protecting democracy itself. Unlike the response to the first problem, which has been largely brushed aside or laughed at by those in a profession often deluded about its own detachment from political influence, a great deal of time and effort has been devoted to trying to understand journalism's economic woes, not least since thousands of jobs were on the line, and thousands more had already been lost.

Whatever anybody says, journalism as an ideal is not dead. And as a basic practice it has not lost its capacity to challenge power and hold it to account. If anything, the necessity for this is more important than ever, and the amazing work that some journalists are doing only proves this. This chapter will explore the tragic contradiction at the heart of journalism's decline in both credibility and sustainability, exploring the connection between this mutual dependency and the concurrent deterioration of its constituent elements — democracy into the market-driven society, and journalism into the crises of credibility and identity that gives us both "fake news" and clickbait.

The Problem with Objectivity

The single most important issue in evaluating the positive or negative impacts of journalism has been the question of the extent to which it is possible for someone identifying their work as journalism to provide a purely informational picture of events — "just the facts" — that allows the viewer to reach their own conclusions without any sort of "nudge" from the content itself. The concept arose after World War I, over wariness towards state propaganda and other official channels that had been part of the war machine (Allan, 1999: 24). Believe it or not, despite the last hundred years, some people still actually believe in journalistic objectivity, which is almost as ridiculous as still believing in the tooth fairy or trickle-down economics. The words "objectivity", "impartiality" and "balance" are thrown around both in the debates about the responsibilities of the news media and in questions of their regulation. All but the most embarrassingly positivist contributors to this discussion concede that "objectivity" is an ideal, rather than an assured outcome, but even here, there is uncertainty about what it actually is. For example, there is disagreement among scholars, and confusion among journalists, about whether objectivity is a feature of the work itself — the journalism that has been produced is or is not objective — or the labour that produced it — the journalism was produced by following objective practices. Journalism scholar Gaye Tuchman, for example (1972), whose quote features at the beginning of this chapter, characterises objectivity as the latter, and particularly as a set of *rituals* that occur in the labour of producing journalism. For other scholars, however, it is a measurable feature of the work itself. Sandrine Boudana argues that "the degree of truth" that characterises a journalistic report is what defines its objectivity: "The higher this degree, the better the performance" (2011: 396).

Boudana argues that if not all Marxists are working class and not all feminists are women, our own subjective positions can also be transcended when it comes to providing an objective account in a journalistic context. While this may be true up to a point, and some studies show that journalism students even overcompensate for their own ideological positions when attempting to produce objective journalism (Drew, 1975, cited in Boudana, 2011), that does not mean that there is such thing as a perfect "performance" of journalistic objectivity — not least because, just like most other media, journalism is first and foremost an act of communication that to varying degrees *constructs* rather than merely depicts the events that it concerns. What is perfectly objective to one person may seem distorted to another, with more, less, or different information, and there is no real consensus about the meaning of anything. This should not be taken as another version of the "everything is relative" argument (which has long been derided as a left-wing cop-out but is actually nothing to do with left-wing politics) but rather, as Stuart Hall has argued, "'Consensual' views of society represent society as if there are no major cultural or economic breaks, no major conflicts of interests between classes and groups" (1978: 58).

Another common mistake is to conflate objectivity with neutrality — something that most first-year journalism students quickly learn not to do, but which continues to pervade some newsrooms and the broader world of media. As Boudana rightly says, "the brainless recitation of the arguments of both sides is not just ineffective at maximizing objectivity; it is an obstacle to it" (2011: 394), but as we will see later in the chapter, the impartiality view of journalistic objectivity remains common and has been particularly corrosive. You cannot be impartial the one hand, and be a pro-democratic public service on the other hand, and the failure to understand this tension has been catastrophic. Rather than rehearse scholarly arguments about the nature of journalistic objectivity, however, more relevant here is simply to acknowledge that providing an account of events that does not in some sense influence or colour the reader's or viewer's perception of those events is at best a struggle, and most often an impossibility.

Another way to look at this influence is to use the three-part taxonomy offered by journalism scholar Daniel Hallin (1986: 116–117) for how journalism represents the world. First, he said that as far as discourse around current affairs goes, there is a "sphere of consensus" — the realm of issues about which few people could reasonably disagree, such as "motherhood and apple pie", in which "the journalist's role is to serve as an advocate or celebrant of consensus values". Next was a "sphere of legitimate controversy", in which expected forms of disagreement such as electoral debates were framed. Last in this taxonomy was the "sphere of deviance", which was "the realm of those political actors and views which journalists and the political mainstream of the society reject as unworthy of being heard". In a more recent context, the establishment's fear of and tendency to reduce available airtime for so-called "left populist" candidates such as Bernie Sanders and Jeremy Corbyn is an example of their location in this sphere, and the power involved in doing so. It is also the sphere where climate change denial and racism belong, although as we will see below, the mainstream news media has taken a long time to realise this.

Beyond purely framing issues editorially, there are also the functional limitations that, in combination with the inescapable ideological influences above, tend to colour the ways that issues are presented: "Given the time and space constraints of broadcasting, decisions about which voices and positions to represent necessarily involves selectivity and significant curatorial responsibility on behalf of the journalist" (Wahl-Jorgensen et al., 2016: 784). A similar limitation applies to print journalists, particularly as newspapers and broadcasters converged online into sophisticated multimedia platforms that look very similar regardless of historical origin — the difference depends on local culture and regulations.

Journalism and mass media are always and inevitably going to be in the position of taking a side to some degree, even if the journalist him- or herself is unaware of this. If defending the world's fragile attempts at democracy was journalism's job in theory, frequently it has taken the wrong side in practice. If objectivity means anything, it should mean reaching a conclusion based on a careful, methodical consideration of the available information, grounded in humility rather than hubris, and the evidence of democracy's decline under market forces has been mounting for some time.

Helping to Destroy Democracy

The influences of journalistic framing and treatment may ultimately be inevitable, but they are also not just random misfirings of whatever happens to be in the journalist's head at that particular moment, or merely a reflection of the political persuasions of whichever individual journalist happened to be assigned the story. As we saw in Chapter Two, when we speak of "ideology" in a formal sense, we mean a system of beliefs that constitute the interests of a dominant group within a particular society, reaffirmed and normalised by the media and culture of that society. Consequently, we can and should anticipate that the "sides" that journalism will pick usually conform to the contours of that shift in the sense the most important analysis of any piece of journalism is that of whose interest it ultimately serves — those supporting the dominant hegemony in some way, and to a lesser extent, those challenging it.

Here, just as in previous chapters, we see that political power has been increasingly transferred to private sector corporate organisations as the market-driven society developed, and this is true in the media too. In the late 1980s, Noam Chomsky and Edward Herman published a detailed account of the mass media in North America, showing the ways that it had repeatedly constituted propaganda for corporate interests or cynical US foreign policy. Much of the pro-system anti-ideology addressed in the last chapter means that this is still a surprisingly contentious claim, but as Stuart Allan (1999) reminded us a decade later, as far as privately owned media channels and outlets, the same is still largely true, both in the US and in Europe. The appointment of the former UK Chancellor of the Exchequer and Conservative MP George Osborne as editor of the *Evening Standard*, a major daily newspaper in the UK's most economically important city, by Russian oligarch Alexander Lebedev, is not particularly helpful if objectivity is the look you're going for.

As Chomsky and Herman also indicated, however, it is not as simple as a straightforward influence of conglomerate parent companies explicitly limiting editorial and journalistic activity out of conscious loyalties. In contrast to the explorations of Chapter Three, however, professionalised journalism is not usually an intentional, organised conspiracy, so much as an amplified oversimplification of the world by people who do not have the time to understand it properly, and whose own timidity, cynicism or bourgeois position probably prefers leaving everything as it is. This is corroborated by Nick Davies in his insider account of journalism's deterioration, *Flat Earth News* (2008). Nonetheless, if one ignores the growing number of smaller, independent journalism outlets such as *Democracy Now!, openDemocracy* or *The Intercept*, which are more transparent about their emphasis on scrutinising those in power in as much detail as possible, it is hard not to get the feeling that mainstream outlets still claiming objectivity are distinctly pro-establishment, however unconsciously, or at the very least have difficulty understanding what political power actually is and how it works.

US and UK media work differently — in the UK, print media tend to be unashamedly partisan, while broadcast media are required by law to provide "due impartiality" in their coverage. In the US, this is more or less reversed, and broadcast media provide a circus of partisanship and speculation while newspapers, with a few exceptions, tend to claim a mantle of relative objectivity. Consequently, it is not worth dignifying most of the British newspaper press or the US broadcast journalism, since any claim to impartiality was abandoned long ago — nobody would be surprised that the *Daily Telegraph* supported Boris Johnson or Fox News Donald Trump, but even in those media that ask to be considered as public service broadcasting, or objective at the very least, examples of journalists either affirming the structures of power or failing to take the opportunity to challenge them are too numerous to list.

By way of illustration it is important to consider a few, however.

One recent example of how mainstream journalism has supported the *de-democratisation* of the Euro-Atlantic world is in coverage of austerity after the 2008 financial crash. Austerity is an economic policy widely discredited by most economists, and which "never had any basis in serious economic theory" (Michell, 2020). It cuts a wide array of different kinds of public spending during moments of economic slowdown and reduced tax receipts for government, rather than increase borrowing. The economist Mark Blythe has described it as "more often than not exactly the wrong thing to do precisely because it produces the very outcomes you are trying to avoid" (2013). Indeed, not only does austerity not usually yield the return to economic growth and government solvency that it is usually intended to bring about, but its human cost when imposed is also disastrous — to the point of being deadly. When it was imposed in Britain by David Cameron's governments after 2010, using the reduced tax income that resulted from the financial crisis as a justification for doing so, the effect was a clear reduction in the provisions of the state that saw a decline in life expectancy and an increase in deaths amongst the elderly and others dependent on the state (Dorling, 2017). After the 2008 financial crash, there was a reduction in government incomes across Europe, compared to expectations that had not taken the looming crisis into account (which very few people did).

It is to be expected that certain publications such as the *Economist* or the *Telegraph*, that have always embraced the market-driven society and supported fiscal conservatism, would have cheer led austerity and taken every opportunity to normalise the sharp reduction in public spending that it involved, despite what most economists were saying. But in the UK, the BBC also played a leading role in affirming that the deficit was the outgoing Labour government's fault without drawing attention to the role of the financial sector in causing the crash (Berry, 2016), and heavily featuring think tanks that, while officially non-partisan, played a major role in "legitimizing the idea that austerity was an unavoidable policy response to the crisis" (Chadwick et al., 2018). In 2020, when George Osborne, who had been UK Chancellor during the austerity years under David Cameron, and whose Secretary of State for Health Jeremy Hunt had presided over austerity-driven cuts and "efficiency savings" to the UK's National Health Service, was interviewed about the COVID-19 pandemic, the BBC completely failed to ask him about the cuts he had made to the healthcare budget in the name of this disastrous policy.

Here we can see that journalism's assistance in the dismantling of the public good can work in two ways: it can work positively to affirm and validate policies that are wholly contrary to the public's interest such as presenting austerity, and it can work negatively and omit any challenge or even open-ended questioning of these policies. In practice, of course, both take place at the same time, as we saw when the BBC presented austerity as mere "cost-cutting" or "balancing the books".

US readers will note that this and many of the examples presented are from a UK or European context, and there are a number of reasons for this. Coverage of austerity is particularly apparent in the UK and Europe partly because the conversation around government spending in the United States is so different anyway, and also because the US's media landscape and national conversation on economic matters is already so polarised that there were no real surprises about who supported austerity and who pointed out its folly. Besides the armed forces, US public spending is also much less prominent because the welfare state in the US never saw quite the levels of joined-up care for its citizens that arose in the post-war years in states like the UK and France in the first place, and so there is not a culture of scrutinising and discussing the paltry crumbs of the United States' social contract on the same terms. But despite the US's traditionally inward-looking focus, it would serve the US Americans well to observe what happens in the countries of Western Europe, particularly Britain, given its common language and rigorous implementation of the market-driven society, because their smaller size and increased centralisation draw attention to processes that are also at work in the US, if harder to see.

In the context of the US broadcast media, it is to be expected that Fox News will take certain positions, but even if we can't call them remotely "objective", the US's newspapers tend to be better at presenting themselves superficially as above the usual fracas of the country's intense political partisanship. A perusal of the *New York Times'* coverage of the debate over Medicare for All confirms a similar picture as the BBC, however: a long list of articles cautious about the policy, arguing that it will never happen, or misrepresenting it in various ways, peppered with a few favourable articles, no doubt for "balance", even though the US paper's coverage of UK austerity was remarkably critical. The paper also supported the 2003 war in Iraq and reiterated the disinformation that that Saddam Hussein held weapons of mass destruction based on dubious sources, for which it later apologised.

The US's other major newspaper of record, the *Washington Post*, owned by Amazon.com CEO and founder Jeff Bezos since 2013, called for one of the most important whistleblowers of the twenty-first century, Edward Snowden, to be tried for espionage. They also repeatedly attacked Bernie Sanders, who had campaigned for Amazon workers amongst others to receive a $15 minimum wage and was proposing a policy often known as the "Amazon tax" which required the corporation and others like it to pay increased taxes to pay for expansions to the US welfare state such as universal healthcare — hardly die-hard communism by the standards of most developed countries, especially given that more than forty million US Americans were on food stamps.

In some ways, cleaving to power is a regular occurrence in journalism. Bloomberg's censure of stories detailing the private wealth of China's premier Xi JinPing in order to protect business interests in the country is a far more conventional example (Fincher, 2020).

One clear-cut, if quantitative example from a more localised context that illustrates clear pro-establishment bias is the two interviews of leading British politicians carried out by Kirstie Wark in January 2019 on the BBC's flagship current affairs interview and discussion programme, *Newsnight*, conducted only two days apart. One interview was with then Shadow Chancellor of the Exchequer John McDonnell, a close friend and ally of Jeremy Corbyn, and thus not in government. The other was with Amber Rudd, then the Secretary of State for Work and Pensions in the Conservative cabinet under Theresa May — very much in government. London-based volunteer-run left-leaning outlet *Daily Politik* examined both interviews with two metrics — how often was the politician interrupted, and how often were they challenged? McDonnell was interrupted twenty-one times and challenged eleven times, while Rudd was not interrupted or challenged a single time. Editor, presenter and timeframe were the same. Again, this is not to suggest any intentional conspiracy, but the difference in tone and treatment is as clear as the lack of "due impartiality".

Peter Oborne, a conservative British journalist widely respected on the left and right for his integrity, has pointed to the fact that the British press as a whole often proved incapable of challenging Boris Johnson's habitual and proven lying in the run-up to the 2019 general election. Johnson claimed forty new hospitals were planned, when the true number was just six, and claimed that 20,000 new police were already in operation when the reality was that it was a planned three-year recruitment programme that would do little more than replace the officers who had been cut by previous Conservative governments as a part of their austerity policies (2019b).

The *Guardian*, once a UK newspaper and now a major global English-language news and media platform with large audiences in the US and Australia, showed an increasingly weak approach to power from 2015 onwards. After its journalists bravely revealed the leaks made by Edward Snowden in June 2013, it began to drift away from such direct challenges to the military industrial complex, under pressure from the UK's security services. Although it did still publish some stories critical of the security services, by mid-2015 it was fully integrated into the UK's "DSMA-Notice" system — a supposedly voluntary arrangement by which the country's media can be requested not to publish materials that may affect national security — with its deputy editor even eventually being invited to sit on the committee until 2018 (Kennard & Curtis, 2019). At the time of writing the *Guardian* still publishes some excellent reporting, but besides a few excellent columnists has been noticeably less sharp-toothed in the defence of the public good, of which it would surely claim to be a part. Barring a few opinion articles to the contrary, the *Guardian* was openly hostile to Jeremy Corbyn's bid to democratise the UK economy, publishing over a thousand articles critical of Corbyn between January 2016 and September 2019 that repeated the claim that Labour, and Corbyn specifically, were anti-Semitic. This is not for a moment to say that there are not issues of anti-Semitism on the British left, which as we saw in Chapter Three, often emerge at best as a sort of perverse, racist, lay critique of capital that reveals as much bigotry as it does its illiteracy. Indeed, although a 2016 report by the human rights lawyer Shami Chakrabarti found that the party "is not overrun by anti-Semitism, Islamophobia or other forms of racism" (Chakrabarti, 2016: 1), it did suggest that "antisemitism has not been taken seriously enough in the Labour Party and broader Left for some years" (ibid.). Rather, it is to say that besides the fact that the anti-Semitic views held by Labour voters were shown by polls to have declined substantially in the first two years of Corbyn's tenure (Rogers, 2018, Graeber, 2019) and that such views were significantly more common among Conservative voters (Gidley, McGeever and Feldman, 2020), to claim that Corbyn and the Labour Party were primarily defined by anti-Semitism became a way for mostly non-Jewish politicians on the right of the party to undermine Corbyn's public legitimacy, aided by the press. Like all racism, anti-Semitism has no place in left-wing politics, but as the anthropologist David Graeber wrote at the time, this "weaponisation" of the issue was "so cynical and irresponsible" that it amounted to "a form of antisemitism in itself" (2019). While this might have been expected from the right-wing press, the *Guardian* very much led the charge, demonstrating perfectly the "politics of shallow understanding" explored in the previous chapter.

In a 2019 study of US financial journalists, results "cast doubt that journalists nowadays fulfil their role as watchdogs [...] with regard to (1) providing guidance for acting upon information or (2) yielding people or the government to take action" and found that:

> when journalists reflected upon the main audience they are writing for, it became evident that most of the journalists report for wealthy, male, well-educated business people or

citizens with a strong interest in investments. Thus, instead of informing the broader public or retail investors as intended by the journalists and described by Usher (2012), financial journalists rather speak to an elite audience, mainly located on Wall Street. (Strauß, 2019)

OK, you could say, financial journalism has become a tailored product for people in the financial world. Perhaps expecting financial journalism to turn to exposing the crimes of its own target audience is a bit optimistic. But the description in this study only illustrates a broader issue that even if journalists believe in theory that their role is as a "watchdog", in practice their work either simply fails to do this job despite this continuing belief, or they are consciously aware that their actual work does not fulfil this role.

Think Tanks and Sources

One of the other ways that the BBC is revealed to have drifted significantly as far as its overall ideological positioning is concerned is in the mentions of think tanks and the uses of their work in the context of factual, news and current affairs programming. A 2017 study of the think tanks used by the BBC found that:

In 2009, there was a broad balance between left and right think tanks [...] In 2015, references to right-leaning think tanks remain [...] while references to left-leaning think tanks are halved [...]. To put it into a broad political context, when Labour was in power, the BBC's use of think tanks was relatively even-handed, but when a Conservative-led coalition was in power, the centre of gravity shifted to the political right.

The study continues that:

News/current affairs programmes on BBC Two very clearly favour right-wing think tanks. This is mainly accounted for by two current affairs programmes, *Daily Politics* and *Newsnight*, where the ratio of right-leaning to left-leaning think tanks is a striking six to one. (Lewis and Cushion, 2017: 13–14)

Another study of the same question — the use of think tanks in news and current affairs coverage on the BBC — found that think tanks are frequently used in a quasi-objective way that it called "assumed authority signalling", in which think tanks are constructed as objective, expert sources. The Institute for Fiscal Studies was found to be disproportionately overused in this way: "in 2009, it made up 47 percent of all references to think tanks in BBC news programs and was mentioned eight times as often as the second-ranked think tank; by 2015, this had reached 54 percent/five times" (Chadwick et al., 2018).

Another problem is the repeated use of anonymous sources, who frequently turn out to be spin doctors from within government. As writer and journalist Gary Younge observed in 2019, "When those quotes are non-attributed — 'a senior No 10 source' or 'sources within the cabinet' — the risk of the journalist becoming an enabler and participant is real" (2019). Even *Sky News* journalist Adam Boulton admitted, "Journalists vie to have the best 'sources' but spin doctors on both sides are using this against them" (2019).

Some journalists have drawn attention to this practice, challenging the complacency, myopia and cynicism of their colleagues. Boulton's words were written in support of fellow British political journalist Peter Oborne, who wrote in detail about an example in which the *Daily Mail* reported that a number of MPs were being "investigated" by the British government for allegedly being paid or otherwise influenced by foreign governments so as to disrupt the process of leaving the European Union:

> I rang [accused MP] Dominic Grieve. He told me he had not sought the help of any foreign government "in drafting and tabling a British statute".
>
> He added that he was "not in receipt of any sources of foreign funding". Nor, he said, had he been contacted by Downing Street or anyone else about any investigation.
>
> I then rang the Downing Street press office, and asked an official whether there was an investigation as stated in The Mail on Sunday.
>
> He told me categorically: "No investigation."
>
> Yesterday a Cabinet Office spokesperson told openDemocracy: "There was never such an investigation."
>
> [...]
>
> There has, however, been no retraction from The Mail on Sunday. As far as the newspaper's readers are concerned, the story remains true and the senior British politicians behind the Benn Act continue to be investigated for suspicious involvement with foreign powers. (2019)

The fact that, besides the woeful reporting by the Daily Mail, even the BBC's senior political correspondent failed to ask the most fundamental question of all — whether there actually was an investigation — should also be instructive. When a story such as this is whipped up, and the same snippets of information circulate from journalist to journalist, this should be treated as an ongoing opportunity to test the verification of the information that the story rests on. But all too often a sort of industry group-think seems to take hold, to which Peter Oborne and a number of other excellent reporters are notable exceptions. In this instance, when the Daily Mail was challenged by Oborne, they doubled down in way that was reminiscent of the hyper-empiricism described in the last chapter: "We stand firmly by our story. Two separate sources in Downing Street told us that officials in Number 10 were gathering evidence about allegations of foreign collusion by MPs opposed to a No Deal Brexit." In other words, we had evidence, we used evidence, but no reflection at all on the fact that perhaps their anonymous "sources" were not as authoritative or appropriate choices as they might have believed.

What all of these examples show, rather than the simple fact that mainstream journalism has tended to facilitate rather than challenge the market-driven society, is an utter illiteracy with respect to political and economic power itself. In one example that encapsulates this nicely, prominent British journalist Robert Peston gave away more than he realised when he said on Twitter that he was "literally gobsmacked" by the disclosure in a *Sunday Times* exposé that Boris Johnson did not prioritise preparation for the then looming COVID-19 catastrophe until March 2020. Was this really such a surprise? If genuine, this could only have been the surprise of someone determined to be blind to all the contextual specifics — Johnson's well-known vanity, incompetence and personal ambition, as well as the government's obsession with making a no-deal Brexit appear inevitable — and to focus instead on the simple fact that Johnson was Prime Minister and that this preparation was his job. This blindness is the same kind of positivist, normative reasoning that we saw in Chapter Four, which is both produced by and productive of the political illiteracy that is at the very foundation of the market-driven society. Journalism became something that was often nominally informational, but both produced and read by people who were illiterate about capital and culturally invested in the market-driven society's continuation.

Everything is "Just a Debate"

Similar to the "free marketplace of ideas" delusion that we saw in the last chapter, there is an annoying and wholly unnecessary tendency for journalism to interpret its obligation to at least attempt objectivity as a sort of game in which every controversial issue is merely a "debate", with seemingly little recognition that the issue under discussion has a very real social or economic consequence for the people it concerns. Indeed, in both the UK and the US — countries where politics is largely dominated by two parties — this tends to be a lazy interaction on the terms of existing political parties and their spokespeople:

> in the case of the BBC, [impartiality] is principally put into practice through the paradigm of impartiality as party-political balance: It is achieved by juxtaposing the positions of the two main political parties — Conservative and Labour — to the detriment of a broader range of opinion. (Wahl-Jorgensen et al., 2016: 782)

The somewhat artificial staging of politics as a partisan affair like some sort of mid-table sports fixture with two equally underwhelming sides, each with their own colour and supporter base, is only one form of this dysfunctional pattern, however. It can also represent fairly clear-cut issues of public safety and wellbeing as being somehow "up for debate", as if the issue is somehow not settled or needs to be revisited. For example, in March 2020, the *Guardian* thought it would be a valid "debate" to discuss whether or not the taxpayer should continue to fund free school meals for children, inviting teachers and other officials from the primary education sector to respond with a "yes" or "no" and give their reasons. The "no" arguments were essentially those that saw austerity as either inevitable or not worth challenging, with one saying, "A hungry child doesn't learn well and it's right that children get a decent meal every day at school. But the government says there's not enough money to do everything." Had he forgotten that the alternative was either a private company *profiting* from a hungry child, or that child just staying hungry? Another managed to bizarrely twist the existence of austerity into a reason why the taxpayer should *not* fund free school meals. It is hard to see how this article made any sort of contribution to the health of British democracy or the welfare of British children, besides appearing to suggest that comparatively small amounts of money required of the taxpayer for feeding potentially hungry children were possibly not worthwhile.

If the thought of hungry children at school in the UK is too specific, or does not tug sufficiently at the heartstrings, a more well-known example is that of the BBC's handling of man-made climate change. Until 2018, the BBC treated it as a political issue, meaning that internal editorial guidelines required a climate change sceptic to be included whenever the matter was discussed, despite a broad agreement among 97% of climate scientists that global warming is caused by human activity. That BBC presenter Mishal Husain was paid to attend oil events did not lend any additional credibility (Moore, 2020).

Another faux-debate technique is to pose questions in a headline, apparently not realising that the whole point about a question is that unless it is rhetorical, it can have more than one answer. For example, on 11 April 2020, the UK's *Telegraph* newspaper tweeted from its book reviews Twitter account the question "Could Hitler ever be considered a 'great' man?" and then in the accompanying graphic: "Hitler's greatest mistake? Believing his own publicity." This was bizarrely insensitive, even for the

Telegraph, which had had a field day accusing Labour of "rampant" anti-Semitism.

Frequently, controversial guests are included in news programming in a manner that does not seem to provide clear objectivity or value to the programme at all. During the COVID-19 pandemic, for example, the TV channel *London Live*, which has the same Russian owners — Alexander and Evgeny Lebedev — as newspapers the *Independent* and *Evening Standard*, invited conspiracy theorist David Icke for an interview, in which, unsurprisingly, he pushed wholly discredited and dangerous theories about 5G causing the illness. In another example, this time from the US, broadcaster CNN invited allowed white supremacist Richard Spencer to discuss and defend Trump's tweets. Spencer and Icke are of course entitled to their opinions, and to express them. But just what planet a production editor has to be on to imagine that these inclusions provide any benefit to the public whatsoever, or that there is no consequence for other vulnerable people in encouraging white supremacy on a mainstream news network, it is difficult to imagine. Climate change, wacky and dangerous conspiracy theories about 5G, white supremacy, hungry children or the "greatness" of Hitler are not a simple "matter of debate", and there is no loss to freedom of expression or objectivity by framing them in suitably definite terms.

In some cases, it may be that journalists have an uncomfortable relationship to vague regulations and the management that apply them, but at least in the UK where it is legally mandated, it is sometimes apparent that neither regulators, the journalists themselves, or their audiences actually understand what "due impartiality" means. In July 2019, Donald Trump suggested that four congresswomen of colour "go back to the totally broken and crime-infested places from which they came". Once the BBC had invited a Trump supporter on air to defend him in the "just a debate" manner described above, BBC journalist Naga Munchetty was asked on-air by her co-presenter how, as a person of colour, Trump's tweet had made her feel. She responded that Trump's language was "embedded in racism" before adding, "Now, I'm not accusing anyone of anything here, but you know what certain phrases mean." Two months later, the BBC's Editorial Complaints Unit found she "went beyond what the guidelines allow for". After widespread outcry, they later backed down, but the issue was reminiscent of how other (predominantly white) journalists in the US had also been reluctant to call Trump's tweets "racist" (Vernon, 2017).

The "just a debate" problem does not just hurt by way of the detachment it demonstrates, however. It also provides useful airtime to ideas that endanger people. As CNN's invitation of Richard Spencer and the *Economist*'s and *New Yorker*'s speaking invitations to Steven Bannon in 2017 also showed, the very inclusion of their opinions on these platforms not only conferred legitimacy on them, it also provided them with a huge amount of what has rapidly become one of the most valuable commodities of the market-driven society: attention. The idea that their carefully polished fascism could be seriously challenged by some jolly good debate was the same noxious misreading of John Stuart Mill that we addressed in the last chapter. Some of this complacency about the scourge of racism may be explained by the fact that people of colour are massively under-represented in British newsrooms. According to a report by the Reuters Institute at Oxford, "UK journalism has a significant diversity problem in terms of ethnicity, with black Britons, for example, under-represented by a factor of more than ten" (Thurman, Cornia & Kunert, 2016: 6).

Journalism and the Far-Right

On the whole it is clear from these slightly bewildering examples that journalists can prove useful to power even when they are ostensibly trying to back up stories, but they are not useful solely to those in power. So far this chapter has argued that journalism as a whole has tended to affirm and reify the market-driven society, and (with important exceptions) has failed to challenge the powerful minority that actually benefits from it, despite this nominally being journalism's primary responsibility. As we saw in Chapter Two, however, misinformation and disinformation not only facilitate the market-driven society in a way that has fanned the flames of far-right anger; they also drive some of that anger directly. A broad version of this picture was also visible in the last chapter, and the same is true with mainstream journalism, in so far as part of the overall political illiteracy and naivety we have seen above has also meant that while the professionalised classes may have mocked the far-right and supported the market-driven society that attacked the right's moralised anchors, they have also been gently supportive of the causes that most resonate with them, however unwittingly.

The possibility of institutional racism within the world of journalism is a topic that could be the subject of an entire chapter in a different book, but the removal by *Associated Press* of Ugandan climate activist Vanessa Nakate — the only black face — from a photo of young climate activists attending the World Economic Forum in Davos in January 2020 was a worrying indication of casual white supremacy at a major global news agency. Even if we are to believe *AP*'s insistence that the photo was cropped "purely on composition grounds", there is still a much more serious and substantial case to be made that mainstream journalism outlets have been enablers of the far-right.

The most obvious example of this is probably the issue of immigration. Research has already shown that the tone and quantity of reporting about immigration varies widely in response to news events, but that journalists do tend to shape the ways that audiences understand immigration (Zerback et al., 2020). In an extreme example, the British tabloid press is infamous for its consistently vile, fascistic coverage of immigrants, describing them as "swarms" and even going so far as to suggest that desperate sea-crossing migrants who run into trouble should be left to drown in their hundreds. The sheer extremity of such hateful and obviously racist coverage, which has a long history of representing immigrants as violent or lazy (see Hall et al., 1978), can distract us from an altogether meeker, ostensibly reasonable type of coverage that acts in symbiosis with these more conspicuous instances. But as with the media's normalisation of austerity, its affirmation that immigration *is an issue* as though it were a matter of fact is already an intervention, especially given conflicting empirical evidence at best as to whether immigrants actually do represent a major threat to the economic opportunities afforded to locally born populations, and strong evidence that they work longer hours, are in general more law-abiding, and make major cultural contributions that go beyond what kinds of takeaway food are available.

A study of immigration coverage in UK general election news coverage between the election of John Major in 1992 and the Conservative victory in the 2015 election (in which even the Labour Party made "controls in immigration" part of its campaign) found that the actual change in migrant numbers over that time period was "not, however, a sufficient explanation for the centrality of debates about immigration within diverse polities. Opinion poll evidence routinely shows the public misperceive levels of immigration" (Deacon and Smith, 2017).

In Chapter Two, we saw an example of how a combination of a TV debate show *Question Time*, facilitated by BBC journalist Fiona Bruce and its use of social media via a Twitter account dedicated to the same show bizarrely served to amplify a wildly inaccurate claim by an audience member without any factual correction whatsoever. This is something of a pattern. In February 2020, a different audience member on the same show launched into an uninterrupted eighty-two-second rant about how Britain was "sinking" because there were too many "people flooding into this country that cannot speak English", calling for a "complete" closure of the UK's borders. Although in the live programme, the audience member was challenged, the BBC saw fit to tweet the clip of her rant with no responses or other context, and without any correction of the many factual errors the audience member had asserted, and the clip received nearly seven million views. The BBC's response was that other clips from the same airing of the show had also been shared via social media but this was not impartiality in any meaningful sense; it was the amplification of vile falsehoods. The same audience member was later revealed to be a supporter of far-right campaigner Stephen Yaxley-Lennon, also known as Tommy Robinson, and was filmed shouting in a different video that "we've had enough in this country" and that "Muslim groups" were "taking over our country".

The related area of Brexit also revealed a degree of bias that the far-right should have been grateful for. Like the US broadcast media, UK print media is usually explicitly favourable to specific political positions, and a report by the Reuters Institute at the University of Oxford found a significant favour for Leave-supporting media, which is useful to have in concrete empirical terms, if no real surprise (Levy, Aslan and Bironzo, 2018). Some journalism academics were reluctant to make any characterisation of the BBC as biased in its coverage of the referendum (Beckett, 2016). This is understandable, since there were a huge number of problems with the Remain campaign that had nothing to do with its media portrayal. However, to claim that the BBC was entirely neutral in its coverage of Brexit would be something of a gloss over the fact that the entire discussion was couched in a language of false equivalence, and that the BBC's elevation of the Brexit movement's most vocal figurehead, Nigel Farage, over many years on programmes such as *Question Time* is arguably a significant part of how the entire issue of the UK's membership of the European Union was able to receive widespread attention (Reynolds & Sweney, 2014). As we saw above, it took a very long time for the issue of climate change to be moved out of Hallin's "sphere of legitimate controversy" and for denial of its man-made origins to be consigned to the "sphere of deviance". In relation to European Union membership, bias can consist of not much more than placing the issue in the wrong sphere. A poll by Ipsos Mori, reported in the *Economist* (2017) showed that the number of people believing that Britain's membership in the European Union was the most important issue facing the country was largely below 10% until 2015, when the referendum date was actually announced. So why was Nigel Farage the most common guest on *Question Time* outside of the major British political parties, having first appeared in 2000? In 2020, after Britain had left the EU, the BBC still insisted on asking Farage his opinion, bizarrely asking him for his thoughts about COVID-19, in an interview on flagship news programme *Newsnight*. But constantly giving airtime to reactionary ideologues is not the only way that mainstream journalism has helped the far-right. It has also serviced a number of other reactionary talking points. Even the BBC's failure to treat the theory of man-made climate change as the same type of reliable scientific conclusion as the theories of gravity or evolution by natural selection was outdone, for example, by UK newspaper *Metro*'s inexplicable promotion in 2018 of the widely discredited "sun spots" theory of climate that asserts a "global cooling" as a simple news story with no caveat whatsoever (Hamill, 2018).

Even when the pretence of objectivity is dropped, and outrage ensues, the resulting attention causes an enormous amplification of whatever far-right talking point has caused such offence, while the entirely incompatible moral registers of the disagreement mean few who already hold an opinion on the matter are swayed one way or the other. Nowhere is this more obvious than the way the US media constantly covered every aspect of Donald Trump: every tweet, every press conference, every detail of his conduct — well beyond his actual responsibilities as president. It was Trump as a personage, as a character, that they were covering. What more could a narcissistic, authoritarian leader want? And yet the media has fallen for this trick all across the world.

This support presents a curious question: given this assistance in mainstreaming their talking points and "debating" their leaders, why do the reactionary right hate the "mainstream media" so much? A well-known T-shirt bearing the phrase "Rope, tree, journalist" surfaced in 2016 to widespread outcry, produced by a US Navy veteran from the southern US who also made no secret on social media of also hating Mexico. The shirts were eventually withdrawn from sale by Wal-Mart but were still available for sale from smaller online outlets at the time of writing. In a similar vein, an August 2017 post from extremist internet forum 4chan told readers: "we eventually have to start killing journalists [...] if civil unrest starts, you know who to go after" (Anonymous, 2017).

Surely, the far-right should be thanking mainstream journalism, not hating it, but the problem is not a taxonomical one: reactionaries have no major problem with journalism or journalists when they are all in agreement, or when they have been invited for a nice chat by Zanny Minton Beddoes. As detailed in prior chapters, the drifting status quo, or "stealth revolution" as Wendy Brown has called it, that allowed the market-driven society to take over also caused a rift between those defending the status quo at any particular moment, believing this to be "objectivity", and those more overtly conservative voices that had a fixed view of the society they wanted and began to seek a *return* to a more traditional past. As a result, the cultural pact between moral conservatism and economic conservatism that was possible in a world where capitalism was one and the same with modernity and the establishment was still worried about communism, broke down as the market-driven society outsourced or automated jobs, eliminated, mocked or commodified traditions, and invited lots of hard-working, honest brown people into the country.

Meanwhile, professionalised journalism blindly supported the status quo out of some performative notion of "this is what objectivity looks like", which increasingly meant not only a disdain for anything that appeared to be left-wing, but also for the right. As we saw in the last chapter, this was partly because the market-driven society preferred to think of itself as not having ideology either. Stubborn defence of a traditional, patriarchal vision of society and blind defence of the current status quo as a misguided implementation of objectivity drifted apart, and instead of being normalised into the establishment and treated as "common sense", traditionalist, moralised right-wing voices were cast out of the temple and marked as ideological, whilst given oxygen in the form of attention and platforms from which to speak to a mainstream audience.

What the Lord giveth, the Lord also taketh away. But while the conservative right increasingly noticed and resented the loss of any historical privileges — whether white privilege, patriarchy or being accepted by the establishment — they remained largely oblivious to the ways that their inclusion in "debates" as part of the requirement for "due impartiality" could be helpful to their cause. Bannon and Spencer are amongst those exceptions who realise that any claim to "objectivity" has already jumped the shark, and corporate mainstream journalism's loud self-association with simplistic, de-economised forms of corporate identity politics did not help.

As any motorist knows, failure to acknowledge the warning lights on the dashboard is a recipe for trouble. Failure to acknowledge how broken the system of democracy is when your job is supposed to be to defend democracy is even more calamitous. However, instead of challenging the erosion of democracy, which would have been both in the "public interest" and in the interests of the industry's long-term prospects, mainstream journalism largely went along with the erosion of democracy into a market-driven society, often failing to analyse or question who was behind that process, and what it meant for the democracy from which journalism itself ultimately derived its legitimacy.

More empirically minded readers will be wondering why, beyond examples of journalism that either woefully fail to challenge anti-democratic ideation or that actually affirm it, I have not presented *proof* that journalism is at least partly responsible for the profoundly sorry state that democracy in the Euro-Atlantic world is in. By way of an answer, I would encourage an equally empirical appraisal of democracy's actual state, in whatever year you happen to be reading this, and then, in light of journalism's orientation in democracy that was described at the beginning of this chapter, rhetorically re-ask my colleague's question in a new context: If journalism's primary role was to defend democracy, and democracy has nonetheless become a hollowed out simulacrum of itself, what *is* the point of journalism? The results would suggest that whoever's job it was to defend democracy has not been successful.

As we turn to examining journalism economically as labour to produce a valuable product in a capitalist economy, it is worth pondering as a kind of pivot that not only did this process evaporate the substantive valuation of democracy and civic engagement in which serious journalism actually had a role to play, but part of the market-driven society whose development journalists have spent decades failing to prevent or question entailed a certain *Schumpeterian* "creative destruction", in which the Marxian observation that the ruling class are constantly trying to revolutionise the means of production is recast into an unqualified positive. But while these changes might have been cast as "progress" or "disruptive tech" when they happened to other people and industries, they were not quite the same moment for celebration when they gutted the oldest forms of journalism, such as the newspaper or radio.

Journalism as "Content"

Next time you are browsing a journalism website and reading an online news article through a small slot in the page, between the GDPR footer politely asking if the website can track your every click for advertising purposes, and a huge banner ad trying to sell you football betting odds or pregnancy test kits (depending on your gender and age), spare a thought for the once-great journalism industry — preferably after you have finished the article and encountered below it a long list of link-bait headlines about disgraced celebrities, life hacks and a single, working mother in whatever city you just happen to be reading in, who has apparently discovered a miracle cure for ageing, to the chagrin of cosmetic dermatologists. Indeed, nothing makes the cooling fans on a laptop spin like the garish Flash-based advertisements displayed on news websites.

A market-driven society like the one whose development this book has traced is governed by the law of supply and demand, perhaps more than some of us are comfortable with. The ruthless thing about such situations is that, by the time our values, institutions and forms of governance are subjected to this harsh system of valuation, it is often too late for us to recover the ideas and values that were important, but uncommodifiable — that is to say, those things that could not or should not be bought and sold because their value is somehow *outside* of the market. These are the things that free-market fundamentalists would often rather pretend do not exist, but there is a case to be made that this is the fate that has afflicted the "watchdog", the "public education" and other roles of journalism that remain important for the functioning of a healthy, informed democracy. As Thomas Patterson (2010) and others have suggested, there needs to be a demand for news, for understanding the world, before people will seek it out. To the extent that producing journalism is largely a private, for-profit activity, this is perhaps a telling reminder of what happens when public services based on the idea of a common good are run strictly according to the principles of the free market and its profit motive — as soon as their "product" is not valued by that "market", an important public service is lost or endangered. This is why, on the whole, we don't privatise the fire brigade (although the Institute for Economic Affairs called for this in 2010). If journalism is supposed to be a valued commodity, and the "use value" of that commodity is derived from its status within a journalistic paradigm that is no longer intrinsically valued by as many people, it does not take an economics degree to understand that the "exchange value" of that product-that-nobody-values will decline. And yet the increasingly frantic conversations about the monetisation of journalism and paywalls that accompanied journalism's precipitous decline seldom appeared to address the question of *why* people no longer wanted to pay for journalism, beyond merely pointing the finger at the web as a technology that had the free exchange of content built into its core. By the time the web came along in 1991, there wasn't much time to find a solution. Data on the diminishing circulation figures from Pew Research Centre shows a high point in the 1990s, followed by a gradual decline that began to accelerate around 2003, and even more so after the financial crash in 2007–2008. By 2018, US newspaper circulation fell to its lowest level since 1940 (Grieco, 2020)

Since news outlets are for the most part businesses, the emphasis in responding to this crisis has been to first think from a revenue perspective, and thus to consider value in an economistic sense. What *will* earn money? The choice is usually between pleasing the consumers of digital journalism and pleasing those advertisers willing to pay for their attention, examined below. Both are models that work better at scale, but the two approaches tend to produce quite different outcomes, with the former emphasising cultivation of a smaller, more loyal audience with quality, and the latter tending to lead to more link-bait type content with mass appeal on account of being driven by metrics such as referrals and click-throughs (Suárez, 2020). Whether the journalists and operational strategists in those stuffy meeting rooms are aware of it, however, the questions really being asked are: To what extent does something claiming to do the job of journalism still permit commodification according to the requirements of an ever more market-driven society, and what kind of commodity will actually be exchanged — truth, feelings or attention?

Paywalls vs Journalism as Public Good?

The paywall model, whilst initially a failure in the early 2000s, saw more success once internet users became more accustomed to paying for content subscriptions. Its early failures were also due to the fact that they constituted a demand for payment for internet content whilst failing to consider how the question of *value* had changed in relation to journalism in light of the market-driven society, and the fact that internet users were overwhelmed with a choice of free content of comparable quality. But even when paywalled journalism does offer significant value, that only revealed other complexities entailed in placing journalism behind a paywall. During the COVID-19 pandemic, an interesting and very instructive controversy arose around paywalls after a damning investigation into the UK government's handling of the pandemic was published in the *Sunday Times*, a "hard-paywalled" website. The *Sunday Times* had tended to be supportive of the conservative elements of Britain's political map, particularly after being bought by Rupert Murdoch in 1981. But in the years following the Brexit referendum, that conservative alliance frayed somewhat as the Conservative Party pulled further to the right, as demonstrated by the expulsion of twenty-one conservative MPs from their party in 2019 over their failure to support a vote on Brexit that Boris Johnson's government lost. That fracture meant that the *Sunday Times*, which had stayed towards the more "liberal" side of the conservative political coalition, appeared to be less inhibited by loyalty from publishing stories that were critical of Boris Johnson's right-populist premiership — the first story being the revelation in the summer of 2019 of his "friendship" with former model Jennifer Arcuri. When they broke the story of the UK government's catastrophic negligence in the five weeks from 24 January to 2 March 2020, during which measures could have been put in place to control or contain the virus, the report remained behind the paywall, whereas similarly important revelations from other paywalled papers such as the *Financial Times* had been made available to the public. The report's critical take on Johnson's right-populist government meant that it was also interesting to readers who were outside the conservative political persuasion, who were far less likely to be subscribers to the joint *Times* and *Sunday Times* paywall, or to be willing to spend money to access even one story from a publication of which they might otherwise have been less trusting. The article was quickly "liberated" and shared via other platforms not subject to a paywall, which in turn caused a backlash from a variety of journalists and journalism scholars who pointed out that the crisis had hit newspapers hard and that essentially pirating their investigative exposés, which are expensive to produce, was counterproductive if the report the *Sunday Times* journalists had produced was valuable. *Guardian* journalist Hadley Freeman wrote: "you are not helping. Newspapers are dying right now. If you want to support journalism, link to the newspaper itself", suggesting that interested readers might want to subscribe to the paper and get "two free articles". Not only did the only access links from the story lead to a paid subscription screen, however, but even if two free articles had been in the offing, this would not have helped the newspaper's bottom line save for the small number of readers who later found that they needed a third and subsequent articles badly enough that they were willing to pay for a paper they may well have previously detested.

These journalists were right that on the whole journalism has costs to cover, and that it is not inappropriate for readers or viewers to contribute towards those costs in principle, as they have for more than two hundred years. But this affair revealed other important factors in how those insisting on payment for the article thought about journalism, or rather, the factors that appeared to be absent from their thinking.

Firstly, the owner of the *Sunday Times* is a business partly owned by Rupert Murdoch — a man who spent more than three decades using his various outlets to prop up Conservative governments whose market-driven policies led to the UK's woeful unpreparedness for the pandemic by stripping back the country's public healthcare system, often under the guise of "efficiency savings". To pay those same outlets to provide information about a crisis that they had indirectly helped to produce understandably felt strange to say the least.

Secondly, to ignore the fact that an article of extremely pressing national importance was inaccessible to the majority of those who might have benefitted from reading it because it was paywalled appeared to overlook the fact that journalism considers itself a public service. Indeed, a precedent already existed for paywalled newspapers to make their most urgent and essential coverage of the pandemic freely available. To forget this aspect of journalism or to assume a subscription fee of £26 per month was negligible was not only to display the kinds of economic blindness described in the previous chapter — it was also to make journalism purely an economic product and to affirm the market-driven society in so doing.

Thirdly, to imagine that sharing one article of especially acute importance would somehow hurt the individual journalists who had worked on the story is to conflate those journalists with their employer. No matter what they might have imagined about the newsroom at the *Sunday Times*, it was hardly a worker-owned co-operative. The paper's owner, News UK, is a subsidiary of American corporation News Corporation, which at the time was valued at almost $10bn.

Finally, it was to assume that those sharing the *Sunday Times* article were not paying for other journalism. Just because you are not a subscriber to the *Sunday Times*, especially given it is a Murdoch-associated paper, does not mean you are not supporting smaller, more independent, more precarious and potentially far more deserving outlets.

This insistence thus showed the limitations at least of "hard" paywalls in a number of ways, and is a reminder of an inescapable public service element of journalism that cannot be easily or beneficially subjected to the rules of the marketplace. It will always be naïve to sell digital media in the same way that you sell a bunch of bananas. But the alternative to paywalls — using advertising to pay the bills and making journalism as attention-grabbing as possible to make advertisers happy — also has its limitations.

Understand Clickbait Using this One Weird Trick

Elsewhere I have written about the compensatory emotional drivers for digital media consumption, including journalism, and the growing *emotionalisation* of journalism and information-based media, particularly when mixed with lots of other media in the context of a social media timeline. In the next chapter, we will look at the intersection of emotion, advertising and distraction more centrally. However, in the context of a discussion about how journalism has sought to create alternative forms of value and revenue as a response to the pressures of a market-driven society that increasingly deprioritises the public interest that has been journalism's core offering, it is worth addressing the importance of that advertising has had for journalism.

Newspapers have contained advertisements at least since the nineteenth century, including some rather bizarre ones such as an ad for a flu cure called "carbolic smoke ball" that became the subject of an important English contract law case. Over much of their history, newspapers have received and spent their own advertising expenditure. The move online, and particularly towards the centralised, metric-driven ad systems of Google, was to change this. By 2010, as journalism scholar Richard Collins wrote, "Advertising revenues, which once funded content production and distribution, including news, are increasingly received by firms which do not produce content – Google, Yahoo, eBay and the like" (2010: 1205). Instead, the goal of website owners became to get as many hits as possible, because, as we will see in the next chapter, clicks and "impressions" (a specific ad loaded once on a person's computer) are where the money is.

Attention and its commodification by advertising has had an important role in shaping the digital landscape. Less often remarked is the role of emotion and affect in directing that attention, but what produces ad impressions better than strangely alluring headlines? In his helpful framing of the attention economy, Tim Wu (2017) tells the story of how "clickbait" developed, particularly in relation to the *Huffington Post* as a publication, but what has happened since then is that all online media platforms have come under pressure to make their content more click-friendly. As Adam Curtis put it, "angry people click" (2016). Journalism scholar Martin Conboy reminds us that journalism "has always incorporated an element of entertainment either in its content, such as human interest or witty writing style, or by its juxtaposition with more distracting pieces alongside the serious" (2004: 187), and from the cultural studies perspective, Stuart Hall and colleagues also suggested that journalists "tend to play up the extraordinary, dramatic, tragic, etc. elements in a story in order to enhance its newsworthiness" (1978: 53–54).

The enormous potential of the attention economy meant that no sooner had some of the earliest "web 2.0" cultural events taken place, new publications and platforms began to arise to exploit this explosive prospect in online media. Above we saw the example of the *Huffington Post*, described by Tim Wu — essentially a collective blog about celebrities but with an air of respectability — but many others were also founded. One of the most prominent was *BuzzFeed*, founded in 2006 by internet entrepreneur Jonah Peretti and former AOL communications director Ken Lerer, who had both helped start the *Huffington Post*, along with entrepreneur John S. Johnson. In its early days, *BuzzFeed* was known for inane, over-the-top articles featuring "listicles" and constant references to mainstream popular culture, and would elicit dismissive eyerolls and criticism from those considering themselves "serious" journalists. But despite moving into "serious" journalism from 2011, the original point of *BuzzFeed* was never intended to be about information or power in the ways that journalism had always claimed to be; the point of its irreverence and tomfoolery was to command *attention*, and it was ahead at least in this regard.

Other publications arose with a similar aim, if different tone. Celebrity news website *TMZ*, which also had an AOL connection, was launched in 2005, and *Upworthy* was founded — with the stated aim of emphasising "good news" — in 2012 by activist Eli Parisier, who had coined the phrase "filter bubble" in a book the previous year. One particularly tragic example of these attention-driven sites is Mic.com, founded in 2011 as *PolicyMic* and later renamed *Mic*, with the expressed aim of engaging younger audiences in social issues. The site quickly displayed fluency in the codified moral language of North American leftidentitarian movements, and featured headlines about various righteous individuals "clapping back" or how various pariahs were "problematic", but as an in-depth investigation of the publication later found, "In retrospect, it looks like *Mic*'s commitment to social justice was never that deep — which surprised and disappointed many of the young ideologues who went to work there. [...] *Mic* chanced upon the social justice narrative, discovered it was Facebook gold, and mined away" (Jeffries, 2017).

This sad tale is just one example of how, as journalism's core purpose of challenging true political power became less valuable in a depoliticised market-driven society, and as that market-driven society relied more and more on distraction from its core workings, there was an increased danger that journalism could function more as a simulacrum — a different kind of commodity that looked like journalism in terms of form, but did not reliably do the work of journalism as far as its message is concerned. Instead, it distracted from or misrepresented the exercise of power, rather than meaningfully scrutinising it.

In some ways, this is only a less extreme version of what happened to US television "journalism". For example, in 2013, Jeff Zucker, a former entertainment producer from NBC who had overseen shows including Donald Trump's *The Apprentice*, became president of CNN. As *Vox* journalist Carlos Maza reported in 2017, Zucker quickly set about organising the network's political coverage as though it were "sport", and fanning the flames of political theatre as played out in the feud between Donald Trump and the network.

When real "fake news" came along, detailed in the next chapter, it was only because those creating it had figured out something about digital journalism that the industry itself should have seen coming: emotion and attention, rather than truth, had become the prize commodities of the digital media landscape, with which you could make thousands of dollars. This is not to say that *all* online journalism was unreliable or became like clickbait. Some of the best reporting has increasingly come from online-only independent outlets that were successful in building a base of loyal supporters. Rather, it is to say that when subjected to the pressures of the market-driven society, veracity was only valuable if you still believed in it from a moral standpoint — a hokey, moralistic standpoint if free markets are your thing.

Digital Journalism as Craft

Finally, in consideration of how digital journalism does or does not offer value in a market-driven society, we must examine the idea of digital journalism as *craft*. As journalism and the broader media shifted online, one of the possible ways that value could have been created for audiences would have been to embrace the creative possibilities of the new HTML medium, which had features that neither print nor broadcast had ever been able to offer. In the mid-1990s, the medium was not yet mature or standardised enough and dial-up connection speeds were still too slow, but by the late 1990s and early 2000s, the possibility arose of creating interactive, visually led media that used web standards such as embedded audio, JavaScript and Scalable Vector Graphics (SVG) — a possibility that was and remains largely overlooked.

When the *New York Times* produced its *Snowfall: The Avalanche at Tunnel Creek* feature in 2012, it was widely shared and used in journalism classrooms as an example of an alternative to what online journalism could look like. While the piece was almost a complete non-story as far as traditional news values were concerned, being published nearly eleven months after the avalanche it covered, the big news was the richly layered multimedia format. But that was only an anomaly because, apart from some innovation at the *Guardian* that helped turn it from a newspaper into a digital platform, and the experimentation of a few smaller platforms, the world of online journalism had spent the last decade ignoring what was actually possible with the web from any sort of creative perspective. In the context of technology's arrival in the newsroom, journalism academics Janet Jones and Lee Salter suggest that "the internet has all too often been regarded as an economic opportunity more than an opportunity to change and improve journalistic practices" (2012: 26). The same could be said of the ways that journalism has responded to the affordances of the web as a digital medium with creative potential.

This disinterest can be explained in relation to a number of factors. The first, unsurprisingly, is that when everything is subjected to market forces, efficiency and low cost tend to be emphasised and craft and artistry tend to be minimised. Richard Sennett has described in detail the emotional investment and communitarian potential of craft, and its tendency to come into conflict with commercial logics (2008). This is an idea that journalism scholar Henrik Örnebring (2010) has also explored, specifically in relation to the theory of *de-skilling* which was proposed by US labour theorist Harry Braverman in 1974 to account for the ways that skilled processes of production were divided up into production lines according to the infamous "scientific management" theories of Frederick Winslow Taylor that gave the world modern production lines. Örnebring concluded that there had not been a de-skilling of journalism so much as a more complex process of re-skilling, and this is hard to dispute in relation to the use of technology to undertake a broader range of journalistic duties in the newsroom. However, the narrower questions of creativity, craft and the appeal of whatever media results from that labour were another matter.

Two of the most important technological developments in the transition to online media were open-source blogging software, particularly WordPress, and early social media platforms, which were loosely grouped together under the conceptual umbrella "web 2.0". As we saw in Chapter One, these both exploded in the early 2000s as digital capitalism sought new areas of value after the disastrous dot-com bubble had burst, and identified users who were looking for easier ways to express themselves and self-publish, as the source of that value. Next to the expensive and technically complex publishing systems that were otherwise on offer, these were appealing, and under the pressures of the market-driven society and the associated need for journalistic outlets and organisations to quickly adapt and become dominant on the internet, they were increasingly adopted.

This blog-centric de-skilled model may have been meant emancipatory self-publishing in a way that prefigured social media, but as far as the *craft* of producing online media, its adoption by professionals was a missed opportunity. A text editing window and a big shiny button that said "publish" implemented almost as Taylorist an approach to the online medium itself as it was possible to have, assuming that the only skills that mattered were older ones that predated the internet such as writing, rather than assisting journalism organisations and other users to implement the range of exciting new technologies and standards that continued to be developed for the web browser. The ongoing compatibility issues of the "browser wars" in which Microsoft's "standards" and the W3C's official web standards often did not align, revealed a second hindrance of the market-driven society on the maturation of visually engaging, interactive web-based media. And journalism's competitive impulses in that market-driven society tended to lead towards getting the story first, rather than in telling it best, which added a third.

One of the later attempts to reverse this disregard for the creative affordances of the web came later in the form of a "pivot to video", which was also motivated by a growing awareness of the attention economy. The idea was that given the saturation of text that journalism consisted of, it was a better idea to embrace video, which was somehow richer and more engaging as a medium. As digital media strategist and journalist Heidi Moore (2017) pointed out, there were quite a few problems with the basic assumptions of this strategy — video is skill-intensive and time-consuming to produce well, which makes it expensive in a professional environment; the user experience of videos online, and particularly given the ways that advertising has been integrated into playback, is poor; and totally different skills were needed to produce good videos than the ones that existing writers often had. But what this transition, which saw outlets like *BuzzFeed* lose a lot of money and audience, also revealed was a reductive understanding of the very object of producing those media in the first place, which was not so much about *which* technology was used, but about how successfully and thoroughly it resulted in an engaging and valuable experience for audiences above all else. The sense that a specific technology or medium such as "video" might be the magic bullet to counter the decreasing fortunes of a struggling online journalism industry caught between the Scylla of declining revenues and the Charybdis of audiences accustomed to getting everything, including the public service of journalism for free, was utterly misguided and simplistic. As some journalists and media-makers have demonstrated on platforms like YouTube and TikTok, video can be an engaging and highly creative medium, if and only if both content and form are carefully considered from the audience's perspective. One illustration of the enduring value of craft is the growth of podcasting, which provides an interesting contrast to the mostly disastrous "pivot to video". Podcasts were invented years before their popularity, but after steady growth in the 2010s, a rich and diverse ecosystem of spoken word media emerged. The number of US Americans aged 12 and over who had listened to a podcast in the past grew almost fivefold from 11% in 2006 to 51% in 2019, with a third having listened in the last month (Edison Research, 2019).

The Troubles in/with Journalism

It may be helpful here to summarise the arguments of this chapter. We know from prior chapters that post-war democratic aspirations degraded into a market-driven society built on the extreme implementation of a free-market ethos. Instead of challenge this process in the name of the public that it claimed to serve, the professionalised world of journalism largely facilitated and sometimes supported this process — whether unwittingly, because of a misguided interpretation of "objectivity" as impartiality, because of its ownership models, or because of its bourgeois addiction to an economic status quo that it did not wish to challenge. Unfortunately, the development of the market-driven society was not good for journalism either, because while journalism is or may sometimes aspire to be a part of the fabric of democracy, democracy and its other constituent parts — economics, social affairs, culture, education and so forth — are also a part of the fabric of journalism. Without them being in a healthy state, journalism also cannot function effectively or be valued properly, and merely becomes just another kind of "content" competing for clicks, attention and advertising revenue. If journalism is "fake", this is only in the sense that it has been reduced to the simulacrum of "content" by a system that it was partially responsible for challenging.

Indeed, all three of the issues explored above — paywalls, attention and craft — point to different commodification pressures on journalism as it both moved online and adapted to the ever-intensifying pressures of the market-driven society. All three also indicate the development of an even more pervasive commodification: the slow transition to "content". The word "content" is used a lot when online media are discussed, but rarely if ever are the implications of its usage really interrogated. What we may have been acknowledging or confirming in our casual normalisation of this word is the metamorphosis of not only journalism but also music, video, photography and commercial copy into an imagined commodity with an extremely interesting and varied set of use values.

Chapter Six
Digital Distortions

We live in capitalism.
Its power seems inescapable.
So did the divine right of kings.
Any human power can be resisted and changed by human beings.
— Ursula Le Guin

The BAFTAs like to think of themselves as the British version of the Oscars. In February 2020, a friend of mine posted a picture of himself posing with a BAFTA to his Instagram account. The caption and hashtags made it clear that he himself had not won a BAFTA, and was merely posing with the physical trophy in a performative, ironic way. Much to his initial embarrassment, my friend, who admittedly has a sizeable online following of his own, began receiving sincere congratulations from various online acquaintances for his having "won" a BAFTA, despite his caption. Initially, he attempted to correct people, clarifying that he had not in fact won the prestigious award, before the volume of congratulatory feedback became too much for him to respond to. He called me for a chat, and we both had a good laugh about the ridiculousness of it. I sarcastically congratulated him on his "award". To these followers, many of who were truly sympathetic and supportive of his work, he had "won" a BAFTA — despite not actually having won it, and there being no official announcement of it anywhere on the internet. But he was powerless to "un-win" it, without painstakingly messaging dozens of people individually to explain what was in the grand scheme of things a small factual misapprehension.

As this amusing encounter suggests, to observe that digital platforms like Instagram have become central to the ways that information, misinformation and disinformation are communicated and shared, is to observe that the Pope might be Catholic. Yet I have left these platforms until the end of the story, as far as this book is concerned, precisely because they are so often made into the beginning of the story of how we explain the prevalence of misinformation and disinformation in our societies — usually at the cost of not properly understanding those issues. For a variety of interesting reasons, there is a tendency towards a way of thinking that scholars call "technological determinism". The sociologist Judy Wajcman defines technological determinism as the "pervasive" view that in its most extreme form assumes that "technological innovation is the most important cause of change in society" (2014: 27). The key words here are "most important". Nobody is denying that technology has an impact. My friend's experience, recounted above, illustrates the distinct and alarming ways in which digital platforms amplify and exacerbate certain forms of misinformation and disinformation. It also reveals the ways in which more official sources of verification are either absent from the forms of interaction common to consumption-driven digital platforms, or overwhelmed by the scale that these platforms enable.

But researchers who study any aspect of technology and society continually have to push back against technological determinism precisely because this way of looking at the world obscures the much more complicated relationship between technology, culture, psychology, politics and economics that is played out when for, example, people's names enter the "trending" section of Twitter or politicians undertake awkward publicity stunts on Instagram. We saw in Chapter Four how technology *positivism* can distort our understanding of what are political questions, but technology-blaming in response to political issues can be just as unhelpful. Either way, the implicit message of a technology-centric argument is a call for more or better technology, rather than understanding and alleviating the thornier and more complex problems and market-driven thinking that often lie beneath.

In earlier chapters, this book told a much broader story about the culturally reproduced forms of misinformation in the market-driven society: about the tendency of political alienation and informational disempowerment to produce conspiracy theories, encouraged by that culture to overlook the dominant economic powers that have led to that disempowerment; about the moral and intellectual bankruptcy of liberal capitalism in its desperation to look anywhere *except* the forms of power that actually need to be challenged in order to make the world fairer and more democratic; about the tendency for some journalists who have imbibed these aspects of our societies to further redistribute and amplify them. These factors hopefully make technology-centric arguments untenable and invite us to make a different kind of analysis which recognises that, even when technology is providing the platform for our disinformation, the networks, the code, the like buttons, the data harvesting and news feed algorithms, and even when its design and features do have significant impact on those processes, we can be sure that our susceptibility to these systems was much longer in the making than any app or website. The unreliability of the information we receive about the world has its origins largely in social, political and economic aspects of how that world is arranged. The question to be examined here is what happens when these existing forces of misinformation and disinformation move online.

Public Conversations and Spaces

In the 1990s, internet utopians loved the idea that the web represented a *separate space*, often called "cyberspace". As law scholar Julie S. Cohen has pointed out, the very idea of the internet or of the early world wide web as a separate space was something of a utopian construct (2007: 216). Like technological determinism, this "cyber-exceptionalism" became a rather embarrassing cliché, and often a marker of intergenerational differences in how digital platforms were understood, particularly when certain voices used to claim that digitally mediated conversations were the "new town square" and similar formulations. Thankfully, there have always been scholars such as Cohen and many others who have ventured more nuanced and sophisticated approaches, meanwhile most of my undergraduate students now begin their studies never even having heard the term "cyberspace", and quite rightly so: the concept simply does not apply to their experience of anything digitally networked. There have always been vibrant subcultures composed of individuals who met online around a common interest, but most of the things that take place on today's digital platforms matter precisely because they are mediations of real-world social, economic and political relations and issues. The key is more in this process of mediation: How are conversations impacted or even distorted by the digital platforms where they take place, and how are those economic, political and social relations themselves impacted by these platforms?

There are in fact some lessons we can at least learn from certain spatial comparisons — provided that we avoid the direct application of spatial thinking to the web. The journalism scholar Karin Wahl-Jorgensen helpfully compares the design of online platforms to the architecture of public spaces in a way that avoids any clichés about the activities themselves, and explores the ways in which design of public space has been used to influence the emotional relationship between the people who gather there, the things that happen there, and the powers that have undertaken that design; for example, in the case of fascist architecture (2019: 147). To centre the relationship between design and people, rather than an amorphous mass of "social media", is a really useful way to approach the problems at issue here because design always entails a degree of intentionality: *somebody* always designs in order to achieve some specific ends, even if there are also unintended consequences from that design. As a process, design also intrinsically involves power over economic relations and social conventions, and the design of public space is a useful comparator partly because of the ways that it explicitly brings this power and intentionality together with that which is *public*.

I have written elsewhere about how the informational and factual potential of social media is undermined by the affect- and emotion-centric design and commercial orientation of social networks, who collect data on what moves you and commands your attention, so that they can sell that attention to their clients, who want to sell you things (2017). If you are looking for media to pass the time, to make you feel better about the world or about your life, or to make you feel anything at all, these are all very different motivations than genuinely looking for information that will shift your understanding of the world. Even if the two are not strictly mutually exclusive, they are very different priorities. Indeed, misinformation can be far more engaging.

Even if the conversations on social media are not always public, and the issues being discussed are not always civic issues, the digital networks where misinformation and disinformation occurs have facilitated a *public sphere-like* interaction, alongside the unending self-promotion and increasingly complex TikTok dance routines. As we examine digital platforms, we need to maintain the nuance and caution of Cohen's and Wahl-Jorgensen's thinking, along with many others. They are both continuous and distinct at the same time: on the whole we should consider them as an *extension* of the world we have built, and as a faithful manifestation of the market-driven society, but there are also important differences in the functioning of these networks as places for public conversation and exposure.

Actual "Fake News"

The most obvious examples of online misinformation and disinformation are probably those whose appearance gave rise to the concept of "fake news" to begin with, before the meaning of the phrase melted and congealed into the various broader meanings given at the beginning of this book: rumours, hoaxes, lies, exaggerations, myths, or the dismissal of accurate, factual information on the basis of its political inconvenience. As is quite widely known, these cases involved individuals distributing shocking but untrue stories which were often picked up and "went viral", leading to considerable people being misinformed. The most notable of these individuals were a US man called Paul Horner and a loose network of young people in the city of Veles, in what is now known as North Macedonia.

Although these instances of online disinformation may have been widely remarked at the time, a brief summary is important here too, so that they can be considered in the broader context provided by prior chapters. Horner, who died in September 2017 from an overdose of opioids, was sometimes described as a "hoax artist", and was insistent that he was doing a public service with his hoaxes. He claimed in an interview on a Russian propaganda outlet that there was "good fake news" and "bad fake news", and that he was the former because he always had some kind of good intention in mind to ameliorate some lesser social ill. The old maxim that "the road to hell is paved with good intentions" comes to mind. In some cases, it is easier to see these good intentions in evidence in what Horner did; for example, in response to the phenomenon of "swatting", in which false police reports would lead an armed police response team to arrive at and potentially raid the victim's address, Horner circulated a false news story about a young man being sentenced to lengthy imprisonment for having done so, in a bid to dissuade others from doing the same thing. But most of the stories he circulated displayed at best a callous disregard for the causes that he claimed they might help, as well as for a broader social and political landscape of which he appeared to have had no idea. Another of his stories that achieved widespread circulation was about an entirely fictional "rape festival" in the region of Assam in northeastern India. As proof of its positive intention and impact, Horner said it had raised $250,000 for the charity *Give India*, although this was never verified. The actual article, which refers to India as a "backwards country" and tells the reader that "men all over India" are looking forward to the festival, points to a very different conclusion about Horner's understanding not only of his own work, but of the world in which he was operating. The story is predicated on the assumption that since there had been a number of abhorrent and brutal sex crimes in parts of India, it was perfectly acceptable to exaggerate these into a wholly inaccurate stereotype of the population and attitudes of the country as a whole. But racist hyperbole dressed as "satire" is not redeemed by raising money for a charity, however worthy, especially if for every person who donates, several more read the article without doing so and are left with the impression that India is a country that would tolerate such a festival. Similarly, in the case of Donald Trump's campaign for the presidency in 2016 when the US was still getting used to the idea that Trump, repeatedly dismissed and written off, actually had a chance of being elected president, Horner published articles that, whatever their intension, arguably would have conferred a degree of legitimacy on Trump, if anything. Examples included the idea that the "Amish lobby" had decided to back Donald Trump — which subtly communicated the endorsement of a peaceful, devout, religious community who have moral rather than material reasons for supporting him — and that supporters of Hillary Clinton had been paid thousands of dollars to disrupt Trump rallies. This latter hoax was later shared by Trump's 2016 campaign manager Corey Lewandowski, which suggested conversely that the reasons for supporting Clinton over Trump might be material rather than moral. At the very least, these attempts at satire, if that is what they truly were, were politically illiterate in the extreme. Horner later admitted that his stories might have assisted Trump in an interview with the *Washington Post*, but his defence was to simply blame people reading his articles for being dumb:

> Honestly, people are definitely dumber. They just keep passing stuff around. Nobody fact-checks anything anymore — I mean, that's how Trump got elected. He just said whatever he wanted, and people believed everything, and when the things he said turned out not to be true, people didn't care because they'd already accepted it. It's real scary. I've never seen anything like it.

Even if this may have been true, besides the total foolishness of blaming your own audience, the more obvious question that he should have been asked by the *Post* was why, if he was aware of the potential harm, he kept doing it? There was some indication of his motivations, however. In the same interview, although Horner claimed to hate Trump, he admitted that targeting conservative voters who "keep passing stuff around" was far more profitable, financially speaking — earning as much as $10,000 from a single story (Dewey, 2016).

This was the same motivation that drove the networks of false content originating in Veles, North Macedonia. Around the time what was happening in Veles was discovered, commentary abounded that portrayed the city as a seedy place full of drugs, vice and corruption, of which the "racket" of "fake news" had become a part. But in a sense, much of this coverage was itself misleading, if not as much as the web content that brought notoriety to Veles to begin with. Those journalists who actually bothered to go to the city and understand it better found a different problem: poverty.

After the dissolution of Yugoslavia in the years following the end of the Cold War, Veles plummeted from being a prosperous, industrial hub supported by a state-controlled economy, well located in the south of Europe, to being extremely poor. Its factories closed, its professionals emigrated, and much of the newer international investment aimed at the newly independent country's capital Skopje, a relatively short drive up a NATO-financed road from Veles (Harris, 2017). The average monthly salary in Veles had been approximately $370 before the inflated earnings of the digital advertising world, explored later in this chapter, began to arrive (Subramanian, 2017). But poverty is not the whole story either. Despite having been hit particularly hard by the breakup of Yugoslavia, "What a passing visitor does not see is the myriad innovative ways people have found to fill the vacuum the state left, the legacy of highly skilled and aspirational citizens and the vibrant, highly cultivated social networks which provide community support" (Harris, 2017). Part of this is a history of digital advertising that predates their infamy, that is more complicated than the narrative of a "fake news goldrush" amongst teenagers that was repeated ad infinitum once Veles was discovered. Before Trump even announced his campaign, there were Macedonian-run websites pushing health and beauty tips — disinformation of a different kind: "An incessant stream of natural remedies you might hear about from your grandmother, repackaged and amplified for the gullible millions worldwide now hungry for instant transformation" (ibid.). Let us not forget the disinformation intrinsic to consumerism — including the world of skincare — explored in the second chapter. One of the more well-known stories from Veles was one in which Pope Francis had endorsed Donald Trump (note the similarity to the "Amish lobby" story in terms of subtext), but much of the content was also plagiarised from US-based alt-right websites and simply re-published.

Within the circles of journalism study, there is an oft-cited article by Johan Galtung and Mari Holmboe Ruge from 1965. Ostensibly an obscure offering in the *Journal of Peace Research*, analysing the presentation of concurrent crises in Congo, Cuba and Cyprus in four Norwegian newspapers, it became one of the most important pieces of scholarly work in the study of journalism for its analysis of an important question: What makes something into news? Galtung and Ruge posited a series of hypotheses, from frequency to negativity to cultural distance, and analysed each one in detail. Both Horner and the young people of Veles figured out essentially the same "news values" as Galtung and Ruge had, but took them to the extreme, minus one important feature: shocking and unusual news that displays a suitable combination of cultural familiarity and distance does not actually have to be true to still conform to the principles of news values. In fact, ironically it can exemplify these values even more by being set free of the obligation to accuracy. And so "fake news" was born.

There are a number of important points to draw out of these examples. As I have pointed out, one of the more important and perhaps obvious is the role of money in both. Even if Horner's social and cultural context were very different from that of the young men and women of an impoverished young republic thousands of miles away in the Balkans, the financial motivations in each case are clear, and will be important later in this chapter. Secondly, and even more importantly, we see that the narrative in which "people do something online, and the system is destabilised" is also simplistic at best — a reminder that much of the way the world responded to the crisis of misinformation and disinformation on digital networks was itself misguided. Horner's work was itself the product of a profoundly misinformed worldview that was likely shaped by the far more serious and prevalent forms of cultural misinformation that are analysed in earlier chapters. Not only did he measure the supposed positive impact of his claim to "satire" in financial terms, but he was also blind to the damaging limitations of his own good intentions.

In the case of Veles, since a technologically determinist argument was less feasible, commentary turned to a moral one, laced with leftover Cold War arrogance: these are poor people who are bad because they were deprived of capitalism! Actually, as is clear from the more detailed and attentive reporting from Veles, much of the "fake news" that was published there was as a means to make a bit of pocket money from a rapidly deteriorating political situation thousands of miles away in order to afford nice cars and holidays — exactly the form of materialistic nihilism that one would expect from a society where the transition to market-driven capitalism was so swift. Veles is not the only place where these types of things occur. There have been numerous reports of a significant operation in Kosovo, again targeting harshly polarised US politics for advertising revenue. One "Police Lives Matter" Facebook page, with over 170,000 "likes" in September 2019 when it was reported, was found to have been run from Kosovo. Despite looking surprisingly convincing in comparison to the genuine, US-run versions of such pages, it was riddled with misinformation and incendiary posts that linked to a website where ads were being shown (Legum, 2019).

The closer we look at these high-profile examples of "fake news", the more obvious it becomes that they were the inevitable outcome of a world that has decided that the accumulation of wealth is the most important thing there is. In 2019, digital advertising was a \$330bn global business, largely dominated by Google and Facebook (Uberti, 2019). For advertisers, there are two important factors: exposure and attention. These can be roughly understood as the difference between seeing and looking. Just as with an ordinary billboard next to a busy highway, an ad may have a high degree of exposure without necessarily commanding much conscious attention or interest, but there is no attention without exposure. Advertisers obviously care primarily about attention, but over the history of the web it has been more difficult to cultivate than expected, because human beings are not robots who give every area of their screens equal attention. As early as the nascent web of the 1990s, the phenomenon of "banner blindness" was observed, in which web users hardly saw banner ads unless looking at them was directly related to the functionality of the page they were on (Benway, 1998).

The key to getting people's attention was not to make better ads — advertising as an art form was perfected long ago. The pioneering strategy of Google from 2000 onwards was not only to build the ads into other attention-intensive activities such as searching the web or, later, reading email, but to use the search terms or email contents as data to ensure the most relevant possible ads to the task at hand are shown, because this is what gives advertisers the best chance of getting a user's meaningful attention.

This strategy is not just applied to Google's own products, such as search and email, however — it is also built into third-party websites, and this is where "fake news" providers enter the picture. Besides search advertising, one of the most common forms of advertising is a system called AdSense, in which any website can have Google-brokered ads installed onto it by the owner, who gets a cut of whatever the advertiser has paid. The owner of any website simply needs to put a piece of code provided by Google on their website, and then Google will replace the code with an ad. Every time the website is loaded, a real-time auction is run between all the different advertisers whose ads are deemed relevant to the user viewing the website, based on the data Google holds about that person. The winning ad is shown, and the owner of the website is rewarded financially with a tiny sum for this exposure, known as an "impression". If the ad is actually clicked, the reward will be greater. The only way to make any money as a website owner is by getting hundreds of thousands of views on your website, and as many clicks on those ads as possible (although click-through-rates are usually below 1%). Obviously, this means that website owners, from professional journalistic outlets to troll sites to cynical hoaxes like those above, are all incentivised to get as many "impressions" and "clickthroughs" as possible.

Not only are the creators of the "fake news" encouraged by the financial gain this system potentially enables, above and beyond the repercussions of the content they may be publishing, it is also essential to interrogate the very structure of advertising that makes the whole arrangement possible. As the digital ethics researcher James Williams has written, "If advertising was previously said to be 'underwriting' the dominant design goals of a medium, in digital media it now seemed to be 'overwriting' them with its own" (2018: 32). Criteria for which users represent an appropriate audience for which ads is based on a large number of factors, all of which are stored by Google as data. Has that pair of shoes you were admiring online been following you from website to website? That is because the products you have viewed are sometimes included in those data, and a technique called "retargeting" or "remarketing" decides to keep advertising you the product it is now established that you were interested in, in the hope that you buy it. This kind of browsing data is collected by companies such as DoubleClick, a Google subsidiary bought in 2007 for over $3bn after a fierce bidding war with Microsoft. But data can also be derived from anything else that Google knows about you from your Gmail inbox or YouTube history. In 2012, Google changed its terms of service so that audience data from things like emails could be shared across the advertising technologies used on all its platforms, and in 2016 their end-user terms of service were amended so that all of this data could be combined with that from DoubleClick.

Attention, as we can see here, truly is the commodity, and data has become the means to command it. As Nick Srnicek puts it:

> there is a convergence of surveillance and profit making in the digital economy, which leads some to speak of "surveillance capitalism". Key to revenues, however, is not just the collection of data, but also the analysis of data. Advertisers are interested less in unorganised data and more in data that give them insights or match them to likely consumers. [...] What is sold to advertisers is therefore not

the data themselves, but rather the promise that Google's software will correctly match an advertiser with the correct users when needed. (2017: 57)

Facebook took this strategy a step further by turning their social network into a complex system designed to gather as much data as possible about the lives and tastes of intended consumers, subject it to sophisticated algorithmic analysis, and then target those intended consumers with ads that are as relevant and culturally and emotionally salient as possible. It became fashionable to say that Facebook "sells your data", particularly after the Cambridge Analytica scandal, but, just as in the case of Google, the primary commodity that Facebook and its subsidiaries and imitators came to be built around was never data, but *attention*. Of course Facebook gathers data, even from private messages, and consumer data is bought and sold by a number of companies known as data brokers, but its value is almost entirely derived from its use in better securing the *attention* of would-be consumers, so that they become more likely to click ads and, ultimately, to make purchases. Far from the cigars and cocktail dresses of period drama *Mad Men*, advertising has become a data-driven world (Leslie, 2018).

Finally, it is important to say something about the audiences of advertising-driven hoax websites that gave rise to the idea of "fake news". It should be clear already that, as far as the inherent flaws in the world of data-driven advertising, and the way that its design meant that *attempts* to short-circuit that system were virtually assured, the major share of responsibility lies with those companies like Facebook and Google, and with those who have used their products to distribute hoaxes and other incendiary content for financial reward. But amidst all of the fear about teenagers in Veles or the misguided "satire" of Paul

Horner, very few people seemed to ask the question of why we were so susceptible to these media in the first place.

Hoaxes have a long history, and are not a digital phenomenon. While their content may tell us something about the moment in history in which they originated, their basic effectiveness is not reflective of the market-driven society any more than any other kind of society. But as I argued in Chapter Two, there are forms of cultural misinformation and disinformation that leave us vulnerable to being misled. Part of this is about how equipped people are to deal with the information they encounter via digital platforms. A 2016 report by the Stanford History Education Group looking at the information literacy of US school pupils across different levels remarked that:

> We would hope that middle school students could distinguish an ad from a news story. By high school, we would hope that students reading about gun laws would notice that a chart came from a gun owners' political action committee. And, in 2016, we would hope college students, who spend hours each day online, would look beyond a .org URL and ask who's behind a site that presents only one side of a contentious issue. But in every case and at every level we were taken aback by students' lack of preparation. (Wineburg et al., 2016: 4)

The following year, however, the study was attempted on a smaller scale by different researchers in Finland, a country that is widely regarded to have one of the best education systems in the world. Although it is probably wise not to take the study as entirely conclusive given its relatively small sample size and different team of researchers, the results appeared to be radically different. Whether it was in the "evaluating evidence", "Facebook argument", or "News on Facebook" categories, students in Finland doing

International Baccalaureate programmes were comfortably ahead of the result from the US study. Furthermore, the study highlighted that there was also a difference between the older and younger age groups in the Finnish education system, suggesting that Finnish school students progress as they get older, whereas the claim of the US study was that "there were no measurable differences between grade levels in their study" (Horn & Veermans, 2019).

However ill-prepared US teenagers may have been to discern unreliable information online, a different study found that there were also significant inter-generational differences. Even when controlling for other demographic factors, one study found that those over sixty-five years of age were nearly seven times more likely to share links to articles on "fake news" websites of the type that would be associated with Paul Horner or set up by teenagers in the heart of southern Europe (Guess, Nagler & Tucker, 2019). Despite finding that very few people overall shared any articles from these websites, the study also found that "Republicans in our sample shared more stories from fake news domains than Democrats", and that "Conservatives, especially those identifying as 'very conservative,' shared the most articles from fake news domains". However, this was caveated with the important observation that "This is consistent with the pro-Trump slant of most fake news articles produced during the 2016 campaign, and of the tendency of respondents to share articles they agree with, and thus might not represent a greater tendency of conservatives to share fake news than liberals conditional on being exposed to it." Either way, this leads perfectly to the next important aspect of online misinformation and disinformation: "filter bubbles" and "echo chambers".

Filter Bubbles and Echo Chambers

Two of the most commonly discussed issues after the seeming eruption of longstanding reactionary politics since 2016 have been the related ideas of "filter bubbles" and "echo chambers", which remain pervasive. Political polarisation, so goes the theory, is driven by the separation of politically divergent positions and communities, so that exposure to information and expression of outrage take place only in contact with those who are already politically in broad agreement. The *Wall Street Journal* published an experiment called "Blue Feed Red Feed" that appeared to demonstrate the phenomenon in a US context: strongly "liberal" articles on one side, supporting Hillary Clinton and a number of common talking points within the US's broad coalition of divergent "blue" voices; and harshly conservative, reactionary positions on the "red" side, depending on the issue chosen. Part of the explanation for how Trump and Brexit were possible, it is alleged, lay in how social networks had fractured what was otherwise a far less dysfunctional public sphere, allowing the populism of Donald Trump and Nigel Farage to spread unchallenged. Numerous commentators have spoken about the dangers of "filter bubbles" and "echo chambers" to society, and held them up as proof of the pernicious effects of social media. US law scholar Cass Sunstein, one of the most prominent voices of warning about "echo chambers", describes the problem by remarking that:

> When people use Facebook to see exactly what they want to see, their understanding of the world can be greatly affected. Your Facebook friends might provide a big chunk of the news on which you focus, and if they have a distinctive point of view, that's the point of view that you'll see most. (2018: 2)

The fear seems to be that, if our social interaction is merged with the means we have for news discovery and political exposure, we will be heavily influenced to see politics in a particular way that is determined by our connections on social media platforms. Perhaps it is already clear what the issues are with this claim, but there are actually three major issues here: the existing fragmentation of the media landscape as far as political ideology is concerned; the tendency for social life more broadly to follow the contours of divisive political issues — as explored in the last chapter; and the actual empirical study of what social networks themselves actually expose us to.

As far as the media landscape is concerned, part of the concern about "echo chambers" and "filter bubbles" has arguably been driven by an implicit desire to protect the simplistic ideal of a "public sphere", discussed in Chapter Two, using technologically determinist arguments, and without noticing that broad public sphere does not really exist anyway. To recall the philosopher Nancy Fraser's critique of the idea of the public sphere, she argued that to the extent there even *was* a singular public sphere, social factors such as racism, sexism and class barriers could limit participation and influence in it. Indeed, the ways that we "meet" online are also highly unequal. Any imagination that Twitter, for example, is a democratic "public sphere" is defeated not only by the abundance of abuse and misinformation, as we will see, but as media scholar Natalie Fenton has observed, that "the top 10% are dominated by celebrities or mainstream media corporations such as CNN. [...] 60% of twitter users have fewer than 100 followers, while those with over 1,000 are in the 97th percentile" (2016: 149).

Meanwhile, the concerns about filter bubbles also seem to be driven by the Enlightenment-style positivism around "debate" and "free speech" within that public sphere, which presupposes that the more opinions a person encounters, the greater the overall benefit to that person and to the overall public sphere in which their political engagement takes place, as if this was some sort of linear, quantitative exercise that could be plotted on a line graph. Sunstein does not even make it to Chapter One of his book on social media and politics without an obligatory quote of Enlightenment philosopher John Stuart Mill, saying that "it is hardly possible to overrate the value, in the present low state of human improvement, of placing human beings in contact with persons dissimilar to themselves" (2018: xi). Again, we saw in Chapter Four and Five that this idea of everything being a "debate" — in a sort of phony-liberal, fascism-friendly way — affords attention to a newly emboldened fascism as it permeates the attention economy that the market-driven society has created, and is actually an inhibition of the very liberty and reason that its proponents hope it will produce.

Obviously, there has always been political diversity in the broader media landscape, and, as Nancy Fraser suggests, democratic participation is probably more likely with a "plurality of competing publics than by a single, comprehensive public sphere" (1990: 68). Most people were choosing the media that they agreed with or felt some kind of affinity with long before Facebook was even imagined, and since it is essentially impossible for a news report *not* to involve some kind of ideological framing, as we saw in the last chapter, the only difference from one outlet to the next is how conscious this kind of ideologically driven media choice is for audiences, and how explicitly it is communicated by producers. Just as Fox News takes certain positions and is watched by viewers who have a preference for the type of positions that the network will take, the same is true with most other TV news, newspapers, magazines and websites — even if they also claim to be "fair and balanced". The fact that journalism has had to think of itself as a *product* in the ways explored in the last chapter does not make this any better.

Beyond ideological fault-lines in the *media* landscape, there is also the issue of whether our ideological preferences on timeline media platforms, specifically, are socially determined in a way that is different enough to older forms of media to justify the panic and discussion that the issue of echo chambers has led to. Even assuming social media channels can comprise "echo chambers" in the strict sense of there being a high incidence of concordant political views, are other means of culturally similar habitual social interaction not also echo chambers? Indeed, Cass Sunstein writes that "in countless domains, human beings show 'homophily': a strong tendency to connect and bond with people who are like them" (2018: 1), but if this is the case, surely the problem he and others are talking about is one that is not actually caused by or unique to social media at all. Even if your political exposure is partially determined by your social relations on Facebook, how is this dramatically different from friends shaping your political views? Is it *so* different from going to a bar or sharing an apartment with close friends? Is the preferred alternative that all of us are primarily or only influenced into thinking by mainstream journalism, rather than by our social relations? Particularly given the issues in the last chapter, this would seem to be a rather naïve, positivist assumption. Not only do mainstream media tend to be a source of influence as well, but there is also a well-studied history to suggest that news consumption has *always* been a social act (Anderson, 2006), and indeed that *all* media consumption is to some extent an inherently social process (Childress, 2012).

When the question of how online "echo chambers" and "filter bubbles" are different to other forms of homophily is posed, the answer that is usually given involves algorithms — decision-making software that in this context is used to automatically choose what to include in a timeline. In contrast to the natural tendency to select media and sources we agree with on social media, which scholars have called "self-selected personalisation", this type of technologically determined exposure to specific content has been called "pre-selected personalisation", because it takes place automatically when a social media timeline is loaded (Zuiderveen Borgesius et al., 2016). Generally, we are right to be suspicious of algorithms that are designed to target users with whichever content will maximise the attractive power of the social media timeline (Gilroy-Ware, 2017). Even if the source code remains secret, repeated news reports have shown that the *intention* in creating these algorithms is cynical and manipulative, and at best is reckless as to the effects this could have as far as learning about political issues and participation in the overall debates that are said to constitute a democracy. Pre-selection is not being offered as a pro-bono curatorial service for internet content because Mark Zuckerberg and his pals are nice guys — indeed, the last few years have shown social media giants, and especially Facebook, to be fundamentally antithetical to the good of the public or of the civic issues affecting that public.

The experiences that people have that drive the filter bubble and echo chamber myths are quite possibly real. When we wake up on the morning of an election, or during a moment of civil unrest, our Twitter or Facebook feeds may well contain an elevated amount of politically themed content. But however much we may rightly distrust social media platforms, the idea that their algorithmic timelines significantly intensify the homophily of our social lives or the pre-selection that we apply both to social media sources and media as a whole is tenuous. Exposure is a crucial aspect of what comprises the online public conversations in which we participate, and to a certain extent there is no denying that algorithmically driven pre-selection feeds us more of what we already like, and its ability to detect our interest in cake-decoration, steam engines or championship boxing before suggesting more of the same is surely obvious to most users. It is well known that Facebook makes calculations about the political orientations of its users, but there is nothing to suggest that their timeline algorithms are sophisticated enough to reliably determine the political leanings of every single piece of content and screen out the ones a user may disagree with on that basis alone. Your partner's righteous and uncompromising anti-fascist militancy and your racist uncle's conspiracy theories will frequently appear side by side, even if the former is a source of pride and the latter one of consistent eye rolls, if not shame. Even if algorithms do amplify the voices we are inclined to agree with, this does not mean that they suppress those that we don't (Zuiderveen Borgesius et al., 2016).

Furthermore, not all timeline media exhibit the same uses and features, and few would argue, for example, that Twitter and Facebook operate in the same way or provide their users with the same types of political discussion. Depending on numerous factors, not least the design features of whichever social media platform you are on, the degree to which you use it, and how important your political views are generally, any political coverage or discussion a user encounters may be concordant to a greater or lesser extent. Indeed, some types of political issues lend themselves to more grouping than others. A 2015 study of Twitter in the journal *Psychological Science* found that more explicitly political processes such as elections and government shutdowns did resemble slightly more ideologically convergent "echo chambers", while discussion of news events such as terrorist attacks did not (Barberá et al., 2015). At most, what this suggests is that, for the habitual processes of already partisan democratic politics, ideologically identified groupings have formed, but this is still not necessarily very different to or separate from those groups who support specific political parties, or choose newspapers or other media that accord with their broad political leanings, and is a long way away from supporting any argument that social media platforms actually produce political polarisation at a societal level.

Probably the most thorough scholarship on this issue to date is by the digital media scholar Axel Bruns, who takes a similarly sceptical view. While those who do consume political media in some form may already be participating in an intrinsically social process, the extent to which people go onto social media themselves to seek out politics or news varies widely and tends to be overstated (Bruns, 2018; Gilroy-Ware, 2017). The fact that those "echo chambers" that have been observed are generally present only during more exceptional political events suggests that when those who are not normally political online are pulled into political engagement by unusual and dramatic events, they are not pulled into "echo chambers". As Bruns writes, studies have tended to suggest that those who are consciously motivated to seek out news and explicitly political coverage on social media are exposed to a *greater* variety of political opinions than they would have been exposed to using other forms of media, because as numerous scholars have observed, social media platforms tend to bring about "context collapse", in which multiple different strands of a person's life — work, friends, family — tend to be merged into a single experience. Above all, the idea of an online conversation, particularly one oriented around explicitly ideological themes, being a sort of saccharine, frictionless repetition of exactly the same political views with no differences of opinion, seems a bit far-fetched to anyone who has actually attempted to discuss politics online. Even in groups where users have come together around a shared interest or purpose, disagreement and challenge are frequent occurrences (Bruns, 2018), particularly given that digitally mediated discussion is on the whole a lot less inhibited than face-to-face interaction (Suler, 2004).

Not only are filter bubbles still largely unproven, but what evidence there is suggests that, far from filter bubbles as they are commonly understood *producing* polarisation or extreme politics, it is extreme politics that tends to lead to separation on social media networks. Where offline networks involve strongly convergent thinking, such as in extreme online communities, the use of online networks will also tend to have some degree of conformity as well. In Bruns' discussion of German far-right party Alternative für Deutschland, for example, he writes that "Only the AfD and its supporters, who reject this consensus-based democratic model in favour of an autocratic and polarising style of politics, inhabit a separate echo chamber of connections around shared populist obsessions, which may also give rise to a filter bubble of exclusionary in-group communication" (2019: 70).

It is understandable that, as people grasp the enormity of what social media platforms mean for our public conversations, they would begin to construct accounts of the world that help to make sense of that predicament. But as we have seen throughout this book in different ways, narratives about the world, whether the darkest conspiracy theory or the blandest shareholder report, tend to be structured by social, economic and political processes, with technology as an assistant rather than an instigator. Rather than social media creating "echo chambers" in the way that is alleged, it is more the case that once political outcomes "liberal" society considered impossible started to happen, the technology that had revealed how polarised society had become behind the thick curtain of technology positivism and Enlightenment thinking became the villain in itself. It is important to scrutinise social media platforms, and as we'll see below, there is much to be criticised about them, but it is also essential that the criticisms we make are accurate, or we fight them with one hand tied behind our back.

Internet Reductivism

Taking all of the caveats and social and political explorations in this book as a foundation, there is nonetheless something to the character of political discussions mediated over the internet that feels extremely reductive. Recall from Chapter Two the idea of "negative entropy" — the tendency for complex, even chaotic issues to be simplified and reduced over time.

Part of this tendency is the way in which technology and culture combine to invite us to say things we perhaps wouldn't express in other forums. As Harry Frankfurt has remarked, bullshit "is unavoidable whenever circumstances require someone to talk without knowing what he is talking about" (2005: 4). But what we see on Twitter or Facebook every day, or any other social network for that matter, is that bullshit is unavoidable even when people are not required to talk about topics they know nothing about. People happily spout bullshit even when there is no obvious need. Of course, this is frequently harmless, and everybody is entitled to an opinion, but on digital platforms where discussion of public issues is more central, and Twitter in particular, conversations frequently appear to be a competition to see who can come up with the most widely applicable generalisation or observation. In a highly reactive political environment, in which the neoliberal logic of the market-driven society invites us to compete with each other, and both social capital and attention are precious commodities, it is not really a surprise that the world has seen a slowly growing incidence of "hot takes", at least according to the volume of Google searches for the term. Foolish talking points such as "The UK's COVID-19 crisis can't be compared to other European countries because it has a city the size of London" or "Peaceful protests are fine, but many of these protesters just hate the police/are just looking for an excuse to loot" are not generated by those platforms, however. They are generated by the kind of emboldened, unselfconscious stupidity that, alongside fascism, is produced by societies that neglect un-marketable values such as critical thinking and solidarity. As with "fake news" and "filter bubbles", what we see is that technology acts at the very least as an enabler, and at the very most an amplifier or an invitation of these tendencies, just as radio or the printing press afforded these same voices historically.

There are a number of interesting forces at work here. For one, there is almost certainly some applicability here of the Dunning-Kruger effect described in Chapter Two: people who are not aware of their own ignorance tend to behave as if they are not ignorant. Those who suddenly become epidemiological "experts" at the start of a global pandemic despite not having studied biology since they were in compulsory schooling, and those who feel qualified to criticise people protesting police brutality without ever having experienced it or taken time to understand the harsh, institutionalised racism of most criminal justice systems, are just two common examples.

It is also generally recognised that, on digital platforms, people tend to be less inhibited than in face-to-face interactions in which they may be challenged or feel more self-conscious about expressing opinions. The psychology scholar John Suler, who came up with the idea of an "online disinhibition effect", divided the phenomenon into two halves: "benign" online disinhibition, which consisted of revealing "secret emotions, fears, wishes" and carrying out "unusual acts of kindness and generosity", and "toxic" online disinhibition, which consists of "rude language, harsh criticisms, anger, hatred, even threats" (2004). But there should at least be one more category: the disinhibition of people who enjoy sharing their opinions without actually having carefully considered the implications or empirical basis for what it is they are saying.

There are social factors to this tendency towards disinhibited bullshit, too. We saw in Chapter Three that there is a way in which conspiracism is exacerbated by a typically, though not exclusively, male tendency to behave as though one has all the answers. Here too, Rebecca Solnit's assertion that *some* men begin to explain things "whether or not they know what they are talking about", seems painfully familiar (2014: 4). But without resorting to technologically determinist arguments, it is also arguable that there is something about the way we experience knowledge and practice knowledge agency on digital platforms that invites a certain kind of ignorance, even when it is not gendered and does not conform to any kind of conspiracist narrative. It is as though the complexities of the past have been drowned out by the "edit wars" of Wikipedia, and those of the present concealed beneath the polished user interface of Twitter. In fact, it is extremely common for the editing of Wikipedia to serve as a political tool. In 2020 for example, amid speculation that the California senator Kamala Harris might be picked as Democratic presidential candidate Joe Biden's running mate, *The Intercept* reported that her Wikipedia page began to be rapidly edited, removing damaging information about her past record. "Presidential vetting operations have entire teams of investigators, but for the public, when the pick is announced, the most common source for information about the person chosen is Wikipedia. And there, a war has broken out over how to talk about Harris's career", wrote the reporter Aida Chávez (2020).

Furthermore, research suggests that, at least in terms of how we engage with news online, this tendency towards oversimplification and amnesia may be a serious problem for how we understand our world. One study found that:

> a usage pattern drawing heavily on social media and push accesses as a source of news (e.g., Facebook newsfeed, email newsletter) and being rather highly driven by entertainment needs has been found to be associated with an overestimation of one's own political knowledge. (Leonhard, Karnowski & Kümpel, 2020)

Here too, we see a Dunning-Kruger-like effect. But there is also the important fact that, while this effect is not caused by technology or social media platforms, it is enabled and encouraged by them, and only mitigated by forms of verification and other applications of media literacy that are optional at best. Ironically this may be part of the reason why online disinformation itself is frequently so poorly understood. Narratives about "fake news" or "echo chambers" causing the rise of populism are easy to understand and to repeat in a way that sounds authoritative and contributes to an overall need to understand and make sense of the world. It is also what makes digital media platforms a natural target for those in the business of spreading misinformation.

Pushing Disinformation

To a certain extent, the issues covered so far in this chapter are all about the capacity for misinformation and disinformation on digital platforms to influence people in one way or another. Does "fake news" cause significant distortions in people's voting patterns? Do filter bubbles? Does bullshit? Actually measuring and proving that what happens online is a determinant of which way people vote is notoriously difficult, since even if people are happy to reveal what they have voted for, it is not easy to say for certain that this ad or that piece of fake news, or even the specific combination that they might have comprised, is definitively what led an individual to vote a certain way, much less large numbers of people.

But this does not stand in the way of our observing that there are certainly very large numbers of people trying to influence our behaviours in all sorts of ways, and a huge amount of money and effort tied up in this. Rather than advertising, which has a commercial connotation, we should really be talking about the *influence industry*.

Of course the commercial world has led the way, in so far as it is much more the case that those with a political agenda are using platforms and techniques developed by the private sector with commercial applications in mind. As the outcry over Cambridge Analytica showed in 2018, nobody really minds if you use targeted advertising to sell cars and ice cream, but they do if you try to sway elections and referendums, and rightly so. But few people at that time seemed to concede that, maybe given the centrality of commerce to everything that is so fundamental to a market-driven society, this should not actually have been much of a surprise.

Whether commercial or political, disinformation and hyperbole are often at the heart of these attempts. In the case of commercial malpractice, we are well trained to ignore these attempts and can in theory refer advertisers to regulators. Dealing with states, on the other hand, is far more difficult.

During Special Prosecutor Robert Mueller's investigation of the Donald Trump campaign in 2018–2019, a lot of extremely interesting information surfaced that was instructive as to how online misinformation and disinformation continue to evolve. Whatever its impact, Russia had invested significantly in trying to bring about a Trump victory in 2016. According to a federal indictment from the US Department of Justice that was part of the Mueller investigation, an organisation based in St Petersburg called the "Internet Research Agency" attempted to influence the elections by:

> posing as U.S. persons and creating false U.S. personas, [the Defendants] operated social media pages and groups designed to attract U.S. audiences. These groups and pages, which addressed divisive U.S. political and social issues, falsely claimed to be controlled by U.S. activists when, in fact, they were controlled by [the] Defendants. (US Department of Justice, 2018: 3)

Funding for this operation was allegedly provided by Russian catering oligarch Yevgeny Prigozhin, known as "Putin's cook", and two companies he controls, Concord Management and Consulting LLC and Concord Catering LLC (ibid.). This is a fascinating, if highly concerning strategy, and there have been repeated reports of Russia attempting to deliberately stoke tensions in Britain and the US. In 2014 Russia was accused of secretly supporting UK environmentalists opposed to fracking, as a means to ensure UK dependency on importing Russian gas (Harvey, 2014). Similarly, there has been suggestion that long before

COVID-19 came along, Russia was deliberately inflaming the conspiracy theories about 5G (Broad, 2019).

Russia is often singled out for its attempts to sow division from outside, or push Russian interests, and these attempts should be condemned in the strongest terms. But the reality is that many states and other actors have attempted to push their interests using similar techniques. A similar strategy to that of the Internet Research Agency was also used by Cambridge Analytica in its attempts to sway politics in a variety of nations across the world. Cambridge Analytica became known for its use of large datasets, partly built from Facebook profile data, that were used to target Facebook users with the issues they were expected to care about most, but this frequent focus on data overlooked the broader network of blogs, YouTube videos and other content that their strategies also relied on.

Brazilian neo-fascist president Jair Bolsonaro was also no stranger to organised disinformation campaigns in his successful bid for office. He was repeatedly accused of creating a "criminal network" to spread disinformation via the WhatsApp messaging service. His son was also widely criticised for spreading a doctored picture of Swedish environmentalist Greta Thunberg that appeared to show her eating her lunch in front of poor black children, whilst simultaneously suggesting that she was financed by Hungarian billionaire George Soros — a frequent figure in far-right conspiracy theories (Harper, 2019).

Social Media and the Right-Wing

As the writers Angela Nagle (2017) and Dale Beran (2017) have documented, there is a vibrant far-right presence online in more peripheral platforms such as 4chan that connects directly to the electoral outcomes of Trump and other reactionary politicians. Given the nominally "liberal" (in the sense described in Chapter Four) outer coating of the technology world, and the tendency for politics of shallow understanding to see technology as the solution to most social and political problems, it may be a surprise that there is a well-established link between digital platforms and the right wing of politics. But as we have seen throughout this book, there is a tendency for the market-driven society to assist the political right wing directly, as well as by merely ignoring or being complacent about the forms of tension in that society that bring about right-wing anger. Here too, we see this double assistance at work.

It is quite well known that certain kinds of digital advertising assisted in Donald Trump's 2016 and 2020 campaigns, at least as far as fundraising. Facebook employee James Barnes, who later left the company, was embedded with the 2016 Trump campaign to help them make the best of Facebook as a platform (Seetharaman, 2019). What is more surprising is that, frequently, conservatives have been able to cultivate a co-operative relationship with Facebook by insisting that they have the opposite — similarly to how British reactionary Nigel Farage manipulated the BBC into giving him preferential airtime for years by accusing them of bias against him.

On the podcast of US comedian and broadcaster Joe Rogan, conservative pundit Ben Shapiro remarked that Facebook should desist from controlling the content on its platform in order to maintain its status as a platform rather than as a publication. The moment they start censoring or controlling the content on ideological grounds, he claimed, is the moment they become editorially responsible for the *entirety* of the content they do allow. While Facebook have undoubtedly manoeuvred themselves into a very difficult situation, as I will explore below, this either-or framing is either pretty disingenuous or pretty stupid. The good that Facebook or any technology company provides in a market-driven society, Shapiro claims, is the product itself: the app, the platform, the operating system. The political gestures of a technology company are not only extraneous, he claims, but tend to suppress conservative political voices because of Silicon Valley's apparently "progressive" politics. It is hard to know where to start with this.

Firstly, it is a perfect example of market-driven thinking: Facebook's entire value and existence is in what they sell. However much profit they make from exploiting disinformation or any aspect of their users' lives that they choose, they apparently have no responsibility to consider their impact in anything other than market terms. Secondly, at its core it is an extreme example of the "free marketplace of ideas" principle, discussed in Chapter Four — an idea that assumes a near-uniform level of education and morality that would protect the forms of exchange and dialogue that it claims to want, but fails to take into account that these anchors have been degraded or removed by precisely the market-driven society that underlies this thinking to begin with. The second that Facebook removes fascism from its platform because it may assist in the emboldening of fascism more generally, is the moment Facebook becomes an anti-fascist platform, apparently. But the truth is that, as we have seen again and again throughout this book, resurgent fascism and nationalism are not "just another opinion", they lead directly to a more dangerous society for those who are already the most vulnerable.

The trickier part, however, is the question of whether removing fascism from Facebook, for example, will help to remove it from the world. According to a quantitative measure at least, the answer would appear to be "yes". Policy researcher Cristina Ariza writes that the decision to "restrict" the YouTube channel of British far-right poster-boy Stephen Yaxley-Lennon meant that "the rate of subscribers has slowed down by half and videos receive 8 times fewer views than before the restriction was applied". Similarly, the Facebook page of the UK far-right party Britain First was the most liked political page in the UK after the Royal Family, until it migrated to right-wing platform GAB (Ariza, 2019). Similarly, in Brazil, a report in *The Intercept* revealed that "of the ten channels that grew most on YouTube Brazil in the period in the run-up to the 2018 election, half were dedicated to promoting Jair Bolsonaro and right-wing extremists like him" (Ghedin, 2019; my translation).

But the popularity of these pages and channels suggests that there are a large number of people who are *already sympathetic*, and who are likely to feel victimised by the removal or suppression of their online communities in a way that could lead to renewed waves of reactionary anger.

This is what happened when the channel of US conspiracist Alex Jones was removed from YouTube: a mixture of jubilation and outrage over "freedom of speech". YouTube CEO Susan Wojcicki eventually buckled, writing that "Without an open system, diverse and authentic voices have trouble breaking through" (Gault, 2019), and InfoWars launched a new channel, "War Room", before YouTube changed tack again, and this channel was deleted.

In late May 2020, while the US was consumed with angry protests over the police murder of African American man George Floyd, an interesting division emerged that further revealed the complexities of this problem. Donald Trump tweeted that he would send the army to deal with the "thugs" who were protesting, and, most concerning of all, that "when the looting starts, the shooting starts". Twitter concealed the tweet behind a notice which said that, although the tweet contravened Twitter's terms of service in relation to glorifying violence, they would not delete it because "it may be in the public's interest" for the tweet to remain. Earlier the same week, the company had added a "fact check" to one of Trump's earlier tweets, leading him to sign an executive order that attempted to remove Twitter's protections under Section 230 of the Communications Decency Act. These warning shots appeared to work, at least as far as Mark Zuckerberg was concerned: the same post on Facebook was not removed or caveated in any way, at Zuckerberg's personal insistence, which led employees at Facebook to rebel, and a number of major corporations to cease advertising on the platform (Hern & Wong, 2020).

Facebook and Zuckerberg's resistance to this kind of intervention is not a surprise, however. Said to be worried about accusations of bias that would potentially lead to more regulation on Facebook (Bertrand & Lippman, 2019), Zuckerberg has made a conscious effort to court the more conservative elements in US politics, hosting dinners and meetings with right-wing journalists, activists and other figures, including L. Brent Bozell, a Tea Party sympathiser and early client of Cambridge Analytica through his conservative organisation America, Inc. (ibid.), as well as Donald Trump himself, in a dinner at the White House with PayPal and Palantir founder Peter Thiel, a vocal supporter of Trump (Democracy Now!, 2019).

What these secret meetings, fluctuations and inconsistencies illustrate is that there is simply no way to get it right, because, as we will see below, the entire model of attention-economy capitalism that YouTube, Facebook and others comprise is flawed.

Follow the Money: A Tension in Attention

As we have seen throughout this chapter, if you are a technology company in the market-driven society, there is almost always money in misinformation and disinformation. I don't mean this in a direct way, although as we have seen, the financial rewards for digital advertising are potentially huge. There is also money in misinformation and disinformation in the sense that if a company is already in a dominant position, its priority will be to maintain and strengthen that position rather than to do the right thing on ethical grounds.

A simple example of this might be to look at something basic and generally uncontroversial like maps. In November 2019, it was reported that Apple had changed its maps technology to recognise Russia's widely condemned annexation of the Crimean Peninsula (BBC News, 2019). Google takes this type of informational totalitarianism a step further. Depending on whether a user is in India or Pakistan, the borders of the disputed region of Kashmir are redrawn to accommodate whichever political perspective is associated with the country where the user is located (Benziger, 2020). Likewise, in 2016 Google was accused of "deleting" Palestine from their maps, but the truth was actually worse: Palestine was never even on their maps to begin with (Cresci, 2016). Why would Google or Apple do this? Is it because they take some sort of ideological position on the political status of Crimea or the existence of Palestine? Perhaps, but the case of Kashmir, which would have cost Google more time and effort than simply drawing the border in a single place, should clarify that there is also another, wholly more likely motivation: angry governments are bad for business. National borders are frequently contested, and there are few issues that better differentiate the spatial, even imperial concerns of sovereign governments and the financial concerns of the modern corporation. Much better to simply misinform people about the border by conforming to the will of whichever political power is dominant in that region, and stay on the right side of a national government, than provide an accurate map that at least reveals the contested nature of any border.

There is also money in other forms of misinformation and disinformation. As we saw in Chapter Three, conspiracy theories arise out of political rather than technological origins, but they also have a long history of being amplified by technology, and this is not that different from digital media platforms. When a mass shooting took place in 2017 in Las Vegas, killing fifty-eight people and injuring nearly five hundred more, conspiracy theory videos quickly appeared on YouTube, which appeared prominently when searching for videos about the tragedy with neutral search queries like "Las Vegas shooting videos". The standard response from YouTube is to "demonetise" content that is deemed offensive rather than removing it, but even this is a manifestation of market-driven thinking, in which money is seen as the only thing that matters. The problem is that even if you demonetise one video, that video and the vile things it contains may still be amplified by the platform's discovery algorithms, and still form part of an overall user experience that is highly lucrative for Google, YouTube's owner. As much as 70% of the viewing time users spend on YouTube is driven by its algorithm-based recommendation feature. Even demonetisation is not uniform. In 2020, a report found that YouTube was still earning advertising revenue from climate science denial videos (Avaaz, 2020). The inevitable conclusion we reach is that there is a financial upside to the resulting misinformation of users using YouTube and other platforms to learn about the world. During the COVID-19 pandemic, YouTube did move to take down videos promoting the conspiracy theory that the disease was caused by 5G radiation, but this should not lead us to conclude that the platform does not benefit from numerous other forms of misinformation and disinformation, just like Facebook, Twitter and others do.

I have written elsewhere that social networks amount to a form of enclosure — the process by which the common lands of the world became privately owned and controlled (Gilroy-Ware, 2017: 151–152). At the very beginning of this book, I quoted Peter Linebaugh's observation that the sixteenth century was the beginning of modern capitalism, and of privatisation (2008: 47), and his work makes an invaluable link between the enclosure of common lands and the rapacious privatisation of the market-driven society. Whereas in previous work I used the idea of enclosure as a metaphor, there is the case to be made that this has not been metaphorical at all, save for the fact that we are not dealing with a spatial problem. What all of the examples in this chapter amount to is a successful attempt at enclosure of both public conversations and private lives in a bid to capture as much of your attention as possible and allow the advertising clients of social media companies to target your attention with data-driven advertising.

The classic definition of an entrepreneur is somebody who takes something from an area of "low value" and finds a way to sell it for "higher value". What we see here is that this relative quantification is misleading, at least in the market-driven society. It is not so much that the input was of "low value" and the output of "high value", but that the input is valuable in some intrinsic manner — something like participation in public debate for its own sake — whereas the output is made valuable primarily to shareholders. What social media platforms have done is to take public conversations that — as we have seen in previous chapters — were already under enormous pressure in terms of the ways that they facilitated and reproduced misinformation and disinformation, and effectively privatise them through enclosure, so that they are less valuable to everybody else, and more valuable to forms of predatory venture capital that are either so naïve or greedy that they see no ethical qualms with this process. The writer Shoshana Zuboff has eloquently called this a "parasitic economic logic" that unlaterally "claims human experience as free raw material for hidden commercial practices of extraction, prediction, and sales" (2019), and this is by no means an overstatement.

There is a tension built into this business model, however — one that has repeatedly produced bad headlines for Facebook and other companies using it. On the one hand, they want to mediate everything that is meaningful in the lives of their users, regardless of the privacy or ethical implications, so that they can garner as much of your attention as possible. Not just public conversations with family and friends — the implication is that anything they know will be meaningful to you and will command your attention should be mediated by their platforms. On the other hand, it has become increasingly clear that many of the most resonant things that make up the complexity of human social, cultural and political life being enclosed are also the most transgressive: sex, terrorism, unending lies, social drama, divisive politics, crippling physical insecurities, drugs, bullying and other serious issues. Save for a number of vaguely defined categories that are beyond the pale of the US's puritan roots, everything must be part of this strategy, including almost every possible meaning of the term "fake news". What they keep discovering, again and again, is that the things they first imagined people might share go well beyond the almost robotic view of human beings that would be required for this business model to run smoothly. When you try to enclose not only the "public spheres", but almost the entirety of human social relations and cultural participation, you capture more than you can handle.

It is hard to tell whether the C-level executives of Silicon Valley actually know this, and are cynically sailing as close to the wind as they can get away with, happy to endure a few hiccups as they follow this overall business model, or if they are so blinded by their quest to become everything to their users that they do not even see that, like Icarus, it is precisely their omnipotence that appears to be causing so many problems.

When Facebook COO Sheryl Sandberg said in 2020 that Facebook just wasn't "capable" of fact-checking political ads, what she meant was that it would hurt the company's operating costs, which it is her job after all to minimise. The line that Mark Zuckerberg has given for this refusal to take responsibility for the outright lying that has been put into place on their platform was that "we think people should be able to see for themselves what politicians are saying". This is either a bizarrely exaggerated form of the positivistic "free marketplace of ideas" construct explored in Chapter Four, or simply an excuse to avoid spending money and taking responsibility for the very mess that Facebook has created.

In the context of YouTube, the historian Heidi Tworek has argued that there is an "upside of ignorance", in the sense that the platform would prefer not to know, and prefer that we did not know, about the prevalence of misinformation and disinformation on their platform and how crucial it is to their business. Indeed, she goes so far as to compare them to the tobacco industry's campaign to ensure that the medical case against smoking appeared as uncertain as possible, examined in Chapter Three (Tworek, 2019).

In May 2020 it came to light that Facebook executives had been warned by their own employees about the ways that the company's algorithms exacerbated political divisions and even led to increased numbers joining extreme groups on the site, but did nothing (Horwitz & Seetharaman, 2020). They did nothing for the same reason that a near-bankrupt farmer selling apples would do nothing if handed a chainsaw in his or her orchard a month before harvest and was told that the only way to save it in the long-term from disease was to cut down half the trees. In a market-driven society, short-term profits are more important than anything else.

Unleashing a Torrent

When I wrote about the exploitative pathologies of social media corporations as far as our emotional lives were concerned, I was asked whether it was possible to have a non-profit alternative, and whether the situation would be ameliorated if we removed Mark Zuckerberg, Jack Dorsey and the other ruthlessly commercial elements from the equation. What if Facebook and Twitter were owned by the people? This is an important thought experiment — one that needs to be periodically restated in relation to new circumstances and developments. But the answer is really only ever a partial amelioration: sure, it would be better if there wasn't a ruthless commercial element guiding the design of these systems. But the very design of technology has historically been guided by those already in a position to be creating technologies to begin with. Like many other technologies throughout history, digital media platforms on which misinformation and disinformation are said to be so prevalent might actually look quite different if they were only designed around public benefit — certainly there'd be a lot less annoying "sponsored" content. But even if we think solely in terms of the abilities they have afforded us — even something as simple as the "retweet" or the share button — it is easy, as a user familiar with these features, to overlook what they have unleashed in a relatively short space of time.

At the beginning of this book I used the metaphor of a dam breaking for the idea that tension built up over time can suddenly release, sometimes with devastating consequences. But what we have already seen in the crises addressed throughout this book is not a single "dam" breaking, but a number of interwoven processes that all fit this profile: the slow hollowing-out of democracy by the market-driven society; the slow drifting apart of social conservatism and market-driven neoliberalism; the slow incorporation of digital technology into ever further reaches of our lives. All involved a slow accumulation of pressure from the flaws that are built into the system, followed by a quick release once that tension becomes too much. Quite possibly, the mounting environmental crisis will also fit this profile unless major changes are made, and made fast.

In conjunction with the political tensions addressed throughout, and the rapid releases of political anger that they led to, in this chapter we have seen that the greed of digital platforms in enclosing essential public conversations about those political and economic matters both exacerbated and was produced by another moment of rapid acceleration. There is an often mis-attributed saying to the effect that "falsehood flies, and the truth comes limping after it", and this feature of how human beings communicate is not new — in fact the phrase can be traced to the early eighteenth century. But the reality is that digital platforms have accelerated and amplified this process, and made billions of dollars doing so. Blinded by the venture capital-funded greed that has come to be so common at the heart of market-driven technological innovation, they made the same fundamental error that those economists made in Mont Pèlerin in 1947, or that "free speech" activists make when they forget how terrifyingly powerful fascism can become when it enters public conversations under the guise of "common sense": that there would be other forces at work to counteract the worst aspects of what is unleashed by their actions.

The gatekeepers of old may no longer have been fit for purpose, and may even have been part of the problem. But when you rapidly accelerate public conversations because it is more profitable to exploit the attention and advertising from the distortions in those conversations, you almost certainly make aspects of those surrounding political tensions worse. What we can see is that the market-driven society did not only produce these tensions at the political level over multiple decades; it also increasingly profited from exacerbating them at the level of media and technology. Where the market-driven society put profit over people and undermined civic participation because the only participation needed was economic — as workers, consumers, shareholders, clients — that same tendency also reduced political conversations themselves into "content" that was imagined along the same lines — consumers seeing ads placed by clients to the benefit of shareholders, all monitored by precarious workers — while political, social and even legal consequences were overlooked, downplayed or suppressed.

When a storage dam collapsed at the Corrego do Feijão iron ore mine in Brumadinho, Brazil, it was not the water released by the dam that was the problem, so much as an acidic, toxic sludge that was a by-product of the iron ore refinery that was taking place there. This is probably a more accurate metaphor as far as the relationship between politics and social media goes. As long as you are commodifying attention by mediating everything in the lives of their users and then harvesting data, the "truth" or genuine democratic participation will never be more than an annoyance, and misinformation will simply be a necessary by-product, like toxic sludge.

Truth in the Market-Driven Society

This book was first published some months after the COVID-19 pandemic hit the world. But it is about a problem that not only exacerbated that crisis but long preceded it, and may continue to be a problem and exacerbate other crises, long after the COVID-19 pandemic has become a matter for the history books. Indeed, the problem I have tried to address here will partly affect *how* the pandemic is even entered into those imaginary, generic "history books".

The problem is not really about social media corporations — it is about our having built a society in which corporations are not only afforded the freedom to put profit over people; they are effectively in charge, because wealth is what affords the most power. Social media corporations merely take this one more step, in the sense that, whether their founders or creators realise it or not, they have evolved essentially to derive value from the destructiveness of capital as a whole. Whereas I argued this from a cultural and psychological perspective in *Filling the Void*, it is also true of the misinformation and disinformation on which the market-driven society depends.

It is all very well to insist positivistically on the importance of "the truth", as many journalists do, but once you realise that this apparently unalienable concept is not compatible with a market-driven society, the problem starts to look rather different. Sometimes, as in the COVID-19 pandemic, the market does not want to hear the truth, because the truth includes the reality that not everything is a commodity.

To blame "politicians" without understanding that the very system that politicians have entered has been increasingly hollowed out into little more than a simulation of democracy is to participate in the very problem you are criticising: the direction of attention and understanding *away* from the anti-democratic nature of the market-driven society.

We can restrict the monopolistic growth of social media platforms, more sensibly regulate other media, and invest heavily in education, but all of these measures ultimately constitute painkillers rather than remedies unless we explicitly take steps to de-normalise the market-driven society and teach people to understand it better. "Fake news", as we now call it, whether it is the reactionary dismissal of accurate information or the variety of misinformation, disinformation, hoax, sensationalism, bias and the like, is at multiple levels a consequence of encouraging us to consider the marketplace and prioritise private accumulation before we value anything else. All are consequences of the same order of priorities in the market-driven society that subordinates all other forms of value to financial value.

So are global warming, nationalism, our lack of preparedness for health crises at both the national and international levels. The environment is apparently only valuable when you can make money from it; accurate information about the world is considered valuable when you can make money from it; pluralistic societies and transnational co-operation — the opposites of nationalism — are valuable when you can make money from them; functional and accessible healthcare systems are valuable when money can be made from them. The pattern is the same.

But as the world discovered from the pandemic, as it is increasingly discovering with mental health crises, climate change, wildfires and species loss, and as it will discover from increased resource wars, hunger, disease and forced migration unless things change, there are things that cannot be traded on any market. If we are to survive these challenges, and to find our way out of or away from them, it is essential that we learn to imagine a future that stops defining freedom in terms of free markets; that stops value being measured in purely financial or individualistic terms; and that centres and embraces those things *outside* the market, like health, love, education, solidarity, peace and the natural environment. Somewhere in there too, is reliable information about the world we collectively inhabit.

Bibliography

Due to the lockdown required for the COVID-19 pandemic, it was not possible to access all books referenced as hard copies, and some books had to be re-purchased as e-books, meaning that some page numbers could not be provided for quoted text.

Addley, E., 2018. *Study Shows 60% Of Britons Believe In Conspiracy Theories*. [online] The Guardian. Available at: <https://www.theguardian.com/society/2018/nov/23/study-shows-60-of-britons-believe-in-conspiracy-theories>.

Adler, D., 2018. The Centrist Paradox: Political Correlates of the Democratic Disconnect. *SSRN Electronic Journal*,. DOI: 10.2139/ssrn.3214467

Adorno, T., 1994. *The Stars Down To Earth And Other Essays On The Irrational Culture*. London: Routledge.

Ali, R., 2017. *The Erasure Of Islam From The Poetry Of Rumi*. [online] The New Yorker. Available at: <https://www.newyorker.com/books/page-turner/the-erasure-of-islam-from-the-poetry-of-rumi>.

Ali, T., 2015. *The Extreme Centre: A Warning*. London: Verso.

Allan, S., 1999. *News Culture*. Buckingham: Open University Press.

Anderson, B., 2006. *Imagined Communities*. London: Verso.

Antonucci, L., Horvath, L., Kutiyski, Y. and Krouwel, A., 2017. The malaise of the squeezed middle: Challenging the narrative of the 'left behind' Brexiter. *Competition & Change*, 21(3), pp.211-229. DOI: 10.1177/1024529417704135

Arendt, H., 1963. *Eichmann In Jerusalem: A Report On The Banality Of Evil*. Viking Press.

Ariza, C., 2019. *Will Online Takedowns Defeat The Offline Radical Right?*. [online] openDemocracy. Available at: <https://www.opendemocracy.net/en/countering-radical-right/will-online-takedowns-defeat-offline-radical-right/>.

Asgari, N., 2020. *One In Five UK Baby Boomers Are Millionaires*. [online] Ft.com. Available at: <https://www.ft.com/content/c69b49de-1368-11e9-a581-4ff78404524e>.

Avaaz, 2020. *Why Is Youtube Broadcasting Climate Misinformation To Millions? (Eng).Pdf*. [online] Google Docs. Available at: <https://drive.google.com/file/d/1Kw0pq7pfeNmVEBt8IbR0zgZmHKBoSGvA/view>.

Bakshy, E., Messing, S. and Adamic, L., 2015. Exposure to ideologically diverse news and opinion on Facebook. *Science*, 348(6239), pp.1130-1132. DOI: 10.1126/science.aaa1160

Balkin, J., 1993. Ideological Drift and the Struggle over Meaning. *Connecticut Law Review*, 25(3), pp.869-892.

Barberá, P., Jost, J., Nagler, J., Tucker, J. and Bonneau, R., 2015. Tweeting From Left to Right. *Psychological Science*, 26(10), pp.1531-1542. DOI: 10.1177/0956797615594620

Bardi, U., 2015. *Why Johnny Can't Understand Climate: Functional Illiteracy and the Rise of "Unpropaganda"*. [online] Resilience. Available at: <https://www.resilience.org/stories/2015-08-31/why-johnny-can-t-understand-climate-functional-illiteracy-and-the-rise-of-unpropaganda/>.

Barkun, M., 2013. *A Culture of Conspiracy*. Berkeley: University of California Press.

Baudrillard, J. and Glaser, S., 1994. *Simulacra And Simulation*. Ann Arbor: University of Michigan Press.

Baynes, C., 2019. *More Than 2.6M Brits Are Holocaust Deniers, Poll Finds*. [online] The Independent. Available at: <https://www.independent.co.uk/news/uk/home-news/holocaust-memorial-day-poll-uk-jews-murdered-nazi-germany-hope-not-hate-a8746741.html>.

BBC News, 2019. *Apple Changes Crimea Map To Meet Russian Demands*. [online] BBC News. Available at: <https://www.bbc.com/news/technology-50573069>.

Beck, U., 1992. *Risk Society: Towards A New Modernity*. London: Sage Publications.

Begum, R., 2018. *For Saudi Women, Freedom to Drive Masks New Crackdown*. [online] Human Rights Watch. Available at: <https://www.hrw.org/news/2018/06/22/saudi-women-freedom-drive-masks-new-crackdown>.

Beirich, H. and Potok, M., 2016. *The Council For National Policy: Behind The Curtain*. [online] Southern Poverty Law Center. Available at: <https://www.splcenter.org/hatewatch/2016/05/17/council-national-policy-behind-curtain>.

Bensinger, G., 2020. *Google Redraws Disputed Borders, Depending On Who's Looking*. [online] Washington Post. Available at: <https://www.washingtonpost.com/technology/2020/02/14/google-maps-political-borders/>.

Benway, J., 1998. Banner Blindness: The Irony of Attention Grabbing on the World Wide Web. *Proceedings of the Human Factors and Ergonomics Society Annual Meeting*, 42(5), pp.463-467. DOI: 10.1177/154193129804200504

Beran, D., 2017. *4Chan: The Skeleton Key To The Rise Of Trump*. [online] Medium. Available at: <https://medium.com/@DaleBeran/4chan-the-skeleton-key-to-the-rise-of-trump-624e7cb798cb>.

Berardi, F., 2018. *Breathing: Chaos and Poetry*. Brooklyn: Semiotext(e).

Berlant, L., 2011. *Cruel Optimism*. Durham, NC: Duke University Press.

Berry, M., 2016. No alternative to austerity: how BBC broadcast news reported the deficit debate. *Media, Culture & Society*, 38(6), pp.844-863.

Bertrand, N. and Lippman, D., 2019. *Inside Mark Zuckerberg's Private Meetings With Conservative Pundits*. [online] POLITICO. Available at: <https://www.politico.com/news/2019/10/14/facebook-zuckerberg-conservatives-private-meetings-046663>.

Best, S., 2019. *Football Club Changes Name to Flat Earth FC In Support Of Conspiracy Theory*. [online] Daily Mirror. Available at: <https://www.mirror.co.uk/science/football-club-changes-name-flat-17291822>.

Blest, P., 2020. *This GOP Senator Conveniently Bought A Ton of Stock in a PPE Company After a Private Coronavirus Briefing*. [online] Vice. Available at: <https://www.vice.com/en_us/article/z3b9ae/this-gop-senator-conveniently-bought-a-ton-of-stock-in-a-ppe-company-after-a-private-coronavirus-briefing>.

Boudana, S., 2011. A definition of journalistic objectivity as a performance. *Media, Culture & Society*, 33(3), pp.385-398. DOI: 10.1177/0163443710394899

Boulton, A., 2019. *Sky Views: Journalists, Don't Be Part of the Government's 'Fake News' Machine*. [online] Sky News. Available at: <https://news.sky.com/story/sky-views-journalists-dont-be-part-of-the-governments-fake-news-machine-11845093>.

Bowcott, O., 2019. *UK Spent £11M Of Public Money Fighting Libya Rendition Case*. [online] The Guardian. Available at: <https://www.theguardian.com/world/2019/apr/24/uk-public-money-fighting-libya-rendition-case-abdel-hakim-belhaj-fatima-boudchar>.

Bown, A., 2014. *Enjoying It*. Winchester, UK: Zero Books.

Branston, J., Gilmore, A. and Hiscock, R., 2018. *The*

Tobacco Industry Plays Price Games To Make It Even Tougher To Quit Smoking. [online] The Conversation. Available at: <https://theconversation.com/the-tobacco-industry-plays-price-games-to-make-it-even-tougher-to-quit-smoking-104356>.

Brenan, M., 2019. *Nurses Again Outpace Other Professions For Honesty, Ethics*. [online] Gallup.com. Available at: <https://news.gallup.com/poll/245597/nurses-again-outpace-professions-honesty-ethics.aspx>.

Broad, W., 2019. *Your 5G Phone Won't Hurt You. But Russia Wants You To Think Otherwise.*. [online] Nytimes.com. Available at: <https://www.nytimes.com/2019/05/12/science/5g-phone-safety-health-russia.html>.

Broderick, R., 2018. *People Think This Whole QAnon Conspiracy Theory Is A Prank On Trump Supporters*. [online] Buzzfeednews.com. Available at: <https://www.buzzfeednews.com/article/ryanhatesthis/its-looking-extremely-likely-that-qanon-is-probably-a>.

Broussard, M., 2018. *Artificial Unintelligence: How Computers Misunderstand The World*. Cambridge, MA: MIT Press.

Brown, D., 2001. *1945-51: Labour And The Creation of the Welfare State*. [online] The Guardian. Available at: <https://www.theguardian.com/politics/2001/mar/14/past.education>.

Brown, G., 2007. *BBC NEWS | Politics | Gordon Brown's Speech In Full*. [online] BBC News. Available at: <http://news.bbc.co.uk/2/hi/uk_news/politics/7010664.stm>.

Brown, S., 2017. *Alex Jones's Infowars Media Empire Is Built To Sell Snake-Oil Diet Supplements*. [online] Intelligencer. Available at: <https://nymag.com/intelligencer/2017/05/how-does-alex-jones-make-money.html>.

Brown, W., 2015. *Undoing The Demos: Neoliberalism's Stealth Revolution*. New York: Zone Books.

———. 2019. *In The Ruins Of Neoliberalism*. New York: Columbia University Press.

Bruns, A., 2019. *Are Filter Bubbles Real?*. Cambridge: Polity Press.

Burns, C., 2008. *Margaret Thatcher's Greatest Achievement: New Labour*. [online] CentreRight. Available at: <https://conservativehome.blogs.com/centreright/2008/04/making-history.html>.

Carr, N., 2010. *The Shallows*. New York: W.W. Norton.

Castells, M., 2011. *Communication Power*. Oxford: Oxford University Press.

Chadwick, A., McDowell-Naylor, D., Smith, A. and Watts, E., 2018. Authority signaling: How relational interactions between journalists and politicians create primary definers in UK broadcast news. *Journalism*,. DOI: 10.1177/1464884918762848

Chakrabarti, S., 2016. *The Shami Chakrabarti Inquiry*. [online] The Labour Party (UK). Available at: <https://tinyurl.com/chakrabarti-inquiry>.

Chávez, A., 2020. *Kamala Harris's Wikipedia Page Is Being Edited*. [online] The Intercept. Available at: <https://theintercept.com/2020/07/02/kamala-harris-wikipedia/>.

Childress, C., 2012. *All Media Are Social. Contexts*, 11(1), pp.55-57. DOI: 10.1177/1536504212436499

Ciabattari, J., 2014. *Why Is Rumi The Best-Selling Poet In The US?*. [online] BBC.com. Available at: <https://www.bbc.com/culture/article/20140414-americas-best-selling-poet>.

Clegg, N., 2016. *Politics: Between The Extremes*. New York: Vintage.

Climate.gov. n.d. *Climate Change: Atmospheric Carbon Dioxide | NOAA Climate.Gov*. [online] Available at: <https://www.climate.gov/news-features/understanding-climate/climate-change-atmospheric-carbon-dioxide>.

Cohen, J., 2007. Cyberspace and/as space. *Columbia Law Review*, 150(1). pp.210-256.

Committee to Protect Journalists, 2019. *Explore CPJ's Database Of Attacks On The Press*. [online] Cpj.org. Available at: <https://tinyurl.com/2019-journ-deaths>.

Conboy, M., 2004. *Journalism*. London: SAGE Publications.

Cortellessa, E., 2018. *Lauder Gave $1.1M To Group Producing Anti-Muslim Ads In 2016*. [online] Timesofisrael.com. Available at: <https://www.timesofisrael.com/lauder-gave-1-1m-to-group-producing-anti-muslim-ads-in-2016/>.

Cresci, E., 2016. *Google Maps Accused Of Deleting Palestine – But The Truth Is More Complicated*. [online] the Guardian. Available at: <https://www.theguardian.com/technology/2016/aug/10/google-maps-accused-remove-palestine>.

Crow, D., 2018. Opioid billionaire granted patent for addiction treatment | Financial Times. *Ft.com*, [online] Available at: <https://www.ft.com/content/a3a53ae8-b1e3-11e8-8d14-6f049d06439c>.

Curtis, A., 2016. *HyperNormalisation*. BBC iPlayer.

Davies, N., 2008. *Flat Earth News*. London: Chatto & Windus.

Davies, W., 2018. *Nervous States*. London: Jonathan Cape.

Deacon, D. and Smith, D., 2017. The politics of containment: Immigration coverage in UK General Election news coverage (1992–2015). *Journalism*, 21(2), pp.151-171. DOI: 10.1177/1464884917715944

Dean, J., 1998. *Aliens In America*. Ithaca: Cornell University Press.

Democracy Now!, 2019. *Facebook CEO Mark Zuckerberg And Peter Thiel Had Secret White House Dinner With Trump*. [online] Democracy Now!. Available at: <https://www.democracynow.org/2019/11/22/

headlines/facebook_ceo_mark_zuckerberg_and_
peter_thiel_had_secret_white_house_dinner_with_
trump>.

DeSmog UK, 2019. *Institute Of Economic Affairs*. [online]
DeSmog UK. Available at: <https://www.desmog.
co.uk/institute-economic-affairs>.

Deuze, M., 2005. What is journalism?. *Journalism:
Theory, Practice & Criticism*, 6(4), pp.442-464. DOI:
10.1177/1464884905056815

Dewey, C., 2016. *Facebook Fake-News Writer: 'I Think
Donald Trump Is In The White House Because Of Me'*.
[online] Washington Post. Available at: <https://
www.washingtonpost.com/news/the-intersect/
wp/2016/11/17/facebook-fake-news-writer-i-think-
donald-trump-is-in-the-white-house-because-of-me/>.

DiFonzo, N. and Bordia, P., 2007. Rumor as Sense Making.
Rumor psychology: Social and organizational approaches.,
pp.113-131.

Dorling, D., 2010. *Injustice: Why Social Inequality Persists*.
Bristol: The Policy Press.

————. 2017. Austerity and Mortality. In: V. Cooper and
D. Whyte, ed., *The Violence of Austerity*. London: Pluto
Press.

Drew, D., 1975. Reporters' Attitudes, Expected Meetings
with Source and Journalistic Objectivity. *Journalism
Quarterly*, 52(2). DOI: 10.1177/107769907505200204

Dugan, A. and Newport, F., 2013. *Americans Rate JFK As
Top Modern President*. [online] Gallup.com. Available
at: <https://news.gallup.com/poll/165902/americans-
rate-jfk-top-modern-president.aspx>.

Dunning, D., 2011. The Dunning–Kruger Effect. *Advances
in Experimental Social Psychology*, pp.247-296. DOI:
10.1016/B978-0-12-385522-0.00005-6

Eco, U., 1995. Ur-Fascism. *New York Review of Books*,.

Edison Research, 2020. *The Infinite Dial 2019 - Edison*

Research. [online] Edison Research. Available at: <https://www.edisonresearch.com/infinite-dial-2019/>.

Embury-Dennis, T., 2017. *Tony Blair's Labour Government Ignored Warnings Over Danger Of Diesel Cars To Air Pollution*. [online] The Independent. Available at: <https://www.independent.co.uk/news/uk/politics/labour-diesel-vehicles-health-warnings-impact-cars-air-pollution-tony-blair-gordon-brown-2000-budget-a8062301.html>.

Enjeti, S., 2019. *Saagar Enjeti: 'Ride Is Likely Over For Kamala Harris'*. [online] TheHill. Available at: <https://thehill.com/hilltv/rising/465008-saagar-enjeti-ride-is-likely-over-for-kamala-harris>.

Eubanks, V., 2018. *Automating Inequality*. New York: St. Martin's Press.

Ewalt, D., 2013. *Thirty Amazing Facts About Private Jets*. [online] *Forbes*. Available at: <https://www.forbes.com/sites/davidewalt/2013/02/13/thirty-amazing-facts-about-private-jets/>.

Ewen, S., 1996. *PR! A Social History Of Spin*. New York: Basic Books.

Fenton, N., 2016. The internet of me (and my 'friends'). In: J. Curran, N. Fenton and D. Freedman, ed., *Misunderstanding the Internet*, 2nd ed. Abingdon: Routledge.

Fernando Toledo, L., do Lago, C. and Sueiro, V., 2018. *Bolsonaro Vence Em 97% Das Cidades Mais Ricas E Haddad Em 98% Das Pobres - Infográficos - Estadão*. [online] Estadão. Available at: <https://www.estadao.com.br/infograficos/politica,bolsonaro-vence-em-97-das-cidades-mais-ricas-e-haddad-em-98-das-pobres,935854>.

Fetzer, T., 2018. Did austerity cause Brexit?. *Warwick economics research papers series (WERPS)*, [online]

Available at: <http://wrap.warwick.ac.uk/106313/>.

Fincher, L., 2019. *Bloomberg Tried To Ruin Me For Speaking Out On China Reporting*. [online] The Intercept. Available at: <https://theintercept.com/2020/02/18/mike-bloomberg-lp-nda-china/>.

Fischer, K., 2018. *The Atlas Network: Littering The World With Free-Market Think Tanks*. [online] Global Dialogue. Available at: <http://globaldialogue.isa-sociology.org/the-atlas-network-littering-the-world-with-free-market-think-tanks/>.

Fisher, M., 2009. *Capitalist Realism*. Winchester, UK: Zero Books.

Flat Earth Society, T., n.d. *FAQ :: The Flat Earth Society*. [online] Theflatearthsociety.org. Available at: <https://www.theflatearthsociety.org/home/index.php/about-the-society/faq>.

Forbes Magazine, 2016. *Forbes List: America's Richest Families 2016*. [online] Forbes.com. Available at: <https://www.forbes.com/families/list/#tab:overall>.

Frankfurt, H., 2005. *On Bullshit*. Princeton: Princeton University Press.

Fraser, N., 1990. Rethinking the Public Sphere: A Contribution to the Critique of Actually Existing Democracy. *Social Text*, [online] (No. 25/26). Available at: <http://www.jstor.org/stable/466240>. DOI: 10.2307/466240

Gallup, 2020. *Congress And The Public*. [online] Gallup.com. Available at: <https://news.gallup.com/poll/1600/congress-public.aspx>.

Gardiner, B., 2019. *Dirty Lies: How The Car Industry Hid The Truth About Diesel Emissions*. [online] The Guardian. Available at: <https://www.theguardian.com/environment/2019/mar/22/dirty-lies-how-the-car-industry-hid-the-truth-about-diesel-emissions>.

Gault, M., 2019. *Infowars Returns To Youtube After CEO*

Said It Will Allow 'Offensive' Content [Updated]. [online]
Vice. Available at: <https://www.vice.com/en_us/
article/59nge8/infowars-returns-to-youtube-after-
ceo-said-it-will-allow-offensive-content>.

Ghedin, R., 2019. *Cinco Dos Dez Canais Que Explodiram
No Ranking Do Youtube Durante As Eleições* São
De Extrema *Direita*. [online] The Intercept Brasil.
Available at: <https://theintercept.com/2019/08/28/
ranking-youtube-extrema-direita/>.

Giddens, A., 1999. *The Third Way: The Renewal Of Social
Democracy*. Cambridge: Polity Press.

Gidley, B., McGeever, B. and Feldman, D., 2020. Labour
and Antisemitism: a Crisis Misunderstood. *The Political
Quarterly*, 91(2), pp.413-421. DOI: 10.1111/1467-
923X.12854

Gilmore, A. and Rowell, A., 2018. *The Tobacco Industry's
Latest Scam: How Big Tobacco Is Still Facilitating Tobacco
Smuggling, While Also Attempting To Control A Global
System Designed To Prevent It. | Blog - Tobacco Control*.
[online] Tobacco Control. Available at: <https://blogs.
bmj.com/tc/2018/06/19/the-tobacco-industrys-latest-
scam-how-big-tobacco-is-still-facilitating-tobacco-
smuggling-while-also-attempting-to-control-a-global-
system-designed-to-prevent-it/>.

Gilroy, P., 2000. *Between Camps: Nations, Cultures and the
Allure of Race*. New York: Allen Lane.

Gilroy-Ware, C., 2017. *Jean-Michel Basquiat, Boom For
Real - The White Review*. [online] The White Review.
Available at: <https://www.thewhitereview.org/
reviews/jean-michel-basquiat-boom-real/>.

Gilroy-Ware, M., 2017. *Filling the Void: Emotion, Capitalism
& Social Media*. London: Repeater Books.

Gitlin, T., 2003. *Media Unlimited: How the Torrent of Images
and Sounds Overwhelms Our Lives*. New York: Owl
Books, U.S.

Glaser, E., 2017. *Anti-Politics*. London: Repeater Books.

Glenza, J., 2018. *Opioid Crisis: Justice Department To Back Local Lawsuits Against Manufacturers*. [online] the Guardian. Available at: <https://www.theguardian.com/us-news/2018/feb/27/opioid-crisis-justice-department-jeff-sessions-taskforce>.

Goldhill, O., 2018. *Propaganda Spread By Data "Bombs" Pushed Brazil's Far-Right President To Power*. [online] Quartz. Available at: <https://qz.com/1659665/fake-news-on-whatsapp-helped-elect-brazil-leader-jair-bolsonaro/>.

Grady, C., 2018. *The Alice Walker Anti-Semitism Controversy, Explained*. [online] Vox. Available at: <https://www.vox.com/culture/2018/12/20/18146628/alice-walker-david-icke-anti-semitic-new-york-times>.

Graeber, D., 2019. *For The First Time In My Life, I'm Frightened To Be Jewish*. [online] openDemocracy. Available at: <https://www.opendemocracy.net/en/opendemocracyuk/first-time-my-life-im-frightened-be-jewish/>.

Graham, J., Haidt, J. and Nosek, B., 2009. Liberals and conservatives rely on different sets of moral foundations. *Journal of Personality and Social Psychology*, 96(5), pp.1029-1046. DOI: 10.1037/a0015141

Gregory, A., 2019. *UN Blames Anti-Vaxxers For Deadly Measles Outbreak As Families Put Red Flags Outside Houses To Request Vaccinations*. [online] The Independent. Available at: <https://www.independent.co.uk/news/world/australasia/samoa-measles-anti-vaxxers-red-flags-houses-vaccination-facebook-a9233911.html>.

Grieco, E., 2020. *Fast Facts About The Newspaper Industry's Financial Struggles As Mcclatchy Files For Bankruptcy*. [online] Pew Research Center. Available at: <https://

www.pewresearch.org/fact-tank/2020/02/14/fast-facts-about-the-newspaper-industrys-financial-struggles/>.

Guess, A., Nagler, J. and Tucker, J., 2019. Less than you think: Prevalence and predictors of fake news dissemination on Facebook. *Science Advances*, 5(1). DOI: 10.1126/sciadv.aau4586

Guyon, J., 2018. *In Sri Lanka, Facebook Is Like The Ministry Of Truth*. [online] Quartz. Available at: <https://qz.com/1259010/how-facebook-rumors-led-to-real-life-violence-in-sri-lanka/> [Accessed 25 August 2019].

Habermas, J., 1989. *The Structural Transformation Of The Public Sphere*. Cambridge: Polity Press.

Hakhverdian, A., van Elsas, E., van der Brug, W. and Kuhn, T., 2013. Euroscepticism and education: A longitudinal study of 12 EU member states, 1973–2010. *European Union Politics*, 14(4), pp.522-541. DOI: 10.1177/1465116513489779

Hall, S., 2011. The Neo-Liberal Revolution. *Cultural Studies*, 25(6), pp.705-728.

Hall, S., Critcher, C., Jefferson, T., Clarke, J. and Roberts, B., 1978. *Policing The Crisis*. New York: Palgrave Macmillan.

Hallin, D., 1986. *The "Uncensored War"*. London: University of California Press.

Halpern, J. and Blistein, D., 2019. *The Deafening Silence of a Pharmaceutical Company In The Face Of The Opioid Crisis*. [online] Literary Hub. Available at: <https://lithub.com/the-deafening-silence-of-a-pharmaceutical-company-in-the-face-of-the-opioid-crisis/>.

Hamill, J., 2018. *Nasa Scientist Says Temperatures in the Upper Atmosphere Are Set To Plunge*. [online] Metro.co.uk. Available at: <https://metro.co.uk/2018/11/16/

nasa-slowdown-8146529/>.

Han, B., 2019. *What Is Power?*. Cambridge: Polity Press.

——— 2017. *Psychopolitics: Neoliberalism and New Technologies of Power*. London: Verso.

——— 2015. *The Burnout Society*. Palo Alto: Stanford University Press.

Hancox, D., 2020. *The 'Street Food' Swindle: Fake Diversity, Privatised Space – And Such Small Portions!*. [online] the Guardian. Available at: <https://www.theguardian. com/commentisfree/2020/feb/23/street-food-swindle-fake-diversity-privatised-space-small-portions>.

Hannen, T., 2019. *The Brexit Disrupters: Beyond Left And Right*. [online] Ft.com. Available at: <https:// www.ft.com/video/bc7ef2b4-a5e2-4313-9341-4e8921d4d0fb>.

Hansard, 2007. *House of Commons Hansard Debates For 06 Nov 2007*. [online] UK Parliament. Available at: <https://publications.parliament.uk/pa/cm200708/cmhansrd/cm071106/debtext/71106-0004.htm>.

Hansard, 2018. *House of Commons Hansard Debates For 23 May 2018*. [online] UK Parliament. Available at: <https://hansard.parliament. uk/Commons/2018-05-23/debates/ F948D8C8-EB41-4807-8D3D-222972C3C626/ NHSOutsourcingAndPrivatisation>.

Harper, P., 2019. *Greta Thunberg: Brazil President Son Shares Fake Twitter Photo | Metro News*. [online] Metro.co.uk. Available at: <https://metro. co.uk/2019/09/27/fury-over-fake-photo-of-greta-thurnberg-eating-lunch-in-front-of-poor-children-10818352/>.

Harris, L., 2020. *Letter From Veles: The Real Story Of Macedonia's Fake News Factory*. [online] The Calvert Journal. Available at: <https://www.calvertjournal.

com/features/show/8031/letter-from-veles>.

Hartigan, J., 1999. *Racial Situations*. Princeton, N.J.: Princeton University Press.

Harvey, D., 2005. *A Brief History of Neoliberalism*. Oxford: Oxford University Press.

Harvey, F., 2014. *Russia 'Secretly Working With Environmentalists To Oppose Fracking'*. [online] the Guardian. Available at: <https://www.theguardian.com/environment/2014/jun/19/russia-secretly-working-with-environmentalists-to-oppose-fracking>.

Hasan, M. and Sayedahmed, D., 2018. *Blowback: How ISIS Was Created By The U.S. Invasion Of Iraq*. Blowback. [online] The Intercept. Available at: <https://theintercept.com/2018/01/29/isis-iraq-war-islamic-state-blowback/>.

Hay, M. 2019. *How To Deal With Cops Who Believe Wild Conspiracy Theories Like QAnon*. [online] Available at: <https://www.vice.com/en_us/article/gy7azb/how-to-deal-with-cops-who-believe-wild-conspiracy-theories-like-qanon>.

Harari, Y., 2020. *Yuval Noah Harari: The World After Coronavirus*. [online] *Ft.com*. Available at: <https://www.ft.com/content/19d90308-6858-11ea-a3c9-1fe6fedcca75>.

Held, D., 2013. *Introduction To Critical Theory*. New York, NY: John Wiley & Sons.

Henry, J., 2012. *The Price of Offshore Revisited: New Estimates For Missing Global Private Wealth, Income, Inequality, And Lost Taxes*. [online] Tax Justice Network. Available at: <https://www.taxjustice.net/cms/upload/pdf/Price_of_Offshore_Revisited_120722.pdf>.

Hern, A. and Wong, J., 2020. *Facebook Employees Hold Virtual Walkout Over Mark Zuckerberg's Refusal To Act Against Trump*. [online] The Guardian. Available at:

<https://www.theguardian.com/technology/2020/
jun/01/facebook-workers-rebel-mark-zuckerberg-
donald-trump>.

Hickel, J., 2019. *A Letter To Steven Pinker (And Bill Gates,
For That Matter) About Global Poverty*. [online] Jason
Hickel. Available at: <https://www.jasonhickel.org/
blog/2019/2/3/pinker-and-global-poverty>.

Higgins, E., 2020. *Leaked Memo Reveals Amazon Execs
Plotted to Paint Fired 'Not Smart' Worker As 'Face Of
Entire Union/Organizing Movement'*. [online] Common
Dreams. Available at: <https://www.commondreams.
org/news/2020/04/03/leaked-memo-reveals-amazon-
execs-plotted-paint-fired-not-smart-worker-face-
entire>.

HM Treasury, 2006. *Leitch Review Of Skills - Final Report*.
London: HM Stationery Office.

hooks, b., 2002. *Speaking Freely: Bell Hooks (09:52)*.
[online] YouTube. Available at: <https://youtu.be/
g2bmnwehlpA?t=592>.

———, 1994. *Teaching to Transgress: Education As The
Practice Of Freedom*. New York: Routledge.

Hopkins, N. and Norton-Taylor, R., 2016. *Blair
Government's Rendition Policy Led To Rift Between
UK Spy Agencies*. [online] The Guardian. Available
at: <https://www.theguardian.com/uk-news/2016/
may/31/revealed-britain-rendition-policy-rift-
between-spy-agencies-mi6-mi5>.

Horkheimer, M. and Adorno, T., 1989. *Dialectic Of
Enlightment*. New York: Continuum.

Horn, S. and Veermans, K., 2019. Critical thinking efficacy
and transfer skills defend against 'fake news' at an
international school in Finland. *Journal of Research
in International Education*, 18(1), pp. 23-41. DOI:
10.1177/1475240919830003

Horwitz, J. and Seetharaman, D., 2020. *Facebook*

Executives Shut Down Efforts To Make The Site Less Divisive. [online] WSJ. Available at: <https://www.wsj.com/articles/facebook-knows-it-encourages-division-top-executives-nixed-solutions-11590507499>.

Hulme, M., 2009. On the origin of 'the greenhouse effect': John Tyndall's 1859 interrogation of nature. *Weather*, 64(5), pp. 121-123. DOI: 10.1002/wea.386

Hume, T., 2020. *Berlin's Anti-Lockdown Protests Are Getting Way Bigger, Crazier, And More Far-Right.* [online] Vice. Available at: <https://www.vice.com/en_us/article/7kzgad/berlins-anti-lockdown-protests-are-getting-way-bigger-crazier-and-more-far-right>.

Ipsos MORI, 2016. *Immigration Is Now The Top Issue For Voters In The EU Referendum.* [online] Ipsos MORI. Available at: <https://www.ipsos.com/ipsos-mori/en-uk/immigration-now-top-issue-voters-eu-referendum>.

———. 2020. *Tolerance Across The Values Divide?.* [online] Ipsos MORI. Available at: <https://www.ipsos.com/ipsos-mori/en-uk/tolerance-across-values-divide>.

Jagers, J. and Walgrave, S., 2007. Populism as political communication style: An empirical study of political parties' discourse in Belgium. *European Journal of Political Research*, 46(3), pp.319-345. DOI: 10.1111/j.1475-6765.2006.00690.x

Jaggi, M., 2008. *Interview: José Saramago.* [online] The Guardian. Available at: <https://www.theguardian.com/books/2008/nov/22/jose-saramago-blindness-nobel>.

Jahn, J., 2013. *Gründungsparteitag Der AFD: Aufstand Gegen Merkels „Alternativlose Politik".* [online] FAZ.NET. Available at: <https://www.faz.net/aktuell/wirtschaft/wirtschaftspolitik/gruendungsparteitag-der-afd-aufstand-gegen-merkels-alternativlose-politik-12148549.html>.

Jameson, F., 1988. Cognitive Mapping. In: C. Nelson and L. Grossberg, ed., *Marxism and the Interpretation of Culture*.

———. 1984. Periodizing the 60s. *Social Text*, (9/10), p.178.

Jeffries, A., 2017. *How Mic.Com Exploited Social Justice For Clicks*. [online] The Outline. Available at: <https://theoutline.com/post/2156/mic-com-and-the-cynicism-of-modern-media>.

Jones, J. and Salter, L., 2012. *Digital Journalism*. Los Angeles: SAGE Publications.

Jones, O., 2019. *It's The People's Vote Of Judea v. The Judean People's Vote*. [online] The Guardian. Available at: <https://www.theguardian.com/commentisfree/2019/oct/28/peoples-vote-labour-brexit-second-referendum>.

Kahan, D., Peters, E., Dawson, E. and Slovic, P., 2013. Motivated Numeracy and Enlightened Self-Government. *SSRN Electronic Journal*,. DOI: 10.2139/ssrn.2319992

Kay, J. and Salter, L., 2013. Framing the cuts: An analysis of the BBC's discursive framing of the ConDem cuts agenda. *Journalism: Theory, Practice & Criticism*, 15(6), pp.754-772. DOI: 10.1177/1464884913501835

Keay, D., 1987. *Interview For Woman's Own ("No Such Thing As Society") | Margaret Thatcher Foundation*. [online] Margaretthatcher.org. Available at: <https://www.margaretthatcher.org/document/106689>.

Keefe, P., 2017. *The Family That Built An Empire Of Pain*. [online] The New Yorker. Available at: <https://www.newyorker.com/magazine/2017/10/30/the-family-that-built-an-empire-of-pain>.

Kennard, M. and Curtis, M., 2019. *DECLASSIFIED UK: How The UK Security Services Neutralised The Country's Leading Liberal Newspaper*. [online] Daily Maverick.

Available at: <https://www.dailymaverick.co.za/article/2019-09-11-how-the-uk-security-services-neutralised-the-countrys-leading-liberal-newspaper/>.

Kimmel, M., 2013. *Angry White Men*. New York: The Nation Institute.

Klein, N., 2007. *The Shock Doctrine*. New York: Metropolitan Books.

Kollewe, J., 2015. *UK Government Wrong To Subsidise Diesel, Says Former Minister*. [online] The Guardian. Available at: <https://www.theguardian.com/business/2015/oct/01/uk-government-wrong-to-subsidise-diesel-says-former-minister>.

Konish, L., 2018. *More Americans Are Considering Cutting Their Ties With The US — Here's Why*. [online] CNBC. Available at: <https://www.cnbc.com/2018/06/27/more-americans-are-considering-cutting-their-ties-with-the-us-heres.html>.

Krajewski, M., 2014. *The Great Lightbulb Conspiracy*. [online] IEEE Spectrum: Technology, Engineering, and Science News. Available at: <https://spectrum.ieee.org/tech-history/dawn-of-electronics/the-great-lightbulb-conspiracy>.

Kronfeldner, M., Roughley, N. and Toepfer, G., 2014. Recent Work on Human Nature: Beyond Traditional Essences. *Philosophy Compass*, 9(9), pp.642-652.

Kunst, S., Kuhn, T. and van de Werfhorst, H., 2019. Does education decrease Euroscepticism? A regression discontinuity design using compulsory schooling reforms in four European countries. *European Union Politics*, 21(1), pp.24-42.

Lacapria, K., 2015. *Fact Check: Did The CDC 'Admit' 98 Million Americans Were Given A 'Cancer Virus' Via The Polio Shot?*. [online] Snopes.com. Available at: <https://www.snopes.com/fact-check/cdc-admits-98-million-got-cancer-polio-vaccine/>.

Lahart, J., 2018. *Obama Builds Ties To 'Chicago School'*. [online] WSJ. Available at: <https://www.wsj.com/articles/SB122610604643110229>.

Lamoureux, M., 2017. *I Watched The 34-Hour Infowars Marathon And It Turned My Brain To Mush*. [online] Vice. Available at: <https://www.vice.com/en_uk/article/kz3y59/i-watched-the-34-hour-infowars-marathon-and-it-turned-my-brain-to-mush> [Accessed 22 April 2020].

Lawless, K., 2017. *The Story Of How Fake Sugar Got Approved Is Scary As Hell*. [online] Vice. Available at: <https://www.vice.com/en_us/article/nzpbkx/the-story-of-how-fake-sugar-got-approved-is-scary-as-hell>.

Lawrence, A., 2018. *Fake Moon Landings And A Flat Earth: Why Do Athletes Love Conspiracy Theories?*. [online] the Guardian. Available at: <https://www.theguardian.com/sport/2018/dec/27/stephen-curry-kyrie-irving-conspiracy-theories-nba>.

Lawrence, F., Pegg, D. and Evans, R., 2019. *How Vested Interests Tried To Turn The World Against Climate Science*. [online] The Guardian. Available at: <https://www.theguardian.com/environment/2019/oct/10/vested-interests-public-against-climate-science-fossil-fuel-lobby> [Accessed October 2019].

Leary, J., 2018. *The Third Way Is A Death Trap*. [online] Jacobinmag.com. Available at: <https://jacobinmag.com/2018/08/centrism-democratic-party-lieberman-ocasio-cortez>.

Legum, J., 2019. *Huge "Police Lives Matter" Facebook Page Run From Kosovo, Pushed Misinformation About U.S. Cops*. [online] Popular.info. Available at: <https://popular.info/p/huge-police-lives-matter-facebook>.

Lemon, J., 2018. *Trump's "Keep America Great" Re-Election Banners Are Made In China And Were Mass Produced To*

Avoid Trade War Tariffs. [online] Newsweek. Available at: <https://www.newsweek.com/trump-keep-america-great-banners-are-made-china-1043692>.

Leonhard, L., Karnowski, V. and Kümpel, A., 2020. Online and (the feeling of being) informed: Online news usage patterns and their relation to subjective and objective political knowledge. *Computers in Human Behavior*, 103, pp.181-189. DOI: 10.1016/j.chb.2019.08.008

Lerner, S., 2019. *How The Plastics Industry Is Fighting To Keep Polluting The World*. [online] The Intercept. Available at: <https://theintercept.com/2019/07/20/plastics-industry-plastic-recycling/>.

Leslie, I., 2018. *The Death Of Don Draper*. [online] Newstatesman.com. Available at: <https://www.newstatesman.com/science-tech/internet/2018/07/death-don-draper>.

Levy, D., Aslan, B. and Bironzo, D., 2018. *UK Press Coverage Of The EU Referendum*. [online] Oxford: Reuters Institute for the Study of Journalism. Available at: <https://tinyurl.com/brexit-coverage>.

Lewis, J. and Cushion, S., 2017. Think Tanks, Television News and Impartiality. *Journalism Studies*, 20(4), pp.480-499. DOI: 10.1080/1461670X.2017.1389295

Leys, C., 2003. *Market-Driven Politics*. London: Verso.
———. 2008. *Total Capitalism*. Monmouth: Merlin.

Littler, J., 2017. *Against Meritocracy: Culture, Power And Myths Of Mobility*. Abingdon: Routledge.

Losurdo, D., 2011. *Liberalism*. London: Verso.

Lubben, A., 2019. *Millennials Have A Right To Be Pissed At Boomers. This Data Proves It.*. [online] Vice. Available at: <https://www.vice.com/en_us/article/zmjpn4/millennials-have-a-right-to-be-pissed-at-boomers-this-data-proves-it>.

Lunden, I., 2019. *Grammarly Raises $90M At Over $1B+*

Valuation For Its AI-Based Grammar And Writing Tools. [online] Techcrunch. Available at: <https://techcrunch.com/2019/10/10/grammarly-raises-90m-at-over-1b-valuation-for-its-ai-based-grammar-and-writing-tools/>.

Luttwak, E., 1994. *Why Fascism Is The Wave Of The Future*. [online] London Review of Books. Available at: <https://www.lrb.co.uk/the-paper/v16/n07/edward-luttwak/why-fascism-is-the-wave-of-the-future>.

Lyotard, J., 1984. *The Postmodern Condition*. Manchester: Manchester University Press.

Madrigal, A., 2019. *The Servant Economy*. [online] The Atlantic. Available at: <https://www.theatlantic.com/technology/archive/2019/03/what-happened-uber-x-companies/584236/>.

Mahler, J., 2018. *How One Conservative Think Tank Is Stocking Trump's Government*. [online] Nytimes.com. Available at: <https://www.nytimes.com/2018/06/20/magazine/trump-government-heritage-foundation-think-tank.html>.

Mair, P., 2013. *Ruling The Void*. London: Verso.

Malik, N., 2019. *We Need New Stories*. London: W&N.

Martin, E., 2018. *Births In England And Wales, 1938-2017 - Office For National Statistics*. [online] Ons.gov.uk. Available at: <https://www.ons.gov.uk/peoplepopulationandcommunity/birthsdeathsandmarriages/livebirths/bulletins/birthsummarytablesenglandandwales/2017>.

Mathis-Lilley, B., 2017. *If Leaked List Is Accurate, Hillary's Cabinet Choices Would Have Enraged The Democratic Left*. [online] Slate Magazine. Available at: <https://slate.com/news-and-politics/2017/01/hillary-cabinet-plans-leaked-sheryl-sandberg-at-treasury-starbucks-ceo-at-labor.html>.

May, R., 2019. *The Yellow Vest Phenomenon and the Radical*

Right. [online] openDemocracy. Available at: <https://www.opendemocracy.net/en/can-europe-make-it/yellow-vest-phenomenon-and-radical-right/>.

Mayer, J., 2016. *Dark Money*. London: Scribe.

McGoey, L., 2019. *Unknowers: How Strategic Ignorance Rules The World*. Zed Books.

McGreal, C., 2019. *Four Big Drug Firms Agree To $260M Opioid Payout Hours Before Trial Set To Begin*. [online] The Guardian. Available at: <https://www.theguardian.com/us-news/2019/oct/21/opioid-makers-drug-industry-trial-cleveland-ohio>.

McGuigan, J., 2009. *Cool Capitalism*. London: Pluto.

Michell, J., 2020. *Coronavirus Reveals The Cost Of Austerity*. [online] Tribunemag.co.uk. Available at: <https://tribunemag.co.uk/2020/04/coronavirus-reveals-the-cost-of-austerity>.

Mijs, J., 2019. The paradox of inequality: income inequality and belief in meritocracy go hand in hand. *Socio-Economic Review*,. DOI: 10.1093/ser/mwy051

Milbank, D., 2003. *Curtains Ordered For Media Coverage Of Returning Coffins*. [online] The Washington Post. Available at: <https://www.washingtonpost.com/archive/politics/2003/10/21/curtains-ordered-for-media-coverage-of-returning-coffins/13375c81-187e-4f91-a565-2ce8f3bf3549/>.

Milner, R., 2016. *The World Made Meme*. Cambridge, MA: MIT Press.

Mishel, L. and Wolfe, J., 2018. *CEO Compensation Has Grown 940% Since 1978: Typical Worker Compensation Has Risen Only 12% During That Time*. [online] Economic Policy Institute. Available at: <https://www.epi.org/publication/ceo-compensation-2018/>.

Monbiot, G., 2011. *Academic Publishers Make Murdoch Look Like A Socialist*. [online] The Guardian. Available at: <https://www.theguardian.com/commentisfree/2011/

aug/29/academic-publishers-murdoch-socialist>.

———. 2006. *Heat: How to Stop the Planet Burning*. London: Penguin.

Mondon, A. and Winter, A., 2017. Articulations of Islamophobia: from the extreme to the mainstream?. *Ethnic and Racial Studies*, 40(13), pp. 2151-2179. DOI: 10.1080/01419870.2017.1312008

Mooney, C. and Dennis, B., 2019. *Trump Always Dismisses Climate Change When It's Cold. Not So Fast, Experts Say*. [online] Washington Post. Available at: <https://www.washingtonpost.com/climate-environment/2019/01/29/trump-always-dismisses-climate-change-when-its-cold-not-so-fast-experts-say/>.

Moore, H., 2017. *The Secret Cost of Pivoting to Video*. [online] Columbia Journalism Review. Available at: <https://www.cjr.org/business_of_news/pivot-to-video.php>.

Moore, M., 2020. BBC presenter Mishal Husain is paid to attend oil events. *The Sunday Times*, [online] Available at: <https://www.thetimes.co.uk/edition/news/bbc-presenter-mishal-husain-is-paid-to-attend-oil-events-9gwkvpln5>.

Morozov, E., 2013. *To Save Everything, Click Here: The Folly Of Technological Solutionism*. Public Affairs.

Moshakis, A., 2018. *Is The Earth Flat? Meet The People Questioning Science*. [online] the Guardian. Available at: <https://www.theguardian.com/global/2018/may/27/is-the-earth-pancake-flat-among-the-flat-earthers-conspiracy-theories-fake-news>.

Mozur, P., 2018. *A Genocide Incited On Facebook, With Posts From Myanmar'S Military*. [online] Nytimes.com. Available at: <https://www.nytimes.com/2018/10/15/technology/myanmar-facebook-genocide.html>.

Murphy, C., 2020. *Former Ellen Employees Confirm What*

You May Already Know About Working On Ellen.
[online] *Vulture*. Available at: <https://www.vulture.
com/2020/07/the-ellen-degeneres-show-described-as-
toxic-by-employees.html>.

Myers, K., 2020. *Amazon Paid a 1.2% Tax Rate On
$13,285,000,000 In Profit For 2019*. [online] Yahoo!
Finance UK. Available at: <https://uk.finance.
yahoo.com/news/amazon-paid-a-12-tax-rate-on-
13285000000-in-profit-for-2019-210847927.html>.

Nagle, A., 2017. *Kill All Normies*. Winchester, UK: Zero
Books.

Nardelli, A., 2018. *The Government's Own Brexit Analysis
Says the UK Will Be Worse Off In Every Scenario Outside
the EU*. [online] BuzzFeed. Available at: <https://www.
buzzfeed.com/albertonardelli/the-governments-own-
brexit-analysis-says-the-uk-will-be>.

NASA, 2011. *Global Mean CO2 Mixing Ratios - SIO Mauna
Loa & South Pole*. [online] data.giss.nasa.gov. Available
at: <https://data.giss.nasa.gov/modelforce/ghgases/
Fig1A.ext.txt>.

nbc4i.com, 2017. *Study Finds Surprising Number Of
Americans Think Chocolate Milk Comes From Brown
Cows*. [online] nbc4i.com. Available at: <https://www.
nbc4i.com/news/u-s-world/study-finds-surprising-
number-of-americans-think-chocolate-milk-comes-
from-brown-cows/>.

Neate, R. and Jolly, J., 2020. *Hedge Funds 'Raking In
Billions' During Coronavirus Crisis*. [online] The
Guardian. Available at: <https://www.theguardian.
com/business/2020/apr/09/hedge-funds-raking-in-
billions-during-coronavirus-crisis>.

Neate, R., 2020. *Amazon Reaps $11,000-a-Second
Coronavirus Lockdown Bonanza*. [online] The Guardian.
Available at: <https://www.theguardian.com/
technology/2020/apr/15/amazon-lockdown-bonanza-

jeff-bezos-fortune-109bn-coronavirus>.

Nicole Rogers, T., 2020. *No, Mike Bloomberg Did Not Spend So Much Money On His Failed Presidential Campaign That He Could've Given Every American $1 Million Instead.* [online] Business Insider. Available at: <https://www.businessinsider.com/mike-bloomberg-couldnt-give-every-american-1-million-2020-3?r=US&IR=T>.

Noble, S., 2018. *Algorithms of Oppression: How Search Engines Reinforce Racism.* New York: NYU Press.

Norton-Taylor, R., 2020. *Declassified UK: Abduction And Denial — The UK's Role In Torture.* [online] Daily Maverick. Available at: <https://www.dailymaverick.co.za/article/2020-02-11-abduction-and-denial-the-uks-role-in-torture/>.

Oborne, P., 2019. *British Journalists Have Become Part Of Johnson's Fake News Machine.* [online] openDemocracy. Available at: <https://www.opendemocracy.net/en/opendemocracyuk/british-journalists-have-become-part-of-johnsons-fake-news-machine/>.

Oborne, P., 2019. *It's Not Just Boris Johnson's Lying. It's That The Media Let Him Get Away With It.* [online] The Guardian. Available at: <https://www.theguardian.com/commentisfree/2019/nov/18/boris-johnson-lying-media>.

O'Carroll, L., 2016. *Dutch Woman with Two British Children Told To Leave UK After 24 Years.* [online] The Guardian. Available at: <https://www.theguardian.com/politics/2016/dec/28/dutch-woman-with-two-british-children-told-to-leave-uk-after-24-years>.

OECD, 2013. *OECD Skills Outlook 2013: First Results From The Survey Of Adult Skills.* [online] OECD Publishing. Available at: <http://dx.doi.org/10.1787/9789264204256-en>.

Office for National Statistics, 2019. *JOBS05: Workforce*

Jobs By Region And Industry - Office For National Statistics. [online] Ons.gov.uk. Available at: <https://www.ons.gov.uk/employmentandlabourmarket/peopleinwork/employmentandemployeetypes/datasets/workforcejobsbyregionandindustryjobs05>.

Oreskes, N. and Conway, E., 2008. *Challenging Knowledge: How Climate Science Became A Victim Of The Cold War*. Stanford University Press.

Örnebring, H., 2010. Technology and journalism-as-labour: Historical perspectives. *Journalism: Theory, Practice & Criticism*, 11(1), pp. 57-74. DOI: 10.1177/1464884909350644

Oxfam, 2017. *An Economy For The 99%*. [online] Oxfam. Available at: <https://oi-files-d8-prod.s3.eu-west-2.amazonaws.com/s3fs-public/file_attachments/bp-economy-for-99-percent-160117-en.pdf>.

Papacharissi, Z., 2015. *Affective Publics*. New York: Oxford University Press.

Petzinger, J., 2018. *Europe's Intoxicating Love Affair With Diesel Is Dying Out*. [online] Quartz. Available at: <https://qz.com/1183779/europes-intoxicating-love-affair-with-diesel-is-dying-out/>.

Pew Research Center, 2020. *Nearly Three-In-Ten Americans Believe COVID-19 Was Made In A Lab*. [online] Pew Research Center. Available at: <https://www.pewresearch.org/fact-tank/2020/04/08/nearly-three-in-ten-americans-believe-covid-19-was-made-in-a-lab/>.

Pinker, S., 2011. *The Better Angels of Our Nature*. London: Penguin.

Pomerantsev, P., 2019. *This Is Not Propaganda*. Public Affairs.

Proctor, R., 2008. Agnotology: a missing term to describe the cultural production of ignorance. In: R. Proctor and L. Schiebinger, ed., *Agnotology: The making and unmaking of Ignorance*. Stanford, CA: Stanford University Press.

Proctor, R., 2012. The history of the discovery of the cigarette–lung cancer link: evidentiary traditions, corporate denial, global toll. *Tobacco Control*, (21), pp.87-91. DOI: 10.1136/tobaccocontrol-2011-050338

Ramsay, A. and Geoghegan, P., 2018. *Right-Wing Think Tank Accused Of Promoting Tobacco And Oil Industry "Propaganda" In Schools*. [online] openDemocracy. Available at: <https://www.opendemocracy.net/en/dark-money-investigations/right-wing-think-tank-accused-of-promoting-tobacco-oil-indu/>.

Ramsay, A., 2019. *Brexit, Dark Money And Big Data*. [online] Eurozine.com. Available at: <https://www.eurozine.com/brexit-dark-money-big-data/>.

Reprieve, 2015. *Secretive Court Orders GCHQ To Destroy Stolen Documents - Reprieve*. [online] Reprieve. Available at: <https://reprieve.org.uk/press/secretive-court-orders-gchq-to-destroy-stolen-documents/>.

Resnick, B., 2019. *The Costs Of Academic Publishing Are Absurd. The University Of California Is Fighting Back..* [online] Vox. Available at: <https://www.vox.com/science-and-health/2019/3/1/18245235/university-of-california-elsevier-subscription-open-access>.

Reynolds, J. and Sweney, M., 2014. *BBC Receives Almost 1,200 Complaints Over Ukip Election Coverage*. [online] The Guardian. Available at: <https://www.theguardian.com/media/2014/may/30/bbc-complaints-ukip-election-coverage-bias>.

Rogers, T., 2018. *Yougov Polls Show Anti-Semitism In Labour Has Actually Reduced Dramatically Since Jeremy Corbyn Became Leader | Evolve Politics*. [online] Evolve Politics. Available at: <https://evolvepolitics.com/yougov-polls-show-anti-semitism-in-labour-has-actually-reduced-dramatically-since-jeremy-corbyn-became-

leader/>.

Rusbridger, A., 2018. *Breaking News: The Remaking Of Journalism And Why It Matters Now*. Edinburgh: Canongate Books.

Schwartz, B., 2019. *Wall Street Democratic Donors Warn The Party: We'll Sit Out, Or Back Trump, If You Nominate Elizabeth Warren*. [online] CNBC. Available at: <https://www.cnbc.com/2019/09/26/wall-street-democratic-donors-may-back-trump-if-warren-is-nominated.html> [Accessed October 2019].

Schwarz, J., 2018. *Lie After Lie: What Colin Powell Knew About Iraq 15 Years Ago And What He Told The U.N.*. [online] The Intercept. Available at: <https://theintercept.com/2018/02/06/lie-after-lie-what-colin-powell-knew-about-iraq-fifteen-years-ago-and-what-he-told-the-un/>.

Seetharaman, D., 2019. *How A Facebook Employee Helped Trump Win—But Switched Sides For 2020*. [online] Wall Street Journal. Available at: <https://www.wsj.com/articles/how-facebooks-embed-in-the-trump-campaign-helped-the-president-win-11574521712>.

Selyukh, A., 2016. *After Brexit Vote, Britain Asks Google: 'What Is The EU?'*. [online] NPR.org. Available at: <https://www.npr.org/sections/alltechconsidered/2016/06/24/480949383/britains-google-searches-for-what-is-the-eu-spike-after-brexit-vote>.

Sennett, R., 2008. *The Craftsman*. London: Penguin Books.

Seymour, R., 2008. *The Liberal Defence Of Murder*. London: Verso.

Sherwood, H., 2019. *Britain's Battle To Get To Grips With Literacy Is Laid Bare In H Is For Harry*. [online] the Guardian. Available at: <https://www.theguardian.com/education/2019/mar/03/literacy-white-working-class-boys-h-is-for-harry>.

Shirley, R., 2015. *Rural Modernity, Everyday Life and Visual Culture*. Ashgate.

Skinner, G. and Clemence, M., 2017. *Politicians Remain The Least Trusted Profession In Britain*. [online] Ipsos MORI. Available at: <https://www.ipsos.com/sites/default/files/ct/news/documents/2017-11/node-357601-357676.zip>.

Smith, G. and Woodhead, L., 2018. Religion and Brexit: populism and the Church of England. *Religion, State and Society*, 46(3), pp.206-223. DOI: 10.1080/09637494.2018.1483861

Smith, M., 2019. *Left-Wing Vs Right-Wing: It'S Complicated*. [online] Yougov.co.uk. Available at: <https://yougov.co.uk/topics/politics/articles-reports/2019/08/14/left-wing-vs-right-wing-its-complicated>.

Solnit, R., 2014. *Men Explain Things To Me*. London: Granta Publications

Song, L., Banerjee, N. and Hasermyer, D., 2015. *Exxon: The Road Not Taken*. [online] InsideClimate News. Available at: <https://insideclimatenews.org/content/Exxon-The-Road-Not-Taken>.

Sönnichsen, N., 2019. *Europe: Diesel Car Sales Share By Country 2013-2017*. [online] Statista. Available at: <https://www.statista.com/statistics/425113/eu-car-sales-share-of-diesel-engines-by-country/>.

Srnicek, N., 2017. *Platform Capitalism*. Cambridge: Polity Books.

Stanley, J., 2018. *How Fascism Works*. New York: Random House.

Starbird, K., 2017. *Information Wars: A Window Into The Alternative Media Ecosystem*. [online] Medium. Available at: <https://medium.com/hci-design-at-uw/information-wars-a-window-into-the-alternative-media-ecosystem-a1347f32fd8f>.

Starbird, K., Maddock, J., Orand, M., Achterman, P. and

Mason, R., 2014. Rumors, False Flags, and Digital Vigilantes: Misinformation on Twitter after the 2013 Boston Marathon Bombing. In: *iConference*. [online] Available at: <https://faculty.washington.edu/kstarbi/Starbird_iConference2014-final.pdf>.

Statista, 2011. *Handset Penetration In North America 1996-2015 | Statista*. [online] Statista. Available at: <https://www.statista.com/statistics/203688/handset-penetration-per-capita-in-north-america-since-1996/>.

Statista, 2019. *UK: Mobile Phone Ownership 1996-2018 | Statista*. [online] Statista. Available at: <https://www.statista.com/statistics/289167/mobile-phone-penetration-in-the-uk/>.

Strauß, N., 2018. Financial Journalism in Today's High-Frequency News and Information Era. *Journalism*, 20(2), pp.274-291. DOI: 10.1177/1464884917753556

Suárez, E., 2020. *How To Build A Successful Subscription News Business: Lessons From Britain And Spain*. Reuters Institute Journalist Fellowship Paper. [online] University of Oxford. Available at: <https://reutersinstitute.politics.ox.ac.uk/sites/default/files/2020-02/Eduardo_Suarez_Digital_subscriptions_fellowship_paper.pdf>.

Subramanian, S., 2017. *Meet The Macedonian Teens Who Mastered Fake News And Corrupted The US Election*. [online] WIRED. Available at: <https://www.wired.com/2017/02/veles-macedonia-fake-news/>.

Suler, J., 2004. The Online Disinhibition Effect. *CyberPsychology & Behavior*, 7(3). DOI: 10.1089/1094931041291295

Sunstein, C., 2018. *#Republic: Divided Democracy In The Age Of Social Media*. Princeton University Press.

Sydbom, A., Blomberg, A., Parnia, S., Stenfors, N., Sandström, T. and Dahlén, S., 2001. Health Effects of Diesel Exhaust Emissions. *European Respiratory Journal*, 17(4), pp.733-746.

Taylor, P., 1992. *War and the Media*. Manchester: Manchester University Press.

Temelkuran, E., 2019. *How To Lose A Country*. London: Fourth Estate.

Thomson, S., 2016. *GDP a Poor Measure of Progress, Say Davos Economists*. [online] World Economic Forum. Available at: <https://www.weforum.org/agenda/2016/01/gdp>.

Thurman, N., Cornia, A. and Kunert, J., 2016. *Journalists In The UK*. [online] Reuters Institute for the Study of Journalism. Available at: <https://reutersinstitute.politics.ox.ac.uk/sites/default/files/research/files/Journalists%2520in%2520the%2520UK.pdf>.

Tiffany, K., 2017. *If A Scientific Conspiracy Theory Is Funny, That Doesn't Mean It's A Joke*. [online] The Verge. Available at: <https://www.theverge.com/2017/10/9/16424622/reddit-conspiracy-theories-memes-irony-flat-earth>.

Tobitt, C., 2020. *Ofcom Launches Investigation Into London Live's TV Interview With Conspiracy Theorist David Icke*. [online] Press Gazette. Available at: <https://www.pressgazette.co.uk/ofcom-assessing-london-lives-tv-interview-with-conspiracy-theorist-david-icke/>.

Tsotsis, A., 2010. *Respect Are Country, Speak English - SF Weekly*. [online] SF Weekly. Available at: <https://www.sfweekly.com/news/respect-are-country-speak-english/>.

Tuchman, G., 1972. Objectivity as Strategic Ritual: An Examination of Newsmen's Notions of Objectivity. *American Journal of Sociology*, 77(4), pp.660-679.

Tuomi, I., 2002. *View Of The Lives And Death Of Moore's Law*. [online] Firstmonday.org. Available at: <https://firstmonday.org/ojs/index.php/fm/article/

view/1000/921>.

Tworek, H., 2019. *Social Media Platforms and the Upside of Ignorance*. [online] Centre for International Governance Innovation. Available at: <https://www.cigionline.org/articles/social-media-platforms-and-upside-ignorance>.

Tyler, I., 2015. Classificatory Struggles: Class, Culture and Inequality in Neoliberal Times. *The Sociological Review*, 63(2), pp.493-511. DOI: 10.1111/1467-954X.12296

Uberti, D., 2019. *Here's How Google Sends Advertising Dollars to Fake News Sites*. [online] Vice. Available at: <https://www.vice.com/en_us/article/8xw575/heres-how-google-sends-advertising-dollars-to-fake-news-sites>.

United States Department of Justice, 2018. *UNITED STATES OF AMERICA V. INTERNET RESEARCH AGENCY LLC And Others*. [online] Available at: <https://www.justice.gov/file/1035477/download>.

Uprichard, E., 2014. *Big Doubts About Big Data*. [online] The Chronicle of Higher Education. Available at: <https://www.chronicle.com/article/Big-Doubts-About-Big-Data-/149267>.

US Bureau of Labor Statistics, n.d. *Bureau Of Labor Statistics Data: Employment, Hours, And Earnings From The Current Employment Statistics Survey (National) - Manufacturing*. [online] bls.gov. Available at: <https://data.bls.gov/timeseries/ces3000000001>.

Valluvan, S., 2019. *The Clamour Of Nationalism*. Manchester: Manchester University Press.

Varoufakis, Y., 2016. *And The Weak Suffer What They Must?*. New York: Nation Books.

Vernon, P., 2017. *Dancing Around The Word 'Racist' In Coverage Of Trump*. [online] Columbia Journalism Review. Available at: <https://www.cjr.org/politics/trump-racism.php>.

Vosoughi, S., Roy, D. and Aral, S., 2018. The spread of true and false news online. *Science*, 359(6380), pp.1146-1151.

Wahl-Jorgensen, K., 2019. *Emotions, Media And Politics*. Cambridge: Polity Press.

Wahl-Jorgensen, K., Berry, M., Garcia-Blanco, I., Bennett, L. and Cable, J., 2016. Rethinking balance and impartiality in journalism? How the BBC attempted and failed to change the paradigm. *Journalism: Theory, Practice & Criticism*, 18(7), pp.781-800. DOI: 10.1177/1464884916648094

Wardle, C., 2017. *Fake News. It's Complicated.*. [online] Medium. Available at: <https://medium.com/1st-draft/fake-news-its-complicated-d0f773766c79>.

Ware, V., 2019. All The Rage: Decolonizing the History of the British Women's Suffrage Movement. *Cultural Studies*, pp.1-25. DOI: 10.1080/09502386.2019.1638953

Waterson, J., 2020. *Broadband Engineers Threatened Due To 5G Coronavirus Conspiracies*. [online] the Guardian. Available at: <https://www.theguardian.com/technology/2020/apr/03/broadband-engineers-threatened-due-to-5g-coronavirus-conspiracies> [Accessed 3 April 2020].

Webster, F., 1995. *Theories Of The Information Society*. Abingdon: Routledge.

Weintraub, S., 2016. *Apple CEO Tim Cook Was Considered By Hillary Clinton As US Vice President Pick According To Leaked Emails - 9To5mac*. [online] 9to5Mac. Available at: <https://9to5mac.com/2016/10/18/apple-ceo-tim-cook-hillary-clinton-vp-email-leaks/>.

Wilford, H., 2003. CIA plot, socialist conspiracy, or new world order? the origins of the Bilderberg group, 1952–55. *Diplomacy & Statecraft*, 14(3), pp.70-82. DOI: 10.1080/09592290312331295576

Williams, J., 2018. *Stand Out Of Our Light*. Cambridge: Cambridge University Press.

Willsher, K., 2019. *The Truth About Chernobyl? I Saw It With My Own Eyes*…. [online] The Guardian. Available at: <https://www.theguardian.com/environment/2019/jun/16/chernobyl-was-even-worse-than-tv-series-kim-willsher>.

Wineburg, S., McGrew, S., Breakstone, J. and Ortega, T., 2016. *Evaluating Information: The Cornerstone Of Civic Online Reasoning*. [online] Stanford University. Available at: <https://purl.stanford.edu/fv751yt5934>.

Wu, T., 2017. *The Attention Merchants*. London: Atlantic Books.

Yglesias, M., 2016. *The Lesson Of Hillary's Secret Speeches Is She's Exactly Who We Already Knew She Was*. [online] Vox. Available at: <https://www.vox.com/2016/10/7/13207286/clinton-speech-transcripts-wikileaks-email>.

Younge, G., 2016. *Another Day in the Death of America*. London: Guardian Faber Publishing.

———. 2018. *Big Business Is Hijacking Our Radical Past. We Must Stop It*. [online] the Guardian. Available at: <https://www.theguardian.com/commentisfree/2018/feb/09/big-business-radical-past-ram-trucks-martin-luther-king-whitewash>.

———. 2019. *A 'No 10 Source' Is The Voice Of Power. Too Many Journalists Simply Parrot It*. [online] the Guardian. Available at: <https://www.theguardian.com/commentisfree/2019/oct/25/deference-powerful-media>.

Zadrozny, B., 2016. *The Man Behind 'Journalist, Rope, Tree'*. [online] The Daily Beast. Available at: <https://www.thedailybeast.com/the-man-behind-journalist-rope-tree>.

Zerback, T., Reinemann, C., Van Aelst, P. and Masini, A., 2020. Was Lampedusa a key Event for Immigration News? An Analysis of the Effects of the Lampedusa Disaster on Immigration Coverage in Germany, Belgium, and Italy. *Journalism Studies*, 21(6), pp.748-765. DOI: 10.1080/1461670X.2020.1722730

Zuboff, S., 2019. *The Age Of Surveillance Capitalism*. New York: Public Affairs.

Zuiderveen Borgesius, F., Trilling, D., Möller, J., Bodó, B., de Vreese, C. and Helberger, N., 2016. Should we worry about filter bubbles?. *Internet Policy Review*, 5(1). DOI: 10.14763/2016.1.401

Acknowledgements

Thanks to my publisher, Repeater Books, and my employer while I wrote this book, the University of the West of England, Bristol, for extremely generous support and flexibility in my preparation of this project. Thanks also to my students for always pushing me further, and to the many researchers and investigative journalists whose work was so vital to this book. Education, research and radical publishing are three bright rays of light in what feels like a very dark world, politically speaking.

There is another, even brighter ray of light in my world, however: my people. They say it takes a village to raise a child, and perhaps the same is true of a book, even if over a far greater spatial distribution. It is tempting to try to name every person who contributed to this book in some way, and it is a great privilege to have the opportunity to name the people whose contributions to my personal and professional life have meant the most. What, ultimately, do we have in life beyond the people we love, and the comrades with whom we stand shoulder to shoulder? In my view, very little. But the list would be too long, too detailed, too personal, and too boring for most readers beyond my social and professional sphere, were I to include it here.

Those amazing human beings who have pushed, supported, listened, challenged, read drafts, sent me links, helped me get around academic paywalls, lent me books, made cups of tea, sent me chocolate, cooked me meals, crossed oceans to sit and talk and work with me, and just been there, especially during the darkest days of lockdown writing, already know who they are. And many of their names are already written in print or in lights, without the need for me to repeat them here.

I hope they also know that nothing I could print here would ever be a fitting expression of the gratitude I feel for their contributions to this work, as well as to my life in general. So for now, I simply say to them: thank you.

Index

Repeater Books

is dedicated to the creation of a new reality. The landscape of twenty-first-century arts and letters is faded and inert, riven by fashionable cynicism, egotistical self-reference and a nostalgia for the recent past. Repeater intends to add its voice to those movements that wish to enter history and assert control over its currents, gathering together scattered and isolated voices with those who have already called for an escape from Capitalist Realism. Our desire is to publish in every sphere and genre, combining vigorous dissent and a pragmatic willingness to succeed where messianic abstraction and quiescent co-option have stalled: abstention is not an option: we are alive and we don't agree.